The Institute of American Indian Arts

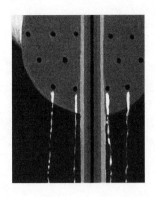

THE INSTITUTE OF AMERICAN INDIAN ARTS

Modernism and U.S. Indian Policy

JOY L. GRITTON

Foreword by Gregory Cajete

UNIVERSITY OF NEW MEXICO PRESS ∎ ALBUQUERQUE

First edition
Library of Congress Cataloging-in-Publication Data
Gritton, Joy L.

   The Institute of American Indian Arts :
modernism and U.S. Indian policy /
Joy L. Gritton. — 1st ed.

      p.   cm.
Includes bibliographical references and index.
   ISBN 0-8263-1878-9 (cloth) —
   ISBN 0-8263-2192-5 (pbk.)
   1. Institute of American Indian Arts.   2. Indian
arts—United States.   3. Indian arts—Southwest,
New.   4. Indians of North America—Cultural
assimilation.   5. Indians of North America—
Education.   I. Title.
   E98.A73 G75 2000
   704.03'97'0071073—dc21

                                        99-050413
Individual illustrations of student artwork, courtesy
of IAIA Honors Collection; all other illustrations,
courtesy of IAIA Archives.

For my grandmother Eunice Mathews Gritton

Contents

ILLUSTRATIONS

Acknowledgments

I am grateful to a number of individuals and institutions without whose assistance this work would not have been possible. Monica Blank of the Rockefeller Archive Center graciously facilitated access to their collections from across the miles, and Martha Derman took time from her busy schedule to act as my eyes and legs in securing the necessary documents. Ramus Suina, formerly a curator at the Institute of American Indian Arts Museum, cheerfully accommodated my initial research with the IAIA Honors Collection and offered valuable insight into the history of the institute from the perspective of a former student. Many IAIA students, past and present, have generously shared their experiences, hearts, and minds with me. Roger Buffalohead, first as IAIA Cultural Studies Department chair and then as Arts and Cultural Studies dean, consistently supported my work and found ways to clear my path to its completion. Alfonso Ortiz afforded me access to his personal collections and provided guidance and direction throughout the entire project. Arnold Rubin believed in the research from the beginning and taught me what responsible scholarship is all about. I am also indebted to UCLA and IAIA for financial support of this project in the forms of a Dickson Fellowship and a faculty development award. My parents, Dr. C. L. and Mrs. Virginia Gritton, have not only encouraged me through the years but also taught me to think critically and use my talents wisely. Many family members, friends, and medical staff have seen me through some difficult times in the writing of this manuscript; without their dedication I would not have enjoyed the health to continue. Finally, my husband, Stephen LaBoueff, has unselfishly given of his own ideas, energy, time, and knowledge. His gifts have enabled me to be a better scholar and teacher, and through him I have learned to live my life whole.

FOREWORD
Gregory Cajete

Joy Gritton has produced a unique contribution toward a more complete understanding of the nature and interplay of U.S. Indian policy, the tenets of modern art, and American Indian arts education. *The Institute of American Indian Arts: A Convergence of Modernism and U.S. Indian Policy* is a hallmark study of American Indian Arts education and the cultural, political, and individual agendas that have formed it in the twentieth century. Yet, it is more than an analysis of the politics of art, the U.S. government, and American Indian arts historical legacy. In a broader context, it exemplifies one of the ways in which modern American education has been used to reconstruct the social reality of minority groups. As such, it also presents an opportunity for raising the consciousness of art historians and educators regarding the "co-opting" of American Indian art traditions to serve ends other than those inherent within American Indian cultures. The focus on themes related to the influence of the Rockefellers' modernist art agenda; the attempt to institutionalize Indian art education and fit it to the mold of assimilationist Indian education policy; and the attempt of the Institute to integrate its paradoxical identities provides both a window and a mirror into the nature and the sources of contemporary Indian education issues.

Joy Gritton's years of work as art historian and instructor at the Institute of American Indian Arts provide the basis for the application of both an "insider's" perception and a comprehensive scholarly study. She applies a mode of art historical analysis that attempts to be transformative in terms of both its approach to analysis and its implications for understanding the social and political dynamics of art in Indian education. Many times, the transformative nature of the work of the art historian/teacher goes unnoticed. Yet, it is an essential element of art education whose ramifications are far-reaching. The work of Joy Gritton should not only be noticed but be actively applied in the multicultural education of art history professionals. Indeed, her work provides the beginnings of a foundation for critical yet constructive analysis of the current circumstances of American Indian arts education. Research such as this also serves to set the stage for the potential revitalization of a truly "indigenous" form of contemporary arts education, with its traditional emphasis on using art to represent and/or reflect upon living a consciously healthy, whole life in meaningful relationship to one's culture and community.

Joy Gritton describes an undercurrent of American Indian education and its all-too-familiar expression of assimilation and political manipulation. The significance of this sort of critical scholarship lies in its promise of a brighter, revitalized future which may begin through the telling of a "truer" history. This promise is evoked through an honest analysis of the origins and underlying premises of a Western ideologically and politically inspired experiment with the education of American Indians—the Institute of American Indian Arts. Joy Gritton achieves this "truer telling" by combining in-depth research of the historical record of IAIA with interviews and analysis of letters, memos, documents, and articles. Her story of the IAIA is further set within the broader context of the history of modern art, American Indian education, and the evolution of thinking regarding contemporary Indian art.

Indeed, as Joy Gritton declares, "the Institute has been characterized by paradox, duplicity and a strange mix of ideological agendas." This work begins with an exploration of the inception of the IAIA as an expression of the "reconstruction" of American Indian art to fit the tastes and philosophy of modern art. The evolution of the IAIA is presented against the background of the modernist movement in art, the "New Deal" politics of the 1930s and 1940s, federal Indian policy, and American Indian education. She outlines the influence of Indian New Dealers such as John Collier and the non-Western cultural art marketing agenda of Rene d'Harnoncourt in providing the social/economic ideology and the strategy of forming American Indian arts to modern art interests and tastes. She describes the roles of the philanthropist and modern art patron Nelson Rockefeller and organizations such as the Rockefeller Foundation and the Indian Arts and Crafts Board in furthering the adaptation of Indian arts to the modern arts canon. She reflects upon the influence of Lloyd New, Charles Loloma, James McGrath, and George Boyce as the first teachers and director of the Institute.

Joy Gritton describes the position of the supporters and nonsupporters of the Institute equally. She explores the attempts at convincing an angry Pueblo Indian community and skeptical Santa Fe public about the intentions and benefits of the Institute. She comprehensively describes the reasons for the opposition of Pueblo Indian leaders to the placement of the IAIA at the Santa Fe Indian School. She relates the early success of IAIA student exhibits and its Indian chorus and dance group, followed by the IAIA's gradual fall from political and BIA graces which, in turn, has led to its struggles to remain open since the late 1970s.

The Institute was officially established on the old Santa Fe Indian School campus in the fall of 1962, following on the heels of the Dorothy Dunn Studio and the tenets of the Rockefeller Foundation–sponsored conference held at the University of Arizona. An underlying ideology of modernist individualism and a process of "legitimization via referencing" with regard to Indian art forms characterized this "New Direction" in American Indian Art through education. It is the analysis of the underlying intent of this "New Direction" which Joy Gritton considers paramount in understanding the complex political agenda of the IAIA and around which she constructs the presentation of the various and complex issues involved in the weaving of a modernist view and approach within the fabric of the cultural and artistic heritage of American Indian cultures. In doing this she opens new avenues for dialogue for revitalizing the Institute and initiating educational change toward a more authentic expression of the evolving tradition of American Indian art.

In her analysis, she advocates a closer look at the culturally problematic modernist agenda, which figures so prominently at the inception of the IAIA. This "closer look" allows for moving beyond the "P.R. curtain" and the myths that have long been perpetuated by and about the IAIA toward a truer picture of the Institute and a clearer view of its potential as a truly Native-centered institution. The inherent potential of the IAIA has remained relatively latent as a serious realm of discussion and research because of the IAIA's "manufactured image" which hides the "colonized" origins of the school. Gritton observed very astutely:

> The decontextualization and appropriation of non-Western arts and the fragments of "primitive" peoples' ways of life were essentially an extension of Euro-American political and economic imperialism. Both

harvests were intended to revitalize and nourish the colonizers. The intellectual and cultural could now sweeten an already rich colonial pot. Modern man was thus sustained by the illusion of the "primitive" that was wholly self-serving.

Given this ideological backdrop, students at the IAIA were encouraged to play the roles of both "primitive" and "modern." They were also encouraged to follow the newly manufactured canon of "modernist" Indian art which dictated a context in which "form took precedence over process, and 'universal' aesthetic [and market] value replaced cultural context."

In a very real way the infusion of the modernist paradigm into the world of American Indian art forms created an illusion which largely denied the deeper cultural reality from which American Indians came. This denial is akin to the implied denial of the lived cultural experience of indigenous peoples throughout the world through the superimposing of Western scientific interpretation on all aspects of their life. This Western interpretation of indigenous art and experience combined with the "sterilization" of the history of conflict and tragedy after European contact in favor of the notion of "ancient roots" formed a foundation for the dissociation of the "new" forms of American Indian art being encouraged at the IAIA from traditional Native values and beliefs. In other words, students were encouraged to use "ancient roots" as inspiration but leave the past behind and create new art in the modernist mode of individualism and "art for art's sake." In the early years, the extent to which IAIA students were able to internalize the modernist credo and express it in their art determined how well their art was received by the modern art world. Thus a kind of Indian artist "star making machine" was created through the early Institute.

Joy Gritton advocates a closer look at the ideology behind the origin of IAIA vs. continuing to perpetuate what has become in the 1990s a dysfunctional myth.

> The Institute of American Indian Arts did not begin its tenure as a place of true exploration of indigenous art education. And those now entrusted with the future art education of generations of Indian students cannot begin to plan effectively for the future without objectively assessing the school's past.

In the final analysis, the IAIA experiment began with the need of its previous financial and political patronage to exemplify their particular view of art. From the New Dealers to the Rockefellers to those committed to social and aesthetic engineering of Native arts through education, the Institute provided a new vehicle to "fit" the American Indian to modern modes of art and economics. As Gritton states, "[the IAIA provided] a program designed to offer the student-artist a means to use his own unique background in meeting the commercial and aesthetic demands of our modern society."

Students were allowed to explore their tribal histories and practice their tribal arts, but the hidden curriculum of IAIA remained focused on "making it" as an Indian artist in the modernist mode.

Yet, the undercurrent of a truer representation of "evolving and tribally based" Indian art forms has always existed at the IAIA. In spite of its assimilationist underpinnings, many IAIA students have found their "cultural and personal selves" at the Institute, and an authentic spirit of cultural revival has been in play at the IAIA since its inception. Many students, faculty, and staff have seemed to know intuitively that the modernist ideology was the antithesis of their deeper sense of cultural orientation and allegiance. It is this tribal sense of spirit which appears now to be surfacing as the guiding paradigm of the IAIA. Given the resurgence of tribal art sensibility, this book has the potential for providing a spring board for a new expression of the IAIA in the twenty-first century.

Expanding the historical consciousness of art and Indian educators, patrons and art historians, educational policy makers, and Indian artists provides one of the motivations expressed by Joy Gritton for writing this book. For it is first and foremost an art historical case study of "an alternative kind," a treatise which presents a story of American Indian education and, in addition, advocates for a change of mindset relative to American Indian arts education. Joy Gritton has produced a case study and an overview of historical events at the IAIA which provide an invaluable resource for Indian educators, art historians, researchers, and policy makers as they attempt to address the challenges of creating Native-centered arts education.

The Institute of American Indian Arts: Modernism and U.S. Indian Policy presents a "seed" for a new vision of American Indian arts education. It underlines the position that through deeper understanding of an educational experiment such as the IAIA it is possible to evoke new creative possibilities, a new and truer dialogue of Indian art, and a more meaningful and culturally responsive paradigm of Indian arts education.

May the Good Spirits guide and keep you as you read this book, for you too are called upon to become a participant in the forging of new, more culturally authentic expressions of arts education in the next century. Be With Life!

Santa Clara Pueblo, New Mexico

INTRODUCTION

The Institute of American Indian Arts (IAIA), which in 1962 replaced the Santa Fe Indian School's "Studio," has been widely credited with revolutionizing and revitalizing modern Indian painting. Encouraged to explode stereotypical expectations and develop strategies for modern applications of traditional forms, institute students' visual vocabulary was from the outset strongly bicultural and their works characterized by innovation in technique, style, and subject. Hailed as a success story of minority arts education and revised Indian policy, the school met with enthusiastic response from the popular press, the federal government, and the international arts community. There were invitations to exhibit in Washington, D.C., and to dance at the White House. Students took top honors at national shows. IAIA traveling exhibitions drew large attendance from Berlin to Santiago, while articles lauding the institute appeared in numerous national periodicals.

The school represented the first attempt in the history of U.S. Indian education to make the arts the central element of a secondary and postsecondary curriculum. A post-Sputnik college preparatory impetus and the GI Bill had not been successful in rectifying the inequities that characterized Indian education. In 1961, the year before the institute enrolled its first students, only sixty-six Indians completed degrees at four-year institutions nationwide. As the arts were perceived as universals that could transcend linguistic and cultural barriers and contribute to a student's sense of accomplishment, the institute proposed arts training as a means of improving cross-discipline academic performance, while retaining pride in cultural heritage.

Yet there is overwhelming evidence to support the contention that the institute was not the cross-cultural refuge it was espoused to be. Those directly responsible for policy and curriculum, such as Director George Boyce, were "old-line" Bureau of Indian Affairs (BIA) educators whose concerns rested not so much with the arts as with "getting the country out of the Indian business." Accordingly, the institute's curriculum stressed those aspects of art education that administrators felt would ease the transition to an assimilated lifestyle and insure commercial success in the non-Indian art market, with course offerings such as "The Artist in Business," "Production," "Sales," and "Advertising Promotion." Students were also coached in "etiquette" and visited Santa Fe homes to observe "family lifestyles." Boyce paid close attention to the students' physical environment and ordered nonstandard BIA furnishings and foods for the institute's living quarters in order that students cultivate "needs" and tastes that would later translate into their adoption of American consumerist habits.

Moreover, Art Director Lloyd New believed it was not possible "for anyone to live realistically while shut in by outmoded tradition" and that the new generation of Indian artists should not resort to a "hopeless prospect of mere remanipulation of the past." Thus the art education theory practiced at the school was one that, as J. J. Brody has suggested, "emphasized the importance of ego satisfaction to the artist," often in direct conflict with Native beliefs. "Traditional" Indian instructors, such as Geronima Montoya, who had directed the arts program at the Santa Fe Indian School for the past twenty-five years, were dismissed, relinquishing their posts to professional artists considered to be more in tune with "mainstream" trends.[1]

While the school carefully constructed a public image of unfettered, culturally pluralistic arts training, the institute's curriculum and the reward system initiated through selective exhibitions, special events, and publications favored a Western, modern aesthetic dominated by individualism and commercial success in the non-Indian art market over indigenous aesthetics distinguished by concern for communal welfare, social mores, and religious proscriptions and practices. Within this framework, the probability of true artistic and intellectual exchange at the school became doubtful. Why, then, has the institute's success story of inventive cross-cultural arts education and revolutionized Native arts remained largely unchallenged? The school's enigmatic reputation has been colored by the special interests that it has served.

First, there is little doubt that the school was perceived as having great potential for demonstrating U.S. leadership in the resolution of racial discrimination and economic repression. This is specifically outlined in the institute's original *Basic Statement of Purpose:*

> A key aim is to present to people of the world—in Asia, Africa, Europe and South America—an American educational program which particularly exemplifies respect for a unique cultural minority.
>
> To the extent that these aims are accomplished, the Institute of American Indian Arts may become a prototype of a practical operating center for upgrading the role of the American Indians in contemporary society. Thus, in many ways, the Institute of American Indian Arts carries the responsibility of being something new in human affairs of potentially great significance.[2]

Five years before the founding of the school the Supreme Court had mandated desegregation with the landmark *Brown v. the Board of Education* decision. Civil Rights sit-ins had begun by 1960, and in 1961, as institute director Boyce was arriving in Santa Fe for preplanning sessions, Freedom Riders were being brutally beaten in the South. The year of the institute's opening, federal troops were on the campus of the University of Mississippi to insure the registration of James Meredith, that institution's first African American student.

Sparks of the fire to come were being ignited in "Indian Country" as well. As early as 1958 Iroquois activists had clashed with state troopers and riot police in New York over the expropriation of Tuscarora reservation land. Indian college students throughout the Southwest had been holding conferences since 1954 to discuss issues crucial to the future of Native Americans. By 1961 they had formed the National Indian Youth Council, which would play an instrumental role in the marches and "fish-ins" of the early sixties. The American Indian Chicago Conference, which brought together Native American leaders concerned about the survival of tribalism in the face of federal termination policy, was also held in 1961. Clearly, amid this atmosphere, there were sufficient political benefits to be reaped from establishing and promoting an educational facility that prided itself on its acceptance, indeed, celebration of "cultural difference."

Paradoxically, the institute also complemented the federal government's interest in mainstreaming Native peoples. Though officially denounced by Secretary of the Interior Fred Seaton as early as 1958, termination continued to enjoy congressional support until the mid-sixties. "Withdrawal" programs for the California rancherías and Menominee, Choctaw, Klamath, and Colville tribes were pending at the beginning of the Kennedy administration, and by 1961 the chair of the Senate Committee on the Interior and Insular Affairs, Clinton P. Anderson, was calling for legislation that would begin the process of dissolving their federal trust status. Between 1954 and 1960 alone sixty-one tribes, rancherías, allotments, and other groups had been terminated. Correspondingly, President Kennedy's task force on Indian affairs recommended that in Indian education "emphasis should be placed on training in the management of money, on the importance of saving, and on ways of locating jobs and of adjusting to many aspects of city living."[3]

At the same time, Indian art was coming to be viewed as both uniquely American and reassuringly modern—two essential components of the international style promoted by the Museum of Modern Art (MoMA) and the Rockefeller Foundation in the trenches of the "cultural Cold War." Indeed, Indian art had played a significant role in the formation of the persona of the new American art, having served as both inspiration and source to a number of the art movement's artists and as validation of its singular identity. Of no insignificant value also was the consideration that Native artists, unlike the abstract expressionists fostered by MoMA, were free from the taint of Communist subversion; this at a time when a proposed national arts council and other arts support legislation were stymied in the House Rules Committee and the U.S. Information Agency was under severe congressional attack for its Moscow exhibit, which displayed works by artists suspected of "Communist sympathies."

A key figure in this coupling of Indian art and modernism was Rene d'Harnoncourt, who was widely known for his marketing strategies based upon "modern applications" of traditional forms. Serving simultaneously as director of MoMA, chairman of the Indian Arts and Crafts Board (IAIA's federal advisory group), vice president of Nelson Rockefeller's Museum of Primitive Art, and first vice president of the Association on American Indian Affairs, it was d'Harnoncourt who initiated the request for the establishment of an Indian art school in the late 1950s. Rockefeller sponsorship of the 1959 Directions in Indian Art Conference and the University of Arizona's Southwestern Indian Art Project (1960–63), from which the institute drew much of its art education methodology as well as several key faculty members and a number of students, cannot be seen in isolation from d'Harnoncourt's own ideological agendas nor separate from Rockefeller political and economic interests.

Jane De Hart Mathews has commented that public patronage is "a cultural issue fraught with symbolic significance." A profile of the Institute of

American Indian Arts' public and private patronage, and its corresponding "symbolic significance," has yet to surface. Yet reconstruction of this complex interweave of sociopolitical, economic, and artistic considerations provides valuable insight not only into the manner in which these at times conflicting special interests were manifested in the very fabric of the institute but also the degree to which these interests influenced public perception of the school and its mission. Moreover, an examination of the historical conditions that determined the institute's very existence and subsequent degree of support raises critical questions regarding the school's ideological roots and ensuing pedagogical philosophy and policies. These questions, in turn, raise the issues of the role of education in cultural change in a multicultural society, state patronage of the arts through education, and Native artistic autonomy versus cultural imperialism.[4]

CHAPTER 1

THE 1959 ROCKEFELLER DIRECTIONS IN INDIAN ART CONFERENCE

The institute's agenda was established well before the school's inception when art educators, administrators, traders, and artists convened at a Rockefeller Foundation sponsored conference in 1959 to discuss "directions in Indian Art." This gathering followed on the heels of a fact-finding tour of the Southwest conducted the previous year by Charles B. Fahs, director of humanities for the foundation. The Rockefellers' interest in Native arts was at least in part an outgrowth of their activities in Third World countries. "In the development of our interest in the arts in the 'undeveloped' areas of the world, the officers have been concerned lest we neglect the comparable problems of some of the less privileged groups in the United States," wrote Fahs in his justification for the conference's funding. "If we do so, we are not only illogical but we also hamper our relations with those interested in such problems abroad. For this reason for several years the officers in Humanities have explored the problems of Indian arts and crafts in the United States."[1]

Fahs was impressed with the work of the Interior Department's Indian Arts and Crafts Board (IACB), but was also cognizant of the fact that federal policy had shifted in the direction of state jurisdiction over Indian affairs and that this threatened to undermine the board's success. "Under these circumstances," reasoned Fahs, "it is of particular importance that the states most concerned develop a responsible interest in the problem." Fahs's attention turned to the state of Arizona, which had a large Indian population. Historically, Arizona had not demonstrated the same support for Indian arts as its neighboring state New Mexico. The Rockefeller Foundation already had ties to the University of Arizona, however, through their financial support of an exchange program between UA and the University of Sonora in Hermosillo, Mexico. Arizona was also recognized for its strong anthropology program. Fahs thus traveled to Tucson in January 1958 to learn just what the university was doing with regard to Indian arts.[2]

Meeting with Academic Vice Pres. David L. Patrick and faculty, Fahs was frustrated by their apparent preoccupation with Sonora and disinterest in the problems of the Indians of Arizona. Even the anthropology program's focus seemed to rest primarily with archaeology, rather than contemporary life. While visiting the Arizona State Museum, Fahs was told by Emil W. Haury, head of UA's Anthropology Department and director of the museum, that they were engaged in some collecting of contemporary Indian art, but Fahs saw little evidence of this. When questioned as to the state's efforts to incorporate Indian arts into the public schools through curriculum development or teacher training, neither Haury nor his colleague professor Edward H. Spicer could offer any concrete information. They thought there was a woman in the Phoenix public schools interested in this area, but neither could remember her name. The only course taught at the university on Indian art was offered by Clara Lee Tanner through the Anthropology Department. Meanwhile, the university's new art gallery showed no interest in Indian art, and their touring exhibits to Sonora had consisted primarily of European fare.[3]

Fahs met the next day in Phoenix with the Cherokee textile artist Lloyd "Kiva" New (see fig. 1), a former teacher at the Phoenix Indian School, and Hopi jeweler Charles Loloma. They viewed the Phoenix Indian School student murals (Fahs learned that the school no longer had an art program), before driving to New's own private crafts center in Scottsdale, where Loloma, together with his wife, Otellie, rented a pottery and silver shop. New had received a bachelor's degree in arts education from the School of the Art Institute of Chicago and before opening the Scottsdale studio, where he marketed his hand-dyed fabrics and leather pieces, had done extensive teacher training for the BIA. The Lolomas had studied at Alfred University.

New and Loloma urged Fahs to consider a new approach to Indian arts, one more appropriate to the realities of post–World War II Indian life. "We criticized the institutions that existed up until then," remembers New,

FIG. 1. Lloyd "Kiva" New.
(Kay Wiest, photographer)

"because they were mostly museum-minded institutions or preservation and cultural conservation-minded institutions, and we had a tendency in our radical way to label all the art school movements up till that point as being more or less dedicated to the preservation of art forms, rather than trying to find out what art forms might suit the dynamics of Indian culture." Among the "institutions" included in their critique was the Indian Arts and Crafts Board. "New says that he is more interested in the projection of the arts into the future, utilizing Indian artistic talents but without being bound by existing materials, patterns, or types of production," noted Fahs. He observed that this approach had served New, personally, well. Textile printing by silk screen methods was apparently a profitable part of New's work in the shop in Scottsdale.[4]

New and Loloma also told Fahs of their dreams for a special small school for Indian arts, noting that they had already interested Frank Lloyd Wright in designing such a facility for them. They envisioned the school being led by a few well-trained craftsmen with ten or twenty young Indian artists of promise working to learn new techniques. This could become "the nucleus for a substantial development," they advised. New inquired about possible Rockefeller Foundation support, but Fahs encouraged him to seek local funding sources, citing the difficulties involved with assisting a completely new organization and the requirements of tax-exempt status. Nevertheless, Fahs left with the firm conviction that "New's work is something worth watching."[5]

Fahs also had meetings with Heard Museum director H. Thomas Cain and with the Southwest representative of the Indian Arts and Crafts Board, Frank Long, before returning to New York. His subsequent note of appreciation for hospitality written to the University of Arizona's president, Richard A. Harvill, assumed the character of both a scathing indictment and a not-so-subtle challenge to action, which included a thinly veiled threat to discontinue the Sonora program:

> If the University of Arizona is to contribute to the further development of the arts of the Southwest or if it is to provide a satisfactory model for attention to the arts in Sonora, should not this Indian contribution become an integral part of work in the arts themselves?
>
> Why should Indian arts be confined to the State Museum with its primary emphasis on anthropology and archaeology and play no role in your beautiful new art gallery? Is there no room for attention to Indian approaches to art in the Art Department and Indian patterns of music in the Music Department? In other words, is there not room for the Indian element in Arizona to be an integral and constructive part of the development of Arizona arts and crafts during the coming years?[6]

The university responded by forming a joint committee on Indian art comprising members from both the anthropology and art faculties (Dr. Haury; Robert M. Church, director of the University Art Gallery; professor Clara Lee Tanner of anthropology; and professor Andreas Andersen of the Art Department). This committee in turn drafted a proposal for an exhibition and conference on contemporary Indian art. With their stated purpose being to "contribute a broader understanding of the esthetic significance of the contribution of the Southwestern Indians to certain of the visual arts of the United States of America," the committee suggested that a "highly selective exhibition, indicating clearly the fine art quality of historical and contemporary works by Southwestern Indians," be installed in the University of Arizona Art Gallery. The Arizona State Museum would cooperate by providing a contextual base for the art of the present through archeological material but would maintain the "same emphasis on art quality." A one-day conference featuring twelve Indian artists would be held in conjunction with the exhibits and a "careful report of conditions important to the contemporary Indian creator assembled."[7]

Unfortunately for Arizona, the proposal's suggestions regarding possible collections to be displayed only served to further emphasize their lack of knowledge and awareness when it came to the matter of Indian arts. Under "contemporary" arts were included small stone carvings from A.D. 1000 to 1300, a Navajo rug, "squaw dress" or Hopi twill "of early date," Hohokam etched and painted shell from the eleventh and twelfth centuries, and Awatovi Kiva murals (replicas) from the fourteenth and fifteenth centuries, as well as basketry, silver, jewelry, and pottery from the Arizona State Museum collections. Watercolors, presumably of the Santa Fe Indian School "Studio" style, were to be borrowed from Denver and Santa Fe. The only reference to a contemporary artist was a suggestion that a piece by Charles Loloma be included to "illustrate new departures in Hopi pottery which are wheel-turned and kiln-baked"! Moreover, the committee showed extreme lack of sensitivity and poor judgment in its plans for a "ceremonial art" component that would have included a re-creation of a Zuni altar with materials borrowed from the Chicago Natural History Museum and kachina masks loaned from other institutions in the East.[8]

Adding to these problems were blunders regarding the conference personnel. Among the "American Indian Craftsmen" to be invited was John Adair, who was listed as "past head of Indian Arts and Crafts Board." Adair was an anthropologist who was, in fact, a recognized authority on Indian silverwork but was definitely not Indian. The committee was also apparently unsure of which Santa Clara potter by the name of Naranjo they wanted to come, and were unclear as to the correct spelling of Charles Loloma's name (listing him as "Lalloma"). Attached to the proposal was perhaps the real reason for the university's interest at all: projected extension programs intended for the Rockefeller-funded Sonora exchange.

The draft's shortcomings did not escape those asked by Fahs to review the project. John Harrison, also of the Rockefeller Humanities Division, noted that there was nothing in the exhibit as described that related the aesthetic significance of the contribution of southwestern Indians to the visual arts of the United States. He also wondered if the Indian artists would be consulted for the conference preparations. "The report probably could be prepared just as well, or better, outside of a conference framework," lamented Harrison, "but I suppose if the exhibit is to have any impact on the public as well as on the Indian craftsmen, some of the best of them would have to be present in Tucson during the exhibit." Oliver LaFarge, an ethnologist who had authored the 1929 Pulitzer Prize–winning novel *Laughing Boy* (a story set among the Navajo) and who was at the time president of the Association on American Indian Affairs, carefully detailed the errors and flaws in the selection of Indian arts and personnel and concluded that the choices reflected "puristic" and "ethnological" thinking and that the project was inadequate "both because it seems too short-term and because those who have drawn it up do not seem to know their subject." He admonished that the University of Arizona people would do well to seek the advice of Rene d'Harnoncourt.[9]

D'Harnoncourt was the Rockefellers' liaison to the world of Indian arts. Serving simultaneously as chair of the IACB, director of the Museum of Modern Art, vice president of Nelson Rockefeller's Museum of Primitive Art, and first vice president of the Association on American Indian Affairs, d'Harnoncourt and his work would ultimately influence the dynamics of the Directions in Indian Art Conference of 1959 on a number of different levels. Not only did the ideological tenets of the conference deliberations seem to follow directly from his promotional work with indigenous art forms in Mexico and the United States, but the very fact that the Rockefeller Foundation was interested in funding such a project revealed yet another aspect of d'Harnoncourt's legacy: a contingent of powerful financial and political backers that d'Harnoncourt had been able to cultivate to support Indian art projects. It is important to note in this regard that d'Harnoncourt's professional activities had been proven to favor not only the public's knowledge and acceptance of Indian arts but also the interests of the Rockefellers (in particular, d'Harnoncourt's friend and patron, Nelson Rockefeller), as well as the Rockefellers' museum, the Museum of Modern Art (MoMA).

Lloyd New later speculated that the direct impetus for the conference itself may have originated with d'Harnoncourt, noting that when Fahs arrived in the Southwest on his investigative mission for the Rockefellers he said only that he was sent by people concerned about what was happening in the world of Indian art. New "wouldn't have been surprised if [d'Harnoncourt's] fine hand wasn't involved in that."[10]

When consulted by Harrison, however, d'Harnoncourt was indifferent about the conference's possibilities. He clearly thought that the Southwest was "the place for support of Indian crafts as art" but did not have confidence that the University of Arizona Art Department had the "intelligent commitment" required to bring about a "true working relationship with the complex and varied strands of the Southwest Indian arts and crafts." Moreover, he expressed reservations about Lloyd New. And at any rate, he felt that a one-day conference of the best Indian artists "with their widely different attitudes towards tradition in Indian art, would result only in an extraordinarily rich expression of parochial opinion." What he did find necessary and of value was that Southwest Indian artists be afforded a "residence board," and he judged the University of Arizona to be the type of institution that could provide this continuity. Assuming that Fahs's assessment of the state's crucial role in Indian arts was correct and that the university's interest was more contrived than real, d'Harnoncourt posed the question, "Does the conference as proposed offer any indication of being an effective first step towards establishing within the University a real sense of responsibility towards Indian art in the Southwest?" He warned that the proposal was no solution in itself and that further support of a more substantial nature would be needed.[11]

In the meantime, Lloyd New and Charles Loloma had been brought in at Fahs's request to plan the agenda for the conference discussion. The conference now had a name, "New Directions for Southwest Indian Art," and an outline of speakers. Session topics included "Status of Southwest Indian Art and Artists," "Southwest Indian Art Today," "Training and Evaluation of the Indian Artist," "The Economics of Southwest Indian Painting," "Acquisition and Preservation of Indian Art," and "Guilds and Special Schools for Indian Artists." The luncheon address was to be delivered by New on the subject of projections in the realm of Indian art, and the banquet speaker was to be Rene d'Harnoncourt, who was to talk on Indian art in American culture.[12]

The proposal supplement promised that the conference would "bring into an organized work conference a group of persons qualified through experience and training . . . to resolve possible ways and means of preservation and development of Southwest Indian arts and crafts." This was to be accomplished through "1. Education of the public in the appreciation of this art, 2. The betterment of the economic conditions of the Indian craftsman and artist, and 3. Opportunities for education of the Indian artist in a period of transition."[13]

Fahs chose to defer a final decision on the proposal until he was able to meet with the Indian Arts and Crafts Board in November. The board members were not especially receptive to the idea of any university program being effective in the realm of "handicrafts" development and, not surprisingly, felt that any such enterprise should be run by the IACB itself. Fahs made a strong case for the advantages of state leadership but left hoping to persuade Arizona to have both d'Harnoncourt and Dockstader share in the conference planning. These sentiments were conveyed to David Patrick, along with the suggestion that the title of the conference be changed to reflect an emphasis on opportunities for direct action, such as "The Role of Arizona and the State Educational System in the Development of Southwest Indian Art." Clara Lee Tanner's keynote address was bumped to make room for Dockstader and the conference was christened "Directions in Indian Art: A Conference on Arizona's Position on Southwest Indian Art Education." The proposal was approved by the Rockefeller Foundation on 12 December 1958.[14]

On 20 March 1959 thirty-one official participants convened in Tucson, only nine of whom were Indian, with approximately fifty guests in attendance. The exhibition of Southwestern Indian arts opened the same day in the University Art Gallery. Discussion in conference sessions focused on ways to expand the ethnic art market so as to increase the income derived from Indian arts and crafts. The problem of marketing Native arts was multifaceted and complex, and included such factors as competition from mass-produced objects, a cash economy that offered better wages for other types of work, and a shift from a Native market to a primarily non-Native one. "How can the Indian live by art?" lamented Apache artist Allan Houser. "The facts discourage him. He has learned that commercial art, which pays well, is a competitor to creative art which offers nothing but starvation." [15]

Moreover, as New had indicated to Fahs, some of the motivations for the promotion of indigenous arts had given rise to a demand for "traditional" items, which obscured the dynamics of Native Americans' past and obliterated any prospect for innovation. Because craft production was viewed as a form of employment that fostered self-esteem and could be carried out in the home, antiassimilation forces had encouraged the revival and promotion of Indian arts as a way of partially staying the tide of cultural erosion, while providing sorely needed income to reservation communities. For example, Indian rights groups organized in defense of Pueblo land claims in the early 1920s, such as the Eastern Association on Indian Affairs, the New Mexico Association on Indian Affairs, and the American Indian Defense Association, all listed the support of Indian arts among their projected goals. The Rockefeller-funded School of American Research and the local chamber of commerce began sponsoring the Santa Fe Indian Market to this end in 1922. In 1927 these efforts were given official sanction with the release of the Meriam Report, which recommended that the Indian Office coordinate the marketing of Indian "handicrafts," guaranteeing genuineness, quality, and fair prices as a "means to an end; namely, the improvement of the economic and social conditions of life." These recommendations were realized in part with the formation of the Department of Interior's Indian Arts and Crafts Board in 1935.[16]

Inherent in this proposition of Native arts as the economic and social salvation of modern Native American peoples was a predisposition to "preserve," which gave rise to a resistance to change. Non-Native activists, collectors, and tourists alike wished to possess only those objects that conformed to their own preconceptions about what constituted Native subject matter, style, or technique. An arbitrary "traditional" ideal was established that was based on the state of the arts during the initial period of external collecting activity. "If these people lived in Basketmaker times," art dealer Tom Bahti complained about the purists among Indian art patrons, "they would object to the development of pottery in the belief that it was not traditional and therefore not Indian." To further complicate matters, artists often found themselves caught between two principal categories of buyers: collectors and museums, who purchased high quality work but did not represent an economically significant portion of the total market, and tourists, who typically consumed large numbers of goods but primarily purchased inexpensive items.[17]

Faced with these considerations, the general consensus that emerged from conference discussion called for a break with tradition and a move from isolation into a more promising modern era. "The future of Indian art lies in the future, not the past," proclaimed New. "Let's stop looking backward for our standards of Indian art production. We must admit that the heyday of Indian life is past, or passing." Citing the promotional and marketing success of certain Scandinavian art forms, as well as the accomplishments of the Indian Arts and Crafts Board, it was suggested that the real future of Indian arts lay in new applications of old techniques and skills to meet the demands of contemporary markets. "The craftsman must make a revision of his own work," explained Loloma. "He must find newer ways of doing things. New forms can come out of Indian backgrounds. People have lots of money, but they have been all over the world and have seen lots of other craft work. It is up to any craftsman to create new things which the buyer cannot resist."[18]

Royal Hassrick of the Denver Art Museum agreed, telling the conference audience that the "pitfalls in the economics of Indian craft production" lay in great part with a simple "failure to understand changes of public whim" and to adapt traditional objects accordingly. Silverwork and textiles could easily find modern uses, he noted. Other art forms posed more difficult "fits" into contemporary society, however. Hassrick warned that basketry, for example, seemed to have no place in non-Indian culture, unless possibly designed for use as waste baskets. Pottery was similarly doomed, except for a "wide potential still unexplored in flower jars glazed within to hold water, or table service, fruit bowls or bean pots."[19]

Providing a non-Native, modern context for Indian arts was not a new concept; it had been championed for more than twenty years by the IACB under General Manager Rene d'Harnoncourt's direction. The full implications of d'Harnoncourt's influence—both direct and indirect—on the conference become apparent only upon examination of his career, for it is only then that the nature of the d'Harnoncourt-Rockefeller connection is made clear and their shared political and economic agendas are revealed.[20]

D'Harnoncourt had been recruited for the post of assistant to the IACB general manager in 1936 by John Collier, Roosevelt's New Deal commissioner of Indian Affairs, after the two had met in Mexico. Austrian by birth, d'Harnoncourt had immigrated to Mexico in 1926, his studies in chemistry at the University of Graz having been cut short when his great-grandfather's estate was appropriated by Czechoslovakia and he was left financially destitute. Unable to find a job as a chemist, d'Harnoncourt worked first as a commercial artist and then as a purchasing agent of arts and antiquities for wealthy American clients such as the U.S. consul-general Alexander W. Weddell and William Green, executive vice president of the Huasteca Oil Company, a Mexican subsidiary of Standard Oil of New Jersey. It was at this time that he also came to know Frederick Davis, the owner of the Sonora News Company in Mexico City, one of the shops that catered to d'Harnoncourt's clients. D'Harnoncourt drew on his diverse purchasing trips throughout Mexico to add contemporary Indian "folk" art and Mexican painting to the Davis store. There, in 1927, d'Harnoncourt organized an exhibition of the Mexican artists Diego Rivera, Jose Clemente Orozco, and Rufino Tamayo.[21]

With the financial backing of Davis, d'Harnoncourt also supplied materials and a market for finished products to Native artists interested in reviving Olinala lacquer work and feather painting. With his reputation for expertise and promotional savvy in the field of contemporary Mexican arts growing, he was invited in 1929 by the Ministry of Education to organize collections of Mexican "folk" art to be shown in U.S. schools. A year later, he was chosen to curate a much larger exhibition of Mexican art, which toured fourteen major American cities in 1930 and 1931. The show was the publicity brainchild of the U.S. ambassador to Mexico, Dwight W. Morrow, one of d'Harnoncourt's most avid patrons. Financed by the Carnegie Corporation, the twelve-hundred-piece exhibition was shown in the Ministry of Education in Mexico City before having its U.S. debut at the Metropolitan Museum in New York.

The exhibit's success led to the continued support of Frederick Keppel of the Carnegie Corporation, who subsequently interceded on d'Harnoncourt's behalf in his attempts to secure U.S. citizenship and offered the young art entrepreneur his first American job—directing the National Broadcasting Company's radio program *Art in America*. This work provided d'Harnoncourt with yet further connections, as some of the scripts for the broadcasts were written by Alfred H. Barr of MoMA.[22] At the same time, Keppel had d'Harnoncourt working as an assistant to the president of the American Federation of Arts, a Carnegie-funded organization that Keppel hoped would assume the role of arbiter and promoter of American art in the absence of an official agency within the U.S. government.[23]

By the time he met Collier, d'Harnoncourt was teaching art history at Sarah Lawrence College, another position arranged by Keppel, who was by then president of the Carnegie Corporation. Collier was able to obtain a partial release from this teaching contract for d'Harnoncourt and funded his work at the IACB through the General Education Board of the Rockefeller Foundation. Less than a year later, d'Harnoncourt was named general manager of the IACB.

D'Harnoncourt lost no time in implementing his vision of the marketing possibilities of Indian arts, a vision first highlighted at the Gallup Intertribal Ceremonial of 1938. There, in conjunction with the United Pueblo Agency, he assembled an exhibit with the theme of Pueblo arts and crafts in the modern home. This was followed by a similar presentation at the American Indian Exposition in Tulsa, Oklahoma, two months later. The concept came to fruition, however, in d'Harnoncourt's celebrated *Indian Art in the United States and Alaska,* an exhibition organized for the Golden Gate International Exposition of 1939 under the aegis of the IACB and the U.S. Department of Interior, in cooperation with the Federal Art Project of the Works Progress Administration. D'Harnoncourt was able to secure additional financial underwriting for the show from his old supporters at the Carnegie Corporation and from the Rockefeller Foundation, the latter providing the funding for a companion text, which was written by George Vaillant through the American Museum of Natural History.

Stating that it was the exhibit's aim "to present to the public a representative picture of the various areas of Indian culture in the United States and Alaska, and at the same time to give the living Indian a chance to find a new market for his products," d'Harnoncourt allocated space within the Federal Building that housed the exhibition to sales rooms and work areas for "Indian artists to demonstrate their skill." An impressive list of some sixty-two prominent Native Americans, the vast majority artists, participated in the exposition, welcoming visitors (including Eleanor Roosevelt) and offering them a firsthand view of everything from sandpainting to totem pole carving. Among the demonstrators was a seventeen-year-old Charles Loloma, who painted one of the wall murals of Pueblo dances for the Gallery of the Pueblo Cornplanters. A temporary gallery at the back of the building was reserved for changing displays of these resident artists' work.[24]

While the main exhibits dramatically depicted the cultural contextual origins of the art forms displayed, d'Harnoncourt viewed the sales rooms, operated in conjunction with the Covelo or Round Valley Indian Community of California, as a "practical laboratory for marketing and merchandising." Accordingly, he purposely installed two contrasting outlets so as to effectively demonstrate the value of an Indian-arts-for-modern-living emphasis:

In the first of these rooms, Indian handicrafts were shown under conditions resembling those of a modern quality gift shop, stressing artistic merit and the quality of every piece rather than its romantic associations. . . . The problem to be overcome here was that the public, by and large, considers all Indian products as souvenirs only and does not associate them with utilitarian purposes. . . . Another salesroom was arranged to look somewhat like the usual Indian Trading Post so as to determine what type of background would prove more stimulating for the purchase of Indian goods. It is interesting to note here that almost all quality sales were made in the shop decorated in the modern gift-shop style.[25]

Recessed into the wall of the "gift shop" were model rooms showing the use of Native-made articles in the modern home. The first of these highlighted Pueblo arts, with pottery, kachinas, basketry, and a drum serving as accent pieces. The second featured products of the Great Plains and Eastern Woodlands, incorporating such diverse items as a cornhusk mask, roach headdress, and breast plate into the interior decor. Both rooms used furniture made in Indian schools but not, D'Harnoncourt was quick to add, in Indian style: "on the contrary, it was consciously designed in the contemporary white style, to show how well Indian articles fit into modern homes." The entire salesroom stressed the decontextualization of Native arts so as to place emphasis on their aesthetic qualities and improve their marketability. "No attention was paid in this shop to tribal origins," d'Harnoncourt explained, "and the articles were grouped in a manner to make the individual pieces appear at their best."[26]

The show was viewed by no fewer than 1.5 million people and vitally influenced the perception and interpretation of Indian arts and cultures by non-Indians for decades to come. Lloyd New was later to credit the direction taken by himself and others in Tucson at the Southwestern Indian Art Project to the inspiration of d'Harnoncourt and this exhibition:

> . . . the instigation of the fair in 1939 in San Francisco, I think, was really the beginning of this movement that we're talking about. It was at that exposition that he organized a show of Indian artifacts, objects that had been considered to be artifacts up to that time, and in this magnificent showing, a show that I don't think has ever been equaled . . . Indian artifacts were really shown to the American public, for almost the first time, as "fine art."[27]

D'Harnoncourt's impetus for the transferal of Indian-crafted items out of the trading posts and natural history museums and into the gift shops and art galleries, had, of course, not been conceived in isolation. Native American arts, initially ignored as rude examples of "material culture," had been "discovered"—together with objects deriving from Africa, Oceania, the European peasantry, children, and the insane—by the European art community in the first quarter of the twentieth century. Welcomed into the fold as kindred sheep, objects as diverse as totem poles and kachina masks were rapidly appropriated to serve as both inspiration and affirmation for postimpressionist attempts to move from a perceptual to conceptual canon of representation.[28]

D'Harnoncourt lost no time in drawing attention to these supposed correlations in the explanatory notes that accompanied the San Francisco exhibit. An Inuit shaman's mask, for example, was described as showing "the surprising affinity between certain phases of modern art and primitive art," noting that this affinity was especially noteworthy given that "founders of the corresponding modern schools were entirely unfamiliar with Eskimo carvings and paintings." An eighteenth-century Iroquois club was characterized as "anticipating modern sculpture in its treatment of balanced masses," while another mask was found to demonstrate the "seemingly illogical grouping of form elements that is also typical of surrealism in modern art."[29]

Since the interfacing between indigenous and modern art forms was at the core of much of the non-Indian redefinition of Native arts and provided the underpinning for the Indian-art-for-modern-living promotional tack, the roots of this cross-cultural shotgun marriage and the soil that nurtured it warrant further investigation. Native American cultures and arts, especially those of Alaska and the Northwest Coast, had emerged in the 1920s as a particular interest of the surrealists, who saw in them expressions of a mythical, universal order lost to Western man. Heavily influenced by the writings of Sigmund Freud and Carl Jung, the surrealists found in the realm of the subconscious a glimpse into the metaphysical realities of indigenous thought and beliefs. For these artists Native American societies represented utopias where creativity was fully integrated into daily life and all beings were balanced in a web of harmony and interdependence.[30]

The surrealists were avid collectors and exhibited with their own works those from which they had derived influence. In 1927, for example, paintings by Yves Tanguy were shown at the Galerie Surrealiste together with Northwest Coast and Pueblo carvings. In the early 1930s an exhibition of Inuit and Northwest Coast art from the Museum of the American Indian in New York was organized by Charles Ratton in Paris. Ratton subsequently loaned four Inuit masks from his collection to the *Exposition surrealiste d'objets* of 1936.[31]

As the popularity of non-Western arts burgeoned, a number of books on "primitive" art appeared. Art history encyclopedic reference works began to include essays on the arts of the peoples of Native America, Africa, and Oceania. By 1926 aficionados were able to read a chapter devoted to "aboriginal American art" in Helen Gardner's classic art history survey.[32]

With the onset of World War II, many members of the surrealist circle immigrated to the United States, several with the assistance of the Museum of Modern Art. First to arrive in 1939, Kurt Seligmann and Wolfgang Paalen both made trips to the Northwest Coast to study the Native cultures there. That same year Seligmann contributed an essay to the surrealist publication *Minotaure* on a conversation he was said to have had with a Tsimshian Indian. Paalen journeyed on to Mexico, where from 1942 until 1944 he edited the periodical *Dyn*, which contained numerous articles on the peoples of the Northwest Coast. In 1943 he devoted a double issue of *Dyn* to the indigenous arts of the Americas, proclaiming that "this is the moment to integrate the enormous treasure of Amerindian forms into the consciousness of modern art." That integration, to Paalen's mind, would lead to a "universal art" that embodied "all those human possibilities hinted at throughout the ages, so often abandoned, refound, and lost again." Other articles on Native arts appeared periodically in publications aligned with the surrealists, such as *VVV* and *View*.[33]

The new immigrants joined an already strong contingent of American artists and writers who were enthusiasts of Indian art and cultures. For those critics, scholars, institutions, and artists endeavoring to give shape and form to an independent American art, American Indian art had come to be touted as the vital root of an untainted, uniquely New World tradition. Exhibitions of Native arts had sprung up in and about New York, many of which directly asserted the Indian role in the evolution of American culture and all of which attempted to forge primal bonds between the aboriginal American and his latecomer modernist brethren.

One of the more ambitious and popular exhibits of this era was the *Exposition of Indian Tribal Arts* at the Grand Central Art Galleries in New York in 1931, which was sponsored by the commissioner of Indian affairs, the secretary of the interior, and the College Art Association. Billed as "the first exhibition of American Indian art selected entirely with consideration of esthetic value," the show included more than six hundred pieces of pottery, jewelry, textiles, sculpture, basketry, beadwork, and paintings. It was organized by John Sloan and Amelia White. Sloan, a New York artist who spent summers in New Mexico, was a longtime patron of Indian arts. As president of the Society of Independent Artists, he had arranged for showings of Indian paintings in conjunction with the society's annual exhibition from 1920 until 1922. Amelia White was secretary of the Eastern Association on Indian Affairs and a founding member of the Santa Fe–based Indian Arts Fund.[34] They worked under the aegis of the Exposition of Indian Tribal Arts, a private organization founded in 1930 with a board of directors that included Mrs. John D. Rockefeller Jr.[35]

The show's catalog was written by Sloan and Oliver LaFarge. They lamented that white Americans had been "painfully slow to realize the Indian's value to us and to the world as an independent artist" and that museums had fostered this ignorance by placing emphasis on scientific knowledge rather than aesthetic excellence, often exhibiting "the choice vase and the homely cooking pot side by side." They hoped that their exhibition of "fine and applied arts, selected from the best material available," would at last give the "Indian a chance to prove himself to be not a maker of cheap curios and souvenirs, but a serious artist worthy of our appreciation and capable of making a cultural contribution that will enrich our modern life."[36]

The exposition toured the United States and Europe, winning rave reviews on both sides of the Atlantic. It became a rallying call for the "American wave" intent upon rectifying the trade imbalance of art exhibitions and sales between the two continents. "The art of the Indians, so eloquent of this land, is American art, and of the most important kind, " wrote Walter Pach in his *New York Times* review of the show; "a hundred years ago, men could not have realized this. Art was then a thing to be seen in the Vatican or in the Louvre."[37]

The supposed affinities between the primal and the modern were again underscored but this time with a uniquely American twist. "Indian abstraction is seen to be something radically unlike that of any of the modern European 'isms,'" chided Edward Alden Jewell. "The Indian artist would not know what to make of cubism and futurism; yet he knows a great deal about simplification and stylization, methods of working that have sprung directly from the employment of symbolic forms."[38] Sloan, in the introduction to the catalog affirms this distinction, setting the Indian artist apart from Old World traditions:

> The Indian artist deserves to be classed as a Modernist; his art is old, yet alive and dynamic, but his modernism is an expression of a continuing vigour seeking new outlets and not, like ours, a search for release from exhaustion. . . . He is a natural symbolist. He is bold and versatile in the use of a line and colour. His work has a primitive directness and strength, yet at the same time it possesses sophistication and subtlety. Indian painting is at once classic and modern.[39]

Noting how extensively the modernists of Europe had borrowed from African sculpture and a "curious analogy" between certain Indian representations of animals exhibited in the exposition and work by contemporary American sculptors, Jewell questioned, "Are we about to witness an enthusiastic borrowing of Indian motif and technique on the part of artists in this country, so alive just now to the American heritage?"[40]

This dialogue only intensified when d'Harnoncourt took the San Francisco show to New York in 1941. Before the doors of the Golden Gate International Exposition had closed, an even more ambitious presentation of the exhibit at the Museum of Modern Art had been planned. The museum gave d'Harnoncourt full use of its facilities for display of the highly acclaimed *Indian Art of the United States*, which now included more than one thousand objects. It was surely no coincidence that that same year Nelson Rockefeller, who had met d'Harnoncourt in the mid-1930s, was elected president of MoMA's Board of Trustees.[41]

Secretary of the Interior Harold Ickes declared the show to be "a picture of the ancient Indian moving out into modern American and world life while holding fast to his ancient genius and devotions." Noting in the exhibition catalog that civil authorities had previously suppressed Indian dances, ceremonials, language, and arts, perceiving all Native traditions to be obstacles to progress, d'Harnoncourt credited the Roosevelt administration with turning the policy tide, commending the New Dealers for not only "cooperating with the various tribes in their efforts to preserve and develop those spiritual and artistic values in Indian tradition that the tribes consider essential" but also making "every effort to help them realize their desire to adopt from the white man such achievements as will make it possible for them to live successfully in a modern age."[42]

Since taking office in April 1933, John Collier had indeed worked closely with Secretary of the Interior Harold Ickes to implement a New Deal Indian policy predicated upon Indian economic and cultural self-determination. Particularly supportive of the arts, the administration had made a number of efforts, prior to d'Harnoncourt's tenure, to increase the exposure and sales of Indian artists. These included an Indian branch of the Public Works of Art Project in New Mexico and Arizona, government displays of contemporary arts at the Century of Progress Exposition in Chicago in 1933–34 and in Atlanta in 1934, a sales promotion of Southwest Indian products at Macy's department store in New York in December 1934, and the establishment of the Department of the Interior's Office of Exhibits in 1936, which sponsored Indian exhibits at the California Pacific International Exposition, The Texas Centennial Exposition, and the Great Lakes Exposition. The San Francisco Golden Gate Exposition and Museum of Modern Art exhibitions were the Indian artist's New Deal come to full maturity.[43]

The Roosevelt administration was certainly no stranger to employing the arts for purposes of promulgating political agendas, including the war of words against totalitarianism. In a radio speech given in honor of the new Museum of Modern Art in 1939, President Roosevelt had declared that "only where men are free can the arts flourish and the civilization of national culture reach full flower," the conditions for democracy and art being one and the same.[44]

The equation of modern art and American democracy having been planted—an equation that was to take a firm hold in the future—it was left to d'Harnoncourt to extend the theorem to include the Native American. "At this time, when America is reviewing its cultural resources," related the foreword to the *Indian Art of the United States* catalog, "this book and the exhibit on which it is based open up to us age-old sources of ideas and forms that have never been fully appreciated. In appraising the Indian's past and present achievements, we realize not only that his heritage constitutes part of the artistic and spiritual wealth of this country, but also that the Indian people of today have a contribution to make toward the America of the future." That contribution was being called into play at a time when world war weighed heavy on the American consciousness. "The show now current at the Museum of Modern Art finds Americans stranded on their own continent in recoil from a beset world," wrote Jean Charlot in the *Nation* in 1941. But he noted perceptively that while "the patriotic angle may well weigh the scales in favor of these hundred-per-centers of American art," the pride in the aesthetic achievements of the Indian should be tinged with introspective compunction, some of the objects having been "collected" by the War Department and the cover of the catalog having featured a shield design that depicts a "bear charging fearlessly into the thick of a salvo of United States bullets."[45]

Calling Indian arts "the most American of any we have in this country," d'Harnoncourt was, of course, keenly sensitive not only to the potential of Native arts to reaffirm and bolster the collective national psyche but also its possibilities for enhancing America's non-Native modern art status abroad by mere association. The effort was not lost on Charlot, who observed, "that a museum dedicated to modern art stages this show is no haphazard event, for Indian crafts are one of the sources of our own modern style."[46] D'Harnoncourt was also careful to note these affinities in the catalog's text:

> Good Indian work, done without the interference of whites, includes restrained colors as well as bright ones, and usually leans to economy rather than complexity of design. It shows a careful balance of design and color, and so is neither restless nor confused. This subtle

control of its elements and the close relationship between function and form are what bring Indian work so near to the aims of most contemporary artists and make it blend with their surroundings that are truly of the twentieth century.[47]

This blending was, of course, central to d'Harnoncourt's plan not only as the exhibition's organizer but also as general manager of the IACB. Though retail sales of Indian arts were not offered by the museum directly, d'Harnoncourt devoted the museum's lower floor to "Indian Art for Modern Living," where items such as Navajo jewelry and floor rugs, Pueblo and Papago pottery, and a Cherokee "wastepaper basket," as well as paintings by Fred Kabotie (who supervised the making of the Awatovi and Kawaika-a mural reproductions for the MoMA exhibit at Haskell Institute in Lawrence, Kansas), Oscar Howe, Munroe Tsa-to-ke, and Harrison Begay were displayed. D'Harnoncourt also contracted with a Swiss clothing designer, F. A. Picard, to incorporate Indian art forms as accents in contemporary apparel. Among the Picard creations exhibited were a "modern evening dress" that sported Pawnee ribbonwork, a cape trimmed with an Osage beaded and braided belt, and an "after-skiing suit" that used a Seminole patchwork blouse as its bodice and had buttons of Navajo hammered silver.

D'Harnoncourt's defense of the new forms was a portent of the philosophy expressed by New and others nearly twenty years later at the Rockefeller conference:

> There are people who have created for themselves a romantic picture of a glorious past that is often far from accurate. They wish to see the living Indian return to an age that has long since passed and they resent any change in his art. But these people forget that any culture that is satisfied to copy the life of former generations has given up hope as well as life itself. The fact that we think of Navaho silversmithing as a typical Indian art and of the horsemanship of the Plains tribes as a typical Indian characteristic proves sufficiently that those tribes were strong enough to make such foreign contributions entirely their own by adapting them to the pattern of their own traditions. Why should it be wrong for the Indian people of today to do what they have done with great success in the past? Invention or adaptation of new forms does not necessarily mean repudiation of tradition but is often a source of its enrichment.[48]

It was a sentiment that had also been sounded ten years earlier in the catalog of the *Exposition of Indian Tribal Arts*, when Sloan and LaFarge had warned, "the Indian, fortunately, is not an ethnological specimen, any more than he is a curio, but a live man with his own initiative. His arts must grow, he cannot be kept from adapting to his own uses such of our materials as suit him."[49]

Indian Art of the United States met with almost uncritical critical acclaim and spawned a number of more modest exhibits, among them *Northwest Coast Indian Painting* at the Betty Parsons Gallery in New York in 1946. This show was particularly significant for the interest in Native arts it revealed among proponents of abstract expressionism, among them Barnett Newman, who organized the exhibit. The gallery itself was on the forefront of the New York vanguard art scene—a nucleus for the emerging abstract expressionists that afforded many of them their first public showings. The exhibit garnered strong support from Mark Rothko and Adolph Gottlieb, who, like Newman, were painters working in the fledgling New York style. All three artists had viewed the 1941 MoMA show, and in a 1943 radio interview Rothko and Gottlieb expounded upon the appeal that "primitive" art in general held for them in wartime America:

> If we profess kinship to the art of primitive man, it is because the feelings they expressed have a particular pertinence today. In times of violence, personal predilections for niceties of color and form seem irrelevant. All primitive expression reveals the constant awareness of powerful forces, the immediate presence of terror and fear, a recognition of the brutality of the natural world as well as the eternal insecurities of life. That these feelings are being experienced by many people throughout the world today is an unfortunate fact and to us an art that glosses over or evades these feelings is superficial and meaningless.[50]

Newman had earlier hinted at an additional motivation, one particularly critical to the members of the Parsons group, who were struggling for recognition. Writing in the catalog for an exhibition of pre-Columbian work at the Wakefield Gallery in 1944, he suggested that, "so great is the reciprocal power of this art that while giving us greater understanding of the people who produced it, it gives meaning to the strivings of our own artists." Newman articulated this need for self-validation more clearly in the Betty Parsons catalog: "Here, then, among a group of several peoples, the dominant esthetic tradition was abstract. . . . There is an answer in these works to all those who assume that modern abstract art is the esoteric exercise of a snobbish elite, for among these simple people, abstract art was the normal, well-understood, dominant tradition. Shall we say that modern man has lost the ability to think on so high a level?"[51]

This carefully delineated association having served its purpose, the following year Newman organized a contemporary show at the Betty Parsons

Gallery, proudly proclaiming that "spontaneous, and emerging from several points, there has arisen during the war years a new force in American painting that is the modern counterpart of the primitive art impulse."[52]

Other painters in the Betty Parsons circle were influenced by Native arts and cultures, as well. Jackson Pollock, who exhibited there until 1951, had made vague references to indigenous forms in his pictographic work of the late 1930s. After visiting the MoMA show in 1941, his appropriation of Native American motifs and materials intensified. Pollock was particularly impressed with the Navajo dry paintings on view in the exhibition and openly credited his later drip painting techniques to their influence. Paalen was to reinforce the ties between Pollock and his sources by reproducing Pollock's *Moon Woman Cuts the Circle* in the Amerindian edition of *Dyn* in 1943.[53]

The interweave between Native arts and the abstract expressionists is especially important to understand with regards to the Rockefeller conference of 1959, because with the return of the surrealists to Europe at war's end, it was the abstract expressionists, and their supporters, who dominated art institutions and arts education in the United States well into the 1960s, thanks largely to the traveling exhibits and educational materials distributed by the Museum of Modern Art. They were the artists favored by Nelson Rockefeller's personal collection of modern art, as well as those championed by his family's museum. This was significant; for while most conference delegates readily subscribed to d'Harnoncourt's redirection of appreciation from the ethnological to the aesthetic and his tactics for cultivating new markets, some were also keen to his savvy melding of New Deal Indian policy with MoMA-Rockefeller modernism.[54]

With the weaning of Native arts from their romantic associations well underway and indigenous arts now free to be judged on an "equal" footing with their Western counterparts, the conference tackled the next logical step on the continuum: the detribalization of the creators of the arts themselves. Admitting that the Indian artist could not be repackaged as simply as his product, several speakers nevertheless remained firm in their conviction that a deep-seated transformation in the relationship between artist and culture was required if Indian arts were to survive and flourish in the modern era. Andreas Andersen, chairman of the Art Department at the University of Arizona, warned that while the transition between "Indian-artist" and "artist" would not be easy, it was nevertheless crucial in order to "force" new forms:

> In order to produce a valid art product, the Indian artist must face the choice of one of two alternatives: either to try to keep his work within the tradition, or to disregard the tradition.

Unfortunately the results in the first direction have become stereo-typed or confused by meaningless repetitions. Artistic quality has been lost and fewer and fewer true artists have developed. In the second case the tradition is lost; no tradition can be preserved when the conditions which fostered it are in change. We do the Indian no service by trying to impede or prevent change because of a sort of nostalgia.[55]

New concurred, challenging the audience to "see that the young Indian real-izes the values of his great and wonderful traditions as the springboard for his own personal creative ideas."[56]

A few speakers, such as anthropologist John Adair, held that the artist could simply divorce his cultural life from that of his professional career. "This is business," contended Adair. "The arts from which the Indian derives his es-thetic satisfactions are another thing, tied to his religion, dancing, costuming, and chanting."[57] Others, however, agreed with Andersen and saw any com-promise with the past as less than satisfactory. Robert Quinn, associate pro-fessor of art at the University of Arizona, summarized these sentiments with the pronouncement:

> It is important for the Indian to realize that being an artist is a mat-ter of being an individual. In many cases tribal customs inhibit this, but I am convinced that only an individually creative approach can bring about a growth in art produced by the Indians, or for that matter by any people. . . . It seems to me that the real problem the Indian artist faces is the insistence that he be an Indian. He should be an Indian only if he simply cannot help it. To dwell too much on his Indianism is to put the emphasis on ethnology rather than art. There should be no effort to contain the Indian within the traditions of his past. He has to realize that he is an artist first and an Indian second if his art and the tradition it rep-resents are to grow. . . . His only alternative is to become a museum piece himself.[58]

The "matter of being an individual," of which Quinn spoke, held far-reaching connotations for the American art community in the spring of 1959, ones seemingly tangential to the world of Indian art. The issues of Western individualism, modernism, and democracy had by the 1950s become tidily conjoined in such a manner that they were deemed synonymous. It was a mystification deliberately propagated by MoMA, the Rockefellers, and d'Har-noncourt in the trenches of the "cultural Cold War," with the abstract ex-pressionists on their front lines. The alliance had a complex and evasive history, and was to have profound consequences for the new "directions in Indian art."

"Modern art is related to the problem of the modern individual's freedom," wrote Robert Motherwell in 1944; "for this reason the history of modern art tends at certain moments to become the history of modern freedom." Disillusioned by the catastrophic events of the war, many artists who in the 1930s had participated in the Federal Art Project and taken up the cause of social responsibility in art had in the 1940s abandoned their liberal political activism for purely individualized aesthetics that they felt better addressed their misanthropic horror at postwar life. The Moscow trials of 1936–38 and the Stalin purges, together with the Nazi-Soviet Non-Aggression Pact of 1939, had deeply marred the political left, as well as the social realist style with which it was associated. Totalitarianism, whether of the fascist or communistic variety, seemed to leave little room for the "modern individual's freedom." Neither did the atomic bomb or the materialism of the capitalistic right. The modernists retreated to an apolitical radicalism. "Modern painting is the bulwark of the individual creative expression, aloof from the political left and its blood brother, the right," declared Paul Burlin at a 1948 MoMA forum on modern art; "their common dictators, if effective, would destroy the artist. . . . He would be the servile creature accepting on bended knee the accolade of the dictator." True to form, the new painters resisted being classified, put into groups or schools, and even balked at nomenclature, rejecting the various attempts made at naming their brand of art.[59]

Amid the milieu of postwar heady nationalism, nuclear terror, and Red hysteria, modern art soon came to be heralded by its proponents as the epitome of individual choice in the free world. "It is obvious that the dilemma of our time cannot be solved by a denial of experimentation whether by directive or by pressure," wrote d'Harnoncourt in 1948. "It can be solved," he continued, "only by an order which reconciles the freedom of the individual with the welfare of society. . . . I believe a good name for such a society is democracy, and I also believe that modern art in its infinite variety and ceaseless exploration is its foremost symbol."[60]

The Cold War had begun to take concrete form in 1947 with the introduction of the Truman Doctrine, which promised economic and financial aid to those countries threatened by "Soviet aggression." The Truman Doctrine was followed a few months later by the announcement of Secretary of State George Marshall's plan for the economic rehabilitation of war-ravaged Europe. Shortly thereafter the overland route to Berlin was closed and a massive airlift begun. The next three years saw the Soviet Union test its first atomic bomb, the formation of the North Atlantic Treaty Organization (NATO), the fall of the Chinese nationalists, and the invasion of South Korea by the North Koreans. By 1951 the lines of espionage and propaganda were well drawn.

In this war of ideas, concern over foreign perception of the United States resulted in the expansion of the government's Information and Cultural Program, first with the Smith-Mundt Act of 1948, then with the creation of the U.S. Information Agency (USIA) in 1953. The arts were deemed a crucial component of this emerging cultural offensive. "We in the United States have fallen into the habit of letting the rest of the world believe in the myth that there is no real cultural base in the United States," Herbert Lehman, a New York Democrat, complained to the Senate as he introduced an omnibus arts package. "The Communists have exploited this myth by propagandizing the peoples of the world with the story that we in the United States are materialistic barbarians." [61]

Eisenhower responded to the challenge by creating the International Exchange Program in 1954, which was funded by a $5-million "Emergency Fund for International Affairs." [62] That same year the president honored the twenty-fifth anniversary of the Museum of Modern Art with a much-awaited public statement regarding the rights and role of the arts in a free society. Stating that freedom of the arts was "one of the pillars of liberty in our free land" and essential to the "healthy controversy and progress in art" that gave rise to "genius," Eisenhower (in an obvious reference to the Soviet Union) added, "How different it is in tyranny. When artists are made the slaves and tools of the state; when artists become the chief propagandists of a cause, progress is arrested and creation and genius are destroyed." [63] His words echoed those of John Hay Whitney, chairman of the board of trustees of MoMA, who, writing in a commemorative book designed to highlight the museum's permanent collections for this same occasion, espoused that institution's contribution to the democratic process:

> Particularly during a time when conformity enforced through authoritarian pressure is a constant threat to the development of a free society, it is most heartening to turn to the arts and to find in them the vitality and diversity that reflects freedom of thought and of faith. We believe that the collection of the Museum of Modern Art and this publication represent our respect for the individual and for his ability to contribute to society as a whole through free use of his individual gifts in his individual manner. This freedom we believe fundamental to democratic society. [64]

The following year Eisenhower called for the establishment of a Federal Advisory Commission on the Arts within the Department of Health, Education, and Welfare (HEW). The bill providing for the commission was drafted by the then undersecretary of HEW, Nelson Rockefeller. Federal support of the arts according to this plan was warranted by virtue of the precepts that "growth and flourishing of the arts depend upon freedom, imagination, and individual initiative," and that "the encouragement of creative activity in the performance and practice of the arts, and of a widespread participation in an appreciation of the arts, promotes the general welfare and is in [the] national interest."[65]

This policy, though never realized in the form of an Advisory Commission on the Arts, became an unspoken guide for cultural correctness in the latter half of the decade. Those supporters of the arts that would find monies for their projects learned quickly to master the rhetoric of the "national interest." For example, in the interest of pending arts legislation New Jersey representative Frank Thompson published an article entitled "Are the Communists Right in Calling Us Cultural Barbarians?" in which he admonished that the time had come for the United States to mount a "counteroffensive" against Soviet violinists, ballerinas, athletes, and chess players. Thompson subsequently introduced his American National Arts, Sports, and Recreation Act on the House floor, declaring that plans should be developed for "getting the peoples of the world on our side through maximum use of sports, the theater, and educational exchanges," for it was "through cultural interchange and development . . . that the real answer to communism must be sought."[66]

Likewise, Lloyd Goodrich, chair of the Committee on Government and Art and associate director of the Whitney Museum of American Art in New York, drew upon the Red paintbrush scare for his testimony in support of arts legislation in 1957, reminding the representatives that "international tensions and our leading role in world affairs have taught us the importance of the arts as an international language and the necessity of giving the world a true picture of American life, American culture, and American democracy." The congressmen probably did not need their memories refreshed. They had heard much testimony regarding the supposed Russian cultural build up, and they had seen the newspaper accounts of increased Soviet funding for the arts.[67]

Government sponsorship of modern art for export was, however, largely rejected by an American public wholly unsympathetic to its elite and esoteric nature and by a legion of American artists who felt disenfranchised by the new movements. Moreover, modern art and its supporters were ironically coming under scrutiny as being less than American and less than patriotic. This opposition was first evidenced in the recall of the *Advancing American Art* exhibit of 1946. Funded by the State Department, the exhibition was a promotion of American "culture" scheduled to tour Europe and Latin America over a five-year period. Vehement and persistent complaints from academic artists (led by the American Artists Professional League) and the William Randolph Hearst publishing empire regarding the content of specific works and the supposed associations of exhibiting artists with Communist fronts resulted in the show's official condemnation and eventual demise. The paintings that had been purchased by the State Department for this traveling showcase were subsequently auctioned off as war surplus property.[68]

The congressional attack against similar federally funded cultural programs was marshaled over the following decade by Michigan representative George A. Dondero, chair of the House Committee on Public Works. Dondero objected not only to the specific content of particular works and the politics of individual artists but also to modern art in general, characterizing it as the work of a highly sophisticated Communist plot. "The art of the isms, the weapon of the Russian Revolution," Dondero told Congress in 1949, "is the art which has been transplanted to America, and today, having infiltrated and saturated many of our art centers, threatens to overawe, override and overpower the fine art of our tradition and inheritance." He went on to explain that while not all of these "isms" were "media of social or political protest," all were "instruments and weapons of destruction":

Cubism aims to destroy by designed disorder.
Futurism aims to destroy by the machine myth. . . .
Dadaism aims to destroy by ridicule.
Expressionism aims to destroy by aping the primitive and insane. . . .
Abstractionism aims to destroy by the creation of brainstorms.
Surrealism aims to destroy by the denial of reason.[69]

In order to refute Dondero's claims, as well as modernism's other reactionary critics in Congress, Alfred H. Barr, then director of collections for the Museum of Modern Art, penned an article for the *New York Times Magazine* entitled "Is Modern Art Communistic?" The essay gave an account of persecution suffered by modern artists at the hands of totalitarian regimes in Russia and Germany, and outlined the rise of social realism in the USSR. "The Modern artist's non-conformity and love of freedom cannot be tolerated within a monolithic tyranny," contended Barr, "and modern art is useless for the dictators' propaganda, because while it is still modern, it has little popular appeal."[70]

The following year, A. H. Berding of the USIA proclaimed that since the agency was interested in art exhibitions only as "a means of interpreting American culture to other peoples," the government "should not sponsor examples of our creative energy which are non-representational." There would be no room for "purely experimental art." Moreover, works by "avowed communists, persons convicted of crimes involving a threat to the security of the United States, or persons who publicly refuse to answer questions of congressional committees regarding connection with the communist movement" would not be exhibited by the USIA.[71]

It is thus not surprising that when two USIA-sponsored shows, *Sport in Art* and *100 American Artists of the Twentieth Century*, came under attack in 1956, support within the agency itself almost immediately faltered. The first was an exhibition organized by the Carnegie-supported American Federation of Arts (AFA) for *Sports Illustrated*. The USIA planned to feature the show at the Olympics being held in Melbourne, Australia, after it toured the United States. When four artists were decried by the Dallas Patriotic Council as having Communist ties, the show's schedule was abruptly interrupted. In quick succession the USIA then canceled a tour of the Symphony of the Air and another AFA exhibit, *100 American Artists of the Twentieth Century*. Both were plagued by accusations of Communist infiltrators, and when the trustees of the AFA voted to withdraw the latter show if any of the artists were not allowed to exhibit, the USIA simply terminated its tour. Afterward, the agency announced that it would no longer sponsor exhibitions of American painting produced before 1917—the year of the Russian Revolution.

Subsequently, the Museum of Modern Art assumed primary responsibility for distribution and promotion of American arts abroad, minimizing the problem of public criticism and control. The "cultural Cold War," with its exportation of American individualism through the vehicle of New York–style modernism, now became primarily a privately funded operation led by the Rockefeller Foundation, with support from other wealthy benefactors, such as d'Harnoncourt's old allies, the Carnegies, as well as the Whitneys. The government support for the arts that remained was, for the most part, a covert operation, with the CIA providing funding through dummy foundations for the Congress for Cultural Freedom, tours of the Boston Symphony Orchestra, and the leftist magazine *Encounter* (among many other organizations) in the interest of influencing European intelligentsia. Thomas Braden, formerly in charge of this CIA campaign, defended its secrecy in an article entitled "I'm Glad the CIA is 'Immoral,'" maintaining that "when the cold war was really hot, the idea that Congress would have approved many of our projects was about as likely as the John Birch Society's approving Medicare."[72]

In 1953 MoMA had received a five-year $625,000-grant from the Rockefeller Brothers Fund for an "international circulating exhibitions program." Porter McCray, on leave from the museum to work with exhibitions for the

Marshall Plan in Europe, was recalled to direct the new project.[73] The museum largely modeled the program after earlier contract work for Nelson Rockefeller's Office of Inter-American Affairs (OIAA) during War World II. The latter had sponsored a variety of sports competitions, technical advisers, and cultural exchanges (including nineteen exhibitions of contemporary American painting) throughout Latin America from 1940 to 1944. The OIAA's Publications and Information Division published an upscale Spanish-language monthly magazine, *En Guardia,* as well as a weekly edition of the *New York Times* for Latin American distribution, and produced a radio precursor to Voice of America that was broadcast on Latin American stations.[74] D'Harnoncourt himself had worked in this office as "acting" art director and had witnessed firsthand the value of American arts in garnishing goodwill among those who held fragile rein over foreign resources—particularly in countries where Rockefeller investments were at stake. He had, in fact, organized a show of Native American art under the OIAA that was exhibited in Mexico City in 1945 at the Museo Nacional de Antropologia.[75]

But MoMA was also no newcomer to the world of transglobal cultural propaganda. The museum had more than modestly met its obligations to the war effort by completing some thirty-eight contracts with the Office of War Information and Library of Congress for "cultural materials," in addition to its work for the Office of Inter-American Affairs. And in 1952, when Representative Fred Busby, a Republican from Illinois, charged that a State Department exhibit of contemporary American prints being shown in the American Embassy in Paris contained works by Communist sympathizers, it was learned that the show had been selected by a curator at MoMA and was actually financed by Nelson Rockefeller, not the U.S. government.[76]

In its first year the International Program was able to send twenty-two exhibitions of American modern art abroad. In conjunction with these efforts, MoMA purchased the U.S. pavilion at the Venice Biennale and from 1954 to 1962 was solely responsible for the American representation there. The museum's success in the international arena, combined with the events of 1956, convinced Nelson Rockefeller and d'Harnoncourt to expand the operation, selecting Mrs. John D. (Blanchette) Rockefeller III to be the first president of a new International Council at the Museum of Modern Art. In announcing the expansion, Mrs. Rockefeller explained that "despite the valuable activities being carried on by the United States Government, and through it private and public organizations receiving Government grants, we feel that in accordance with American traditions a large share in the initiative for patronage of the arts and for sending exhibitions abroad should be the responsibility of privately sponsored organizations." The reorganization primarily was designed to increase funding, with the council operating as a separate membership corporation charged with wooing the private patriotic sector into contributing the thousand dollars a year required to become a member. Responsibility for the preparation of exhibits still rested with the museum's International Program under McCray.[77]

In March 1959, as participants at the Directions in Indian Art Conference debated the value of the artist as an individual, MoMA's *New American Painting* exhibition, organized by the International Program under the auspices of the International Council, was about to close a two-year European tour in London. "Of the seventeen painters in this exhibition," wrote Alfred Barr in the catalog's introduction, "none speaks for the others any more than he paints for the others. In principle their individualism is as uncompromising as that of the religion of Kierkegaard whom they honour. For them, John Donne to the contrary, each man is an island."[78]

D'Harnoncourt claimed that the exhibit had been organized "at the request of European institutions for a show devoted specifically to Abstract Expressionism in America." Dorothy C. Miller, who had given the abstract expressionists their first museum show at MoMA in 1946, was chosen to direct the exhibit. Of the foreign response to the show, McCray wrote, "whether enthusiastically, hesitantly, in the form of back-handed compliments, or of real hostility, it was acknowledged that in America a totally 'new'—a unique and indigenous—kind of painting has appeared, one whose influence can be clearly seen in works of artists in Europe as well as in many other parts of the world."[79]

These larger activities of the Museum of Modern Art, the Rockefellers, and d'Harnoncourt cannot be seen as unrelated to the patronage of the Directions in Indian Art Conference. For Indian art had played a not-insignificant role in the formation of the persona of the new American art. Its powers of validation had been called into play at its birth, and however misunderstood and blatantly appropriated, it had served as inspiration and source to not a few of the new movement's artists. Moreover, according to d'Harnoncourt, Native American art itself could now be promoted as both reassuringly modern, as well as uniquely American.

It should also be remembered that the ideological tenets of modernism, MoMA style, had been consciously and effectively disseminated among and adopted by the American art education hierarchy. Since 1939—the year of the San Francisco Golden Gate Exhibition—when the Rockefeller Foundation had given MoMA a grant to fund exhibitions for "smaller institutions with limited funds," the museum had developed a legion of shows (and other instructional materials) specially designed for the classrooms and exhibition spaces of the nation's schools. The University of Arizona and its faculty had certainly not remained immune to this influence.[80]

In a similar vein, it was to education that some speakers at the Rockefeller conference turned as the medium most capable of propagating the far-reaching reforms proposed during the meeting's discussions. "Today Indian artists compete with all other artists in America," reasoned Clara Lee Tanner. "Their training must be adequate to meet this competition, with secondary schooling which looks forward to college." There were, however, dire assessments of the state of Indian arts education. Charles Minton of the New Mexico Association on Indian Affairs warned that "soon there will be no art at all in Indian high schools. . . . There is little or no exposure to wider artistic traditions. Without some encouragement from somewhere there will be less rather than more Indian art." Margaret Handlong, a Phoenix art teacher, reported that Indian art was not taught to any extent in the public schools and then only in accordance with the interests of individual teachers.[81]

As a partial solution Pablita Velarde, a Santa Clara Pueblo artist, called for a state or federal art center where Indians could work and develop their arts. Hopi artist and educator Fred Kabotie, a teacher at Oraibi High School in Arizona, urged, however, that sensitivity be exercised in any proposed arts education. "We are indebted to any organization which promotes Indian art and culture. But teachers in public schools should not go too deep into the meaning and making of kachina figures and masks," cautioned Kabotie, "because this would disturb the Hopi tribe and make them discourage such teaching. But the teaching of such things as basketry, silver work, or modeling in clay is all right."[82]

Dorothy Dunn of the School of American Research in Santa Fe characterized the desired genre of arts education as "guidance" that would "establish in the student a sense of values by widening his view of art" and "develop skills and resourcefulness in the creation of individuality and . . . self-reliance." This guidance, concluded Dunn, so urgent "if contemporary Indian painting is to last out the life of Indian culture," was the responsibility of the Indian schools.[83]

Dunn was widely known as the coordinator of painting classes held at the Santa Fe Indian School from 1932 until 1937, known collectively as the "Studio." A former teacher at the Santo Domingo Pueblo day school, Dunn had inquired about teaching at the Santa Fe boarding school in 1931, at a time (the Exposition of Indian Arts was touring the country) when both popular public opinion and official federal policy favored the fostering of Indian arts.[84]

Following the release of the Meriam Report of 1928, which had contained a searing critique of Indian education, Commissioner of Indian Affairs

Charles J. Rhoads, under considerable pressure to initiate reform, appointed W. Carson Ryan, a professor at Swarthmore College and one of the authors of the Meriam Report, to the post of director of Indian Education. A proponent of the progressive education movement, Ryan worked to replace the "uniform course of study"—English classics, algebra, geometry, and ancient history—with subjects relevant to the student's cultural background.[85]

To this end Ryan enlisted Native teachers whenever possible to teach a variety of traditional techniques. Santa Fe Indian School students, for example, were instructed in pottery by Pueblo masters such as Maria Martinez of San Ildefonso. When John Collier became Indian Commissioner in 1933 he continued this trend, selecting as Ryan's successor Willard W. Beatty, another progressive educator. As emphasis came to be placed on returning the student to the Native community, rather than preparing him or her to "succeed" in the non-Indian world, the arts began to appear in boarding school curricula. The first full-fledged art department to be established in a bureau school during this period began in 1931 as part of the vocational training offered at the Santa Fe Indian School. Students there were offered silversmithing, woodwork, weaving, embroidery and beadwork in a newly built arts and crafts facility.[86]

The program quickly attained national recognition in the summer of 1932, when a series of murals was completed by several adult Indian artists and eight students in the dining hall of the school. Santa Fe artist Olive Rush, who had acted as a coordinator for the project, promoted the murals with articles in *Contemporary Arts* and *Theatre Arts*, and the artists' talents were touted highly in a number of other national publications. Some of the project's participants went on to form the Mural Guild, which subsequently exhibited moveable panels at the Corcoran Galleries, Rockefeller Center, and the Century of Progress Exposition in Chicago.[87]

Dunn began the separate painting classes in 1932, with the following as her objectives:

> 1. To foster appreciation of Indian painting among students and public; 2. To produce new paintings in keeping with high standards already attained by Indian painters; 3. To study and explore traditional Indian art methods and productions in order to continue established basic painting forms, and to evolve new motifs, styles, and techniques only as they might be in character with the old, and worthy of supplementing them; 4. To maintain tribal and individual distinction in the paintings.[88]

It was the third policy that was to earn Dunn considerable criticism in the intervening years between her tenure at the Studio and the Rockefeller conference of 1959. By her own account, Dunn had one fixed principle that was absolute: "the painting would have to be Indian."[89]

Definition of that quality was dictated by Dunn's knowledge and understanding of certain "established basic painting forms," in particular petroglyphs and painted pottery of the southwestern tribes, the Pueblo kiva murals excavated in the mid-1930s, and the much-publicized easel paintings of Pueblo artists—such as Fred Kabotie, Awa Tsireh, and Tonita Pena—working in the first third of the twentieth century. From her study of these Dunn concluded that "devices associated with European painting were needless in Pueblo painting where objective aspect was subordinate to vital idea." "In the use of perspective," continued Dunn, "scientific laws of optics were unexplored, yet convincing spatial relationships were achieved intuitively through relative placements rather than through mechanically determined position and scale. The employment of light and shade was ordinarily made unnecessary by manipulation of contour through skillful line rendering in situations where suggestion of a third dimension was desirable." In addition, only natural palettes were used, thereby eliminating any concern for laws of color harmony, and subject matter consisted primarily of that related to nature.[90]

Dunn then set about maintaining a "traditional" ideal that did not deviate from these principles. In the Studio she kept Bureau of American Ethnology reports, Sloan and LaFarge's catalog to the *Exposition of Indian Tribal Arts* show, a set of Field Museum of Natural History portfolios entitled *Design in Nature,* and a Peabody Museum publication, *Mimbres Pottery Designs.* Prints from Hartley Burr Alexander's *Introduction to Pueblo Indian Painting* portfolio were hung in the Studio's room and students were exposed to the collections at the Laboratory of Anthropology and the Museum of New Mexico, as well as to objects borrowed from other museums for the Studio's instructional use. Class work included sketching pictographic figures and free-line brush practice. Borrowing of motifs or styles from other tribal groups or from non-Indian sources was discouraged. Subject matter was evaluated for "appropriateness in particular settings," with accuracy of costume, activities, and symbolism deemed essential.[91]

The Studio works that emerged were, in Dunn's view, "in character with the old." Paintings were executed in flat, outlined color. Ceremonial, hunting, and domestic scenes were the favored themes. Perspective was implied through placement, with backgrounds typically eliminated. The construct meshed with that which developed out of Oklahoma institutions to create a style that was pervasive in Indian painting until the late 1950s. Prominent Native American artists who studied at the Studio include Joe Herrera,

Pablita Velarde, Jose Rey Toledo, Geronima Montoya, Allan Houser, Oscar Howe, George Keahbone, Harrison Begay, Gerald Nailor, Quincy Tahoma, Andrew Tsihnahjinnie, Fred Kabotie, and Narciso Abeyta. Montoya, a painter from San Juan Pueblo, assumed leadership of the program after Dunn's retirement in 1937 and directed the art component of the Santa Fe Indian School's vocational curriculum for the next twenty-five years—until the advent of IAIA. Toledo and Abeyta also taught at the school after completing their own studies.[92]

With the active support of prominent Santa Feans, the school launched national and international exhibits of student work, including a large showing of watercolors at the Musee d'Ethnographie at the Trocadero in Paris arranged by French artist Paul Coze, the opening of which drew a crowd of one thousand, including the U.S. ambassador to France. There were frequent visits to the Studio by foreign dignitaries as well as local citizens. The school was invited to participate in the local Works Progress Administration program, with two students, Velarde and Tsihnahjinnie, contributing paintings to a national exhibition of the Santa Fe WPA projects at the Corcoran Galleries in Washington, D.C.[93]

Dunn's critics charged that at best she was imposing a stereotypical, ahistorical Indian painting absolute on her students, and at worst she had created the style from non-Native sources. (Hollywood animated cartoons, book illustrations of the 1930s, midwestern regionalist painting, and Persian miniatures were all suggested.) Dunn adamantly denied the allegations, insisting that she had introduced only Indian influences and that her teaching role was "somewhat like that of a gardener encouraging natural growth to a flowering of plants by the elimination of weeds."[94]

By 1959 Dunn had become symbolic of the old guard of Indian painting and those attending the Rockefeller sessions at the University of Arizona were sharply divided into pro-Dunn and anti-Dunn camps. Stating that Indian painting needed to "advance in quality and quantity more than in kind," Dunn appealed to the conference audience to refurbish the old Santa Fe Indian School program. "The period of teaching art at the Santa Fe Indian School was productive of most of the best known names in Indian painting today. Why should not this school be reorganized along the best of its former lines and expanded to include more arts and crafts courses plus more supporting courses?" This sparked Robert Quinn to reply that he deplored the Santa Fe school, which "in the process of producing an Indian artist, actually taught him a style of painting derived from the Persian miniatures." Quinn concluded that the Studio style was either "unwarranted eclecticism" or an outright "fraud."[95] This verbal attack on Dunn initiated what one participant was to remember as an "unproductive phase" of the conference, in which a few people dominated the discussions and productivity of sessions declined.[96]

The dispute was not out of character with the divergence of ideologies represented at the conference—New Deal cultural and economic policies, modernism's love affair with the "primitive" and with it d'Harnoncourt's redirection of appreciation from the ethnographic to the aesthetic, the fledgling American artists' promotion of individualism and their own uniquely American art (interests in accord with those of the Rockefellers and the U.S. government), the practical considerations of developing a profitable ethnic art market, and very real concerns for the survival of indigenous art forms and Native cultures. Amid the competing agendas, it was the call for educational reform that was to hold the conference organizers' attention and evoke their continued support, culminating in the Rockefeller-sponsored Southwestern Indian Art Project of 1960–63.

CHAPTER 2

THE SOUTHWESTERN INDIAN ART PROJECT, 1960–1963

Four months after the final Directions in Indian Art sessions, Lloyd New telephoned Charles Fahs to convey his assessment of the conference's shortcomings. While the gathering in Arizona had been of limited benefit, New maintained that nothing that was likely to take place in a university setting would meet the real need of Indian artists. Once again he made a pitch for his Indian art school. Real Indian artistic talent was not likely to show up among those otherwise qualified for college entrance, he claimed. In September, New wrote to Fahs, further outlining his position. Noting that much conference discussion had focused upon a perceived "lack of appreciation on the part of the public in general of Indian life and cultural values" and the resultant difficulties in marketing Indian art, New insisted that none of these considerations were "the real problems" and were factors that in any case were not easily remedied. "The public would appreciate Indian art," he maintained, "when it has vitality and purpose." Referencing the Rockefeller conference discussions, New related that he was "delighted when Charles Loloma answered the spokesman from the Navajo guild, who was crying because people wouldn't pay proper prices for Indian art products, by suggesting that there was always a proper market for the really fine art piece, and if they created more deserving things they wouldn't have that problem." For, New concluded, "production and marketing problems—who can really help with these? Devices in this direction always seem to undermine the natural pattern of supply and demand and they exist healthfully so long as the subsidy is healthy."[1]

It was, rather, only through education of the Indian artists, not the non-Indian consumer, that real solutions could be effected:

> Since talking with you when you were in Scottsdale I am convinced more than ever that a special art educational program is the only answer to the total Indian arts and crafts problem. Whether we have an Indian expression as long as we have Indians depends upon whether they will maintain their will to express Indian ideas. After the conference at Tucson I am more of a belief that the main concern for Indian arts and crafts expression should be in a program which is concerned with the evolution of Indian artists doing honest Indian art. And by honest Indian art I mean he should be trained to personal creativity in an area of Indian tradition not limited to the rehashing of old forms or pursuing the effective cliche.[2]

New described to Fahs a special school where Indian youth could be "steeped in the beauties of their own traditions, where their creative talents can be awakened, where their individual taste levels will be raised and adapted to the world into which they ultimately must fit." There, New planned, students would also learn the essentials of economics vital to their artistic pursuits, such as production, cost accounting, finance, and sales presentation. No universities or colleges presently existed, maintained New, that were equipped to accommodate the needs of the Indian art student and no opportunity for arts or crafts training was provided by BIA educational programs. "I am sure as a result of the conference," related New, "[that] they at Tucson are awakened to the need and would like to do something about it, but I dare say they wouldn't have the slightest idea of how to go about meeting the special needs of Indian artists, namely a heightened pride in their own traditions, and a specific plan for opening up creativity with reference to this particular background."[3]

Two weeks later, New was included in a grant proposal submitted to the Rockefeller Foundation by the University of Arizona to fund a series of summer workshops for southwestern Indian students. The proposal, entitled "An Exploratory Workshop in Art For Talented Younger Indians," recounted how following the Rockefeller conference the University Committee on Indian Art had met several times to determine their next phase of action. Lloyd New and Charles Loloma attended at least two of these sessions. In their attempt to "translate the conference proceedings into terms which would aid and guide future efforts," they took as their "primary working text" excerpts from New's banquet keynote address on Indian art education. "They are statements to which the committee returned constantly in all later discussions," the proposal stated, "probably because Mr. Kiva [New] summarized the greatest single problem faced by southwestern Indian artists and craftsmen: 'The future of Indian art lies in the future, not the past—let's stop looking backward for our standards of Indian art production.'"[4]

The proposal made clear the grant writers' lack of confidence in indigenous communities' abilities to equip their own youth for the rigors of the modern art world:

> The consensus of those who participated in the conference was that if Southwestern Indian art is to survive, it must take new directions. Few believe that the force needed to produce this impetus could be generated wholly within Indian cultural circles. . . . There is an obvious need for closer educational and working relationships between young Indian artists and non-Indian professional groups capable of assisting the development of indigenous talent. . . . The changing economic status of southwestern Indians together with the conflict between traditionalism and progress places the artistic young Indian in a confused setting. Such conditions generate an atmosphere in which creative activity needs guidance rarely available at the tribal level.[5]

While acknowledging that opinion was divided on the benefits of an ethnocentric arts education versus a curriculum that combined indigenous influence with recognized methods of non-Indian art training, the proposal cited a statement made by artist Fred Kabotie expressing hope for a revival of Hopi art as evidence that "even when a sizable number of the Indian population are traditionalists, as is true of the Hopis, tradition alone is not sufficient stimulus to encourage young artists and craftsmen."[6]

Proceeding on the assumption that the future of Indian art in the Southwest would be determined not by the talents or efforts of established adult Indian artists but rather by the "direction in which the budding talent of younger Indians is guided," the University Committee on Indian Art once again relied upon New's words for leadership:

> Let's try to find challenging opportunities for the young Indian mind. Let's be more concerned with the evolution of arts rather than of art products. Let's see that the young Indian realizes the values of his

great and wonderful traditions as the springboard for his own personal creative ideas. Indian art of the future will be in new forms, produced in new media and with new technological methods. The end result will be as Indian as the Indian.[7]

The committee believed that the new directions outlined by New clearly called for programs in which the major objective would be "individual training in more than traditional Indian techniques" and that the training should be conducted in an "environment of creative activity not exclusively Indian in nature." Of equal importance, they added, was the need to "encourage traditional sources of inspiration while seeking broadened forms of expression."

To this end the University of Arizona proposed to bring a select group of twenty to twenty-four talented college-age southwestern Indian students together on the Tucson campus for six-week-long summer workshops. They requested a three-year budget totaling $62,700 from the Rockefeller Foundation to cover transportation of participants to and from campus, meals, instructional costs, materials, and faculty salaries. The university was prepared to provide all studio facilities and equipment, as well as housing for the visiting students and personnel. Tuition charges were to be waived, and students would be able to participate in all regular summer session extracurricular activities free of charge.[8]

The workshops were to integrate non-Indian art methods with traditional Indian sources of inspiration by offering classes in Indian culture together with studio work in three areas—painting, ceramics, and metalwork. Instruction in the elements of design were to "relate to the specific problems of the Indian artists." Principles and problems of marketing were also part of the tentative curriculum. The faculty was to include both Indian and non-Indian personnel, with Sidney Little, dean of the College of Fine Arts, serving as coordinator, and Lloyd New and Andreas Andersen, head of the Department of Art, as codirectors.[9] The university Indian art committee was to act as a general coordinating group. Each workshop was to culminate in an exhibit of work completed during the six-week period, as well as a critique to which selected participants in the 1959 Rockefeller conference were to be invited.

The proposal concluded with "significant questions," on which the workshops were expected to shed "reasonably definite information," if not genuine light:

1. What are the capabilities of young Indian artists to adapt to a creative situation in which traditional Indian cultural concepts are modified to meet contemporary forms, media, and methods in the studio? Can the fundamentals of design be absorbed under such conditions?

2. What is the effect on the young Indian artists of association with lecture material and how will he apply it to tradition-inspired work? Is critical analysis of creative production achieved under dual instruction helpful to the artist? Does lecture material on traditional culture and archaeology, plus work in design principles, serve as a point of departure for creative work? Does creativity increase or decrease in such an environment?

3. Does this type of student group adjust to academic learning and still produce personally created work of quality? Determination of this point will have direct bearing on the future possibility of regular offerings at the University, or perhaps establishment of a permanent training center for Indian artists under sponsorship of the University of Arizona.[10]

The questions seem to make assumptions that are paternalistic at best. Most Indian artists had for centuries—including before the time of contact—been adapting traditional Indian cultural concepts to meet contemporary forms, media, and methods. Native arts often recognized by non-Indians as "traditional," such as Plains and Woodlands bead and ribbon work, Navajo weaving and silversmithing, Northwest Coast button blankets, and Plains star quilts, were all ingenious adaptations to change in availability of materials and tools and to evolving lifestyles. Moreover, the fundamentals of design—from the Native perspective—had always been taught in Indian communities and "absorbed" under varying conditions, including those of cultural change. Likewise, many young Indian artists had already been tutored by their elders in "traditional culture and archaeology" and that knowledge was reflected in their creative expression in one manner or another.[11] Clearly, the writers were either ignorant of, or blatantly chose to ignore, this rich history of Native aesthetics and indigenous education models that taught the arts in an integrated fashion as one component of larger cultural worldviews and belief systems. The proposal's ahistorical construct also suggests that the "traditional sources of inspiration" were stagnant in nature, their intellectual, philosophical, and spiritual meanings lacking the vitality and fluidity of living cultures. The final implication that "this type of student group" might be unable to adjust to academic learning and "still produce personally created work of quality" betrays racist undertones typical of many Indian education policies of the period.

While the proposal was being reviewed at the Rockefeller Foundation in New York, John Harrison from the foundation's Humanities Division traveled to Arizona to discuss details of this project for "educating the Indian artist and attempt[ing] to bring him into the mainstream of contemporary art without dropping his Indian heritage" with the university Indian art committee and university gallery director Robert Church. Harrison also visited Lloyd New and Charles Loloma in Scottsdale to discuss the "Indian art situation," as well as the University of Arizona workshops. New followed up with a letter outlining the two artists' perspective on the matter. He noted that the Rockefeller conference had served to draw attention to the crisis of rapid change facing Indian cultures. Because Indian creative expression was one manifestation of a tribal way of life that was threatened as "youngsters become educated in greater numbers, and as Indian parents relinquish Indian values in their continual adjustment as minority members in a fast moving majority world," warned New, certain art forms were doomed to decline unless a "substitute incentive" was found to encourage use of artistic abilities in a nontribal existence. The young Indian of today may not "in truth, subscribe to the same methods of expression as his forbears, and he has no encouragement to find himself as an artist in the personal sense." [12]

The University of Arizona workshops, New advised, would specifically tackle some of these problems. By providing a school for talented Indians, with special consideration for the needs of those from typical reservation backgrounds, they would fill a void left by the Bureau of Indian Affairs' educational programs and "normal institutions" geared only to the general development of artists without regard to specific cultural needs. This experimental arts program could serve to restore pride in Indian heritage, as well as to prevent segregation of the Indian artist by presenting him with a broad perspective in the arts.

Of critical importance to New was that the new school introduce the "personal creative approach" to the Indian artist and that the Indian artist be encouraged and allowed to "find himself" as a "creative artist":

> Under the present boot-strap operation of self-training and misguided helpers we find many potential artists grinding out the "acceptable thing" in a pseudo-artistic career, of no real value as art, however faithful, anthropologically speaking. Encouraged to test new media and to experiment with new methods we may expect Indian art to flourish only in proportion to its validity. This validity would contain truth of expression based upon tradition, but not necessarily limited to it; it would involve true creativity, and not slavish reproduction of old Indian form. [13]

Such a school, in New's mind, could be expected to provide leaders to set the pace for Indian art and would serve as a model for meeting the special needs of Indian students at other educational institutions. While enabling Indian artists to find themselves socially, culturally, and artistically, the school would also provide "new hope for an extension of Indian thought as a contribution to the American cultural scene." "How joyous it would be," concluded New, "to know that as each area of traditional expression dies out for natural and just reasons, that Indian youngsters may have discovered new forms of equal merit in new media, tapestry, sculpture, fabric design, mural work, ceramics, jewelry, weaving, mosaics, leather, and the fashion arts!"

In early February, Frederick Dockstader, director of the Museum of the American Indian and a member of the Indian Arts and Crafts Board, was asked to review the proposal. Dockstader felt that art was an excellent choice of subject area for an educational effort "because it will be easier for the Indian to acquire professional self-respect while in contact with his white counterparts than in most other fields. This is because they have something to say artistically and can readily recognize the validity of their work when it is placed next to the product of white students." He commended the inclusion of Indian artists on the faculty and noted that the participation of New, who had been both commercially as well as artistically successful, would be of particular importance. But he advised that New's presence could also lead to certain problems. His business posed somewhat of a conflict of interest, in that he would be in a position to hire Indian artists trained by the program. "Some people would criticize this aspect of the program saying Kiva [New] would take personal advantage of his connection to use the best of the artists within his own commercial enterprises," Dockstader warned. He also confided that, "Lloyd Kiva for all of his talents, perhaps because of them, was not personally popular with all of the faculty at the University of Arizona or with others who have concerned themselves with the problem of Indian arts and crafts over a long period of time." Moreover, he was concerned that New would prejudice the selection of students based upon their probability of being able to support themselves as full-time artists. "He will not be sympathetic to the Indian artist with something valid to say who will produce this art on a part-time basis." [14]

On 26 February the executive committee of the Rockefeller Foundation voted to award the University of Arizona $93,100—a full $30,400 more than originally requested—to establish special facilities for the professional training of Southwest Indian artists. [15] The funds were to be allocated in decreasing amounts over a four-year period ending in June 1964, with the assumption being that the university would gradually absorb the costs of the program. In addition to the series of summer workshops, the university was to supervise annual exhibits of traditional and contemporary Indian art that were to be shown at the University Art Gallery before and during the course of the workshops, as well as exhibits of selected pieces made by student participants in the summer sessions. Both exhibits would travel throughout Arizona and neighboring states. "This process," explained the Rockefeller resolution, "through its cumulative effect and the quality of the pieces shown, is calculated to make the public conscious of the best in contemporary Indian painting, design, and crafts to a degree not previously possible." The university subsequently made retention of one work produced by each student participant for its own permanent collections and one work for the period of one year for the purpose of the traveling exhibitions a condition of acceptance into the summer programs.[16]

The proposed program, according to the executive committee's resolution, represented a "new and unique approach to the problem of enabling the young Indian artist to make use of his abilities in a nontribal existence and still draw upon his heritage of spiritual and artistic values." The historical documentation for the proposal read like a verbal *End of the Trail,* with dire warnings of the endangerment of tribal cultures and impending doom that faced Native artistic traditions if outside intervention was not forthcoming:

> The traditional political status of the Southwest Indian as a ward of the state has kept him in a largely isolated and dependent position. This situation is now being fundamentally altered. The social change accompanying this process is particularly marked in the Southwest where the reservation system has in the past been more rigid and has involved a greater number of Indians than elsewhere in the United States. It is in the Southwest also where art has been most pervasive as an expression of tribal values. As the tribal core gradually disintegrates, the traditional art loses its meaning, function, and vitality. The young Indian artist must seek new forms of creative expression that draw upon his cultural heritage without slavishly reproducing old Indian forms the value of which both as art and as an expression of moral and social standards no longer exists.[17]

Further paraphrasing Lloyd New's 29 January letter to Harrison, the resolution went on to conclude that the University of Arizona workshops would "enable Indian artists to find themselves socially, culturally, and artistically" and would "provide new hope for an extension of Indian thought as a contribution to the American cultural scene," while providing leaders to "set the pace for other Indian artists."

Dean Little immediately sent letters to those who had attended the Rockefeller conference—as well as other interested individuals—announcing the

Southwestern Indian Art Project and seeking names of nominees to attend the first workshop, to be held 6 June through 16 July. Applicants were required to be between seventeen and twenty-four years of age, and successful candidates would receive room and board, materials, travel to and from Tucson, and tuition. "The objects of the program," read the letter, "are to give young potential artists a thorough knowledge of their own artistic heritage and traditions, of the great world art traditions, of design as it applies to their own art products, and of contemporary tools, materials and techniques. It is, in sum, a program designed to offer the student-artist a means to use his own unique background in meeting the commercial and aesthetic demands of our modern society." With this in mind, the students' interest in art as a career was one of the criteria for their selection.[18]

Lloyd New conducted interviews with applicants in the Phoenix area and western Arizona, while Andreas Andersen covered the agencies and schools of northern Arizona and New Mexico. Joe Herrera, from Cochiti Pueblo, arranged for Andersen's interviews in Taos, Santa Fe, and Albuquerque. Herrera had been a participant in the Rockefeller Tucson conference and was to join the project's faculty as a painting instructor. The son of noted San Ildefonso painter Tonita Peña, Herrera had received his B.A. in art at the University of New Mexico in 1953, after attending Dorothy Dunn's Studio. At UNM he had studied with modernist painter Raymond Jonson, and the two had simultaneously developed modern visual vocabularies derived from Pueblo pictographs and kiva murals. Herrera's innovations had won him widespread acclaim, a one-person show at the Museum of New Mexico, and numerous awards. At this time Herrera was also employed by the State of New Mexico's Department of Education as a guidance and placement officer.[19]

Though the project was limited to the Southwest, recommendations for prospective students came from all over the country, including Alaska. By the opening week twenty-seven students selected by the workshop directors and university committee from more than one hundred applicants had arrived in Tucson. Most were high school seniors, and while many had had experience in the areas of painting or silversmithing, few had worked in pottery or weaving. They were greeted by a faculty comprised of Lloyd New (fabrics), Andreas Andersen (painting), Ruth Brown (fabrics), Maurice Grossman (silverwork and ceramics), Joe Herrera (painting), Charles Loloma (silverwork), Otellie Loloma (ceramics), Mable Morrow (fabrics and fashion design), Andrew Rush (films and lecture), and Clara Lee Tanner (traditional Indian art and anthropology). Of these, four were Indian (New, Herrera, and the Lolomas). The majority of the non-Indian faculty had little or no previous experience teaching Indian students.[20]

The first session consisted of viewing the newly installed exhibit of traditional and contemporary Indian art, with accompanying commentary by gallery director Robert Church and Lloyd New. The collections on display included Hopi kachinas and a woven sash, Pueblo pottery, a Chilkat blanket, Navajo textiles and jewelry, and basketry from various southwestern tribes, all intermingled with contemporary Indian painting and New's own textiles. The remainder of the week was concerned with general orientation and intensive lectures on southwestern and pre-Columbian cultures and the fundamentals of design. This was supplemented by a marathon showing of films, including an "experimental" group—*Energies, Boundary Lines, Begone Dull Care, Poulette Grise, Art and Motion,* and *Rhythm in Paint*—dealing with abstract art principles and design, as well as five "ethnic" films from the university on history and Indian tradition—*Lascaux, Prehistoric Images, Story of Prehistoric Man, Pre-Columbian Mexican Art,* and *Indians of Early America.*[21]

The typical curriculum thereafter was divided between the morning lecture series and afternoons spent in the studios. Lecture topics included Indian art and archaeology, the history of world art, and design fundamentals. Students could then choose to work in any medium, with studios being kept open from 8 A.M. to 11 P.M. daily. Faculty instructed by participation and demonstration, and were discouraged from imposing any particular style or approach. There was a concerted effort, however, to encourage students to try something new.[22] The film series continued with a group of nonobjective studies in color, shape, and rhythm—*Yantra, Obmaru, Sophisticated Vamp, Raga,* and *Logos*—and a selection of titles from Western art history surveys, supplemented with documentary films on modern masters provided by the Museum of Modern Art.

In addition to their work in the classrooms and studios, faculty held informal discussion sessions at meals, and some invited students to their homes for activities. Concerts, a visit to the astronomical observatory, movies, and excursions to the mountains were included in the project's schedule. The university's report glows with photos of students enjoying themselves in the pool at Dean Little's desert home and at patio parties given by UA president Harvill.

At the close of the workshop, Frederick Dockstader, director of the Museum of the American Indian and the keynote speaker for the Rockefeller conference in Tucson, was invited to visit the campus and offer his critique of the program and the exhibition of student work displayed in the University Art Gallery. His written report was submitted to the Rockefeller Foundation in September 1960. On the whole very complimentary, Dockstader's evaluation praised those involved with the workshops for their dedication and accomplishments. He found the university very supportive and nothing spared in terms of equipment, studios, supplies, and general working conditions. Students, Dockstader observed, were enthusiastic, worked well together, and demonstrated remarkable potential. They were not reluctant to experiment, and Dockstader concluded that one of the greatest values of the workshops was the opportunity afforded the participants to explore new techniques and materials. Faculty allowed students free rein and did not dictate styles. Proof of their success in this regard was to be found in the quality and nature of the closing student show. "To the surprise of many," wrote Dockstader, "so-called 'traditional' Indian art was not overwhelming in this display, nor was it a completely 'modern art' exhibit. Actually, the exhibit showed a healthy balance, with works which would have been completely eligible as a demonstration of the art program of any school on a comparable level." [23]

Of particular merit, commended Dockstader, was the faculty's ability to facilitate the critique process among the participants. "For an Indian student to learn to accept criticism of his work is unusual. . . . It was a pleasure to sit in on the critique sessions and watch the reactions of the class as various works were examined, criticized by the faculty and students, and note the degree to which the artist understood, and accepted, these comments." At least one student remembers these sessions somewhat differently, however. Hopi artist Michael Kabotie, one of the two youngest participants in the 1960 workshop, vividly recalls one particular critique that was less than the ideal witnessed by Dockstader. With much of his time and energies being consumed by Tucson movie theaters rather than studio work, Kabotie had been visited midway into the program by Lloyd New, who threatened to send him home and talk to his father (Fred Kabotie) if his conduct did not improve. He then tried to hurriedly make up work before his scheduled critique:

> I remember, like they had this unusual habit, where you did some things and they put it up on the chalkboards and everybody said, well, oh, yeah, that's good, that's great, this is not art, and all of that. I guess they call it critiques. And that was something foreign to me, new to me, and I remembered the following day was my turn, to have my works critiqued, but I was enjoying John Wayne killing those Osage and Cherokees who spoke Navajo, downtown.
>
> But I remember this visit from Lloyd New . . . so I sat up all night that night, and when you're about 16 or 17, you know . . . and you're in that cartoon stage of your life, where you draw nothing but cartoons, and that's what I did. I sat up all night drawing these kachina clowns and kachinas with tennis shoes and with ropes, and things like that, and I remember the following day I went into class and I put them on a chalk-

board. And there was this old sort of like a Marine sergeant art teacher there named Andrew Rushing. I put them up and everybody sat down, and he gets up and looks at them and says, "This isn't art." And he gets up and he grabs all of my works and threw them into the trash can. And that was a real shocker for me. And I sit there and I'm stunned by this whole thing.[24]

Thereafter, Kabotie was taken under the wing of Joe Herrera, who talked with the bewildered youth about his Hopi tradition of painting and shared examples of Herrera's work derived from kiva murals. Kabotie then began working on his own adaptations in chalk.

Dockstader criticized the curriculum as far too ambitious for a short-term program and for "students with such serious background limitations." Faculty expectations, he explained, were unrealistic. "There had been a strong anticipation of working with mature, artistically developed individuals who would readily respond to any stimulus. Instead, the program proved one of how to reach people with a latent (or only occasionally well-developed) talent, but who had never enjoyed a sense of encouragement in their art, or an exposure to non-Indian art experiences." Dockstader also advised that greater care be exercised in the selection of students so as to minimize problems caused by an unwieldy age span (seventeen to twenty-nine) and a broad spectrum of attitudes and competency in the arts. "This session . . . made it obvious," wrote Dockstader, "that 'political' selections should be avoided; those few students who had been chosen because of parental importance in the arts were also the ones who proved less successful."[25]

Dockstader's recommendations concerning the nonstudio components of the curriculum were dominated by his low assessment of students' knowledge and preparation. With regard to the design lectures, Dockstader claimed that, "previously, most of these people had never realized that such a thing existed, and the problem of thinking of design . . . was a troubling novelty." The faculty had, nonetheless, made progress in overcoming barriers of terminology, reported Dockstader, and were able to persuade students to "think about art in formal and objective terms." The art history course work was equally problematic, according to Dockstader. "As far as the Lecture Series is concerned, I have the impression that the European background became too dominant. It seemed to be too ambitious an attempt for this group, and of questionable value. These people need primarily to discover where they fit into the American picture—they need orientation to assist them to meld into the art of America, both Indian and non-Indian." Dockstader recommended that the following year consideration be given to presentation of the Indian and non-Indian arts of North America.[26]

By far Dockstader's greatest concern, however, was with the general lack of clarity or understanding of the program's principal goals. "The sense of confusion communicated itself to the students," he observed, "and resulted in some insecurity and bewilderment." His own perception of the workshop's purpose was that it was to allow promising Indian students interested in the arts an opportunity to experiment in various media and learn new techniques and approaches to be used in later work. They were to take all this back to their respective homes, resulting in a "healthy spread of influences" that could provide "a stimulus for Indian Art throughout the Southwest in time to come."[27]

Dockstader added that he believed the program was intended to go beyond simply turning out a given number of Indian artists or presenting certain factual or visual material to a select group of students. It was also designed to teach the teachers, allowing educators to "experiment, explore techniques, and devise methods which would enable them to more successfully handle the problems of the Indian Art student." The participants represented, Dockstader explained, a unique minority, unlike any other group, and "unless those unique features are discovered and thoroughly understood, and a way found to cope with them, not only will Indian education in the arts (and the non-art fields as well) be affected, but any hope of developing a strong Indian citizenry will be adversely affected. Perhaps a way can be found through such a seemingly minor field as Indian Art training."[28] Not only were these goals not commonly understood by faculty, according to Dockstader, but some seemed to be in opposition to them:

> As a final word, I cannot help but remark that too often I encountered expressions designed to indicate a feeling that there was not complete harmony in the presentation of the curriculum. This seemed to spring from a feeling that some of the Faculty were relatively unsympathetic with the basic premises of the Workshop, even though they gave willingly and thoroughly of their time and energy. Unfortunately, Indians are extremely sensitive to this point; mayhap overly so. But it must be considered, and if not obliterated, at least more carefully concealed.[29]

Lloyd New later characterized the differences between faculty as falling along ethnic lines, with the Indian faculty finding the non-Indian faculty's views "controversial." "The way it turned out," New recalled, "was that the Indian group moved on up to the Institute of American Indian Arts and did their own thing. We didn't pay much attention about their ideas, about European values."[30]

Indeed, at this early stage in the project, the proposed new school in Santa

Fe was already raising questions and quandaries in the minds of those involved in the workshops at Tucson. In a portion of his report entitled "What of the Future?" Dockstader wondered what relationship the Rockefeller program would find with this new Indian art school. "Much of the answer lies with Santa Fe," he reasoned, "and the direction in which the latter develops may well make this question academic. But it would seem most practicable for the Workshop to develop into something of a 'graduate course' for the more talented students after they go through the Santa Fe school." The matter was not of immediate concern, however, and Dockstader concluded his report on a promising note: "The six weeks just past gave a whole new view of art to twenty-seven Indian artists. Many of these will spread this influence to their fellows. I eagerly await the results of this expanding horizon, and look forward to the conclusion of next year's Workshop with every confidence that these students, too, will emerge with an even greater degree of enthusiasm and sense of achievement."[31]

Project faculty also submitted evaluations of the program's success. The summaries of these did not necessarily reflect the cultural split described by New. Andreas Andersen readily acknowledged that basic misunderstandings regarding the philosophy of the project had developed early. "This revolved around the proportion of appreciation of Indian art to be taught in relation to world art in general," noted Andersen. "The main point of difference was whether to break away immediately from the traditional Indian form or to use it as point of departure or to maintain it and build upon it." Andersen recommended that regardless of the end result, "traditional identity" should be the starting point in the project's studios. "The project would not serve its purpose were we to demand an immediate break with Indian tradition and attempt to impose an alien (Anglo) tradition upon them," he cautioned.[32]

New likewise maintained that "Indian art whatever its variations from art in its multiargumentative broad sense is the very core of the project. Indian art may be a craft art, a folk art, a primitive art, but whatever it is it should be honored and accepted as it is and used as a firm basis for all the artistic experiences of these Indian youngsters." New contended that if the foundation were laid for the students' cultural identity, they would be prepared to make their own decisions about the course their art would take. "Against this personal strength then [the student] is in a position to absorb or reject all other artistic experiences in a plus or minor [sic] sense." But he insisted that the concept of Indian art as a "moving art" should be emphasized, and "the artistic should be stressed to the point where all other considerations are secondary." Joe Herrera noted that students exhibited "some resistance to change from the conventional and highly decorative stylization to the new and strange art of which they were completely unfamiliar either from personal experience or observation" but added that the young people who had participated were talented and "deep inside them is the basic Indian attitude of life which directs them consciously and unconsciously."[33]

Most of the faculty, both Indian and non-Indian, seemed frustrated by the maturity level of the students, with some recommending the age limit be increased and others calling for more stringent applicant screening. Several complained about the inordinate emphasis placed on drawing and painting—in the selection of applicants, in the collections chosen for display, and in the organization of the sessions—which hampered their efforts in clay, textiles, and jewelry. Dissatisfaction with the lecture series was nearly unanimous. Closer integration between the lectures on Indian traditions, world arts, and the principles of design, as well as better facilitation with studio work, was demanded.[34]

The university committee on Indian art included in its final report to the Rockefeller Foundation ten recommendations for the 1961 session based on these faculty concerns. The age range was to be between eighteen and twenty-five. All applicants were to personally interview with New, Andersen, or Dean Little before being awarded a scholarship so as to "be sure that the individual's motivation for art as a career is reasonably high and also that he has some valid experience in art before he comes to the project." Enrollment was to be limited to twenty-five students to prevent overcrowding in the craft areas. Weaving was to be eliminated as a division of instruction, and fashion design was to be omitted as a separate course. The exhibition of traditional Indian material designed for student use "as inspiration" was to be adjusted so as to have a better balance between painting and "craft." More emphasis was to be given to design and its integration within the studio activity, in part by requiring all students to attend basic design studio work. In order to effect better coordination of the lectures, it was decided that the subjects of world art and Indian traditions would become the responsibility of one instructor, rather than three. Moreover, the non-Indian faculty was to be increased, with the additional instructor to work in either ceramics or metal.[35]

The report otherwise extolled the project's success, claiming that "both the quality and quantity of student work was far better than originally had been anticipated." Reflecting upon the project's origins and goals, the committee noted, "These students would presumably have had little contact with world traditions or with contemporary movements, and little awareness of the varied forms of Indian arts expression. Each would be a talented person who might, without training and guidance, remain a craftsman in his tribal or area tradition." It was hoped that the workshop would help students to develop an "individual creative consciousness," exploring to its fullest potential their talent in art without the loss of pride in being Indian. The committee claimed that students seemed to grasp the purpose of the project earlier than expected and that participant reaction to the methods and scope of instruction was favorable to the extent that all but two expressed the desire to return the following year. "The exhibition which was installed consisting of student work indicated visually that the anticipated goal for the first year had been reached," concluded the report.[36]

The second year, seven returning students joined sixteen new recruits on the Tucson campus. Changes reflecting the faculty's evaluations were newly in place. The lecture program had been consolidated under one instructor and had been revised so as to reflect a more contemporary focus, with Roy Sieber from Iowa State University being brought in to replace Clara Lee Tanner. There had been some criticism of Tanner's lectures, which according to Lloyd New, left students "on the verge of coming out from the Stone Age period" and going around saying, "Hey, Joe, did you bring your stone ax today?" A number of faculty had complained that too much class time had been devoted to anthropology at the expense of adequately addressing issues of Indian identity. Sieber's classes, New happily reported to the Rockefeller Foundation, consisted of presentations on Indian and non-Indian art "with emphasis upon the aesthetic qualities as opposed to the anthropological or historical point of view" and "served as an excellent basis for an understanding of the universal principles of design."[37]

The lectures were greatly enhanced by a more diverse and extensive opening exhibition and Native art objects provided for use in the classrooms. In February, Dean Little and Andreas Andersen had traveled to New York to consult with Dockstader on selections from the Museum of the American Indian to be loaned for these purposes.

The film series continued virtually unchanged. This drew positive reviews from many students and faculty alike. "The concentrated film program," wrote Lloyd New in his concluding evaluation, "dealing with subject matter in areas of art processes, biographies of artists, sound and motion series, and other cultures seemed to help in the orientation of these young aspiring artists to the world into which they would find themselves as artists— craftsmen." The material "presented to these young kids," he was to later relate, was such that it "couldn't do anything but unsettle them so badly that they would have to find out who they were, in order to survive." Fritz Scholder, who interrupted his education at Sacramento State College to participate in the 1961 workshop, also recalled these sessions as particularly impactive. "We were subjected to a real bombardment program. Films every day and banquets every night. We must have seen ten movies a day. Everything from Museum of Modern Art films to some really experimental stuff. The students in the program represented a wide spectrum of Indian artists—from city Indians, like me, to really traditional artists. The program blew a lot of minds, especially the more traditional ones." [38] George Burdeau, a Blackfeet filmmaker who was sixteen when he attended the second Rockefeller workshop, concurred:

> It was really difficult for, I think, most of the Indian students who were there in that classroom to sit in this sort of very foreign setting and to have to be exposed to these images in the way that we were exposed. But I have to say, that in many cases in talking to some of the members afterwards, when we have talked about that period of time, there were a lot of things that happened in that room, that when we saw Picasso or we saw Henry Moore, or whatever, classical architecture, it really was eye-opening for us. It did something for what was going to happen later in a lot of the work that came out. [39]

Faculty seemed to find the coordination between the lectures, design program, and studio work greatly improved. With respect to the studio curriculum, print making had been added as a minor subject and painting was now integrated with UA's regular summer session classes. This latter move was in anticipation of the university's agreement to assume full responsibility for the program at the end of the Rockefeller funding period. S. Radakovich, a personal friend of the Rockefeller Foundation's John Harrison, had joined the faculty to teach metalwork. Students were now housed in regular university dormitories, rather than having separate facilities, but a special dining area was maintained in the student union, allowing the joint faculty and student informal discussion sessions in the evenings to continue.

The format of the student terminal exhibition was changed to employ a series of photographic panels explaining the pedagogical concept of the project in the entrance gallery, with a photograph of each student accompanied by individual exhibits in two additional galleries. Students were responsible for the selection and display of their pieces. Examples of older Indian arts were, meanwhile, interspersed among the student work. The show drew a crowd of four hundred to its opening. Printed programs for this preview included a brief introductory statement by Dean Little that emphatically stated the project's objectives and proclaimed its success: "This exhibition of student work demonstrated clearly that traditional tribal expression and a progressive contemporary approach are compatible. During the development of these studies the students have been urged to maintain their pride of heritage as Indians while working with natural forms in a contemporary spirit. The results testify that in so doing each student has begun to express professional talent in the art media of his choice."[40]

Frederick Dockstader, invited once again to evaluate the program and critique the final show, was more tempered in his assessment. While he deemed the majority of the work shown to be "quite excellent," he was disturbed by the degree of faculty influence evident in some of the student art. "This is certainly unavoidable in any teaching situation . . . and yet there was a sameness in certain expressions which seemed to my eyes unduly related to similar work for which the particular teacher was known. This seemed true in both the textile, ceramic, and metal fields." Of greater concern to Dockstader was a perceived lack of any discernible quality of "Indianness":

> It is a paradox that this exhibit could well be presented in any gallery in the country, without any identifying title, and there would be little indication of the ethnic origin of the show. This is both good and bad. It is certainly a tribute to the faculty to achieve such freedom of expression that a traditional art basis is not forced through, willy-nilly. On the other hand, it is certain that there is yet a great challenge ahead for the teacher to find out how to inculcate the artistic concepts of our contemporary world while at the same time not cause the artist to lose those very qualities of identification which are so highly prized.[41]

Similar reservations were expressed by Lloyd New in his 1961 evaluation. While New had been the prime exponent of a "personal creative approach" freed from "slavish reproduction of old Indian form," and still recommended that "emphasis should be on experiences of handling painting materials, rather than undue concern about whether they paint in the so-called Indian style," he also harbored certain misgivings about the direction of the project:

> I think we should again take stock at this point to see where we are heading with reference to our obligation to the special nature of an art project dealing with young Indians exclusively. And while our stated purpose is to see how young Indian artists and craftsmen react to formal instructional methods designed to help them discover individual personal creative powers, and to learn about art in its universal sense, are we not primarily interested in seeing how much of the resulting expression may be uniquely Indian, reflecting the particular qualities of a different culture? . . .
>
> It worries me sometimes that we sometimes take the attitude in our approaches to the program here that our first responsibility is to fit the

Indian artist into the world of art in general, and the sooner he gets into the mainstream of the universality of art, the better off he will be. . . . From the point of view that this program is exploratory by nature, I prefer not to take the stand at this particular time that this is our primary objective.

It may be that the real values of this project will be, with further study and analyses of the driving forces of these youngsters, that of finding out there is a legitimate culturally different expression to be considered. This is not to say that the culturally different expression should carry artificial merit just because of its existence, or that it should not be judged by the rules of universal art. My fear is we may unduly hasten assimilation in artistic expression by subtle means at our command, and in doing so jeopardize the hopes implied by this project that there is a contribution to be made by Indians to the general cultural stream. Our job is to find out what form it takes, if any, how different is it, is it honest, etc.[42]

Dockstader ended his report enthusiastically, proclaiming that the project had become "more than just an experiment"; it was now an enterprise with a "strong feeling of confidence concerning goals to be achieved, and a greater degree of skill in accomplishing those goals." He cautioned, however, for the need to follow up on workshop participants, noting that once a student left "he may or may not continue a healthy development." No contact was maintained with former students, other than with those who returned for successive workshops. Paternalistically, Dockstader charged that, "those who continue on their own may be swallowed up by the reservation and these six weeks prove to be no more than a pleasant interlude, with little beneficial results."[43]

The university's report concluded by saying that the following statement drawn from Lloyd New's evaluation expressed the philosophy and goals for the project held by both the university committee and the teaching faculty:

Orient these Indian youngsters with pride through knowledge of their own cultural history, having them identify with their particular artistic heritage and understand it better by having a knowledge of world arts. Teach them the secrets of creative expression based upon a thorough knowledge of the universal principles of art. . . . Encourage them to use this knowledge of cultural tradition as a springboard for personal creative artistic expression. If a youngster is a product of a living tribal culture, and he identifies with that culture, then I would expect his art to be less creative and more within the style of that group. With the purely creative minded Indian youngster I would hope for reflections of his heritage. If no reflections were there then I would hope that he had some strong identity with his own private world, and I would help him find his creative strengths as an artist with reference to this background, Indian or not.[44]

Those connected with the workshop agreed, wrote Dean Little in the report's introduction, that "a workable approach to this special problem has been found and that the young Indian student can be trained to work and to think in a contemporary manner, without apparent sacrifice to his tribal traditions."[45]

Plans were readied to send the student exhibition on tour with stops in New York City at the Rockefeller Foundation headquarters and the American Craftsman Museum, as well as showings in Native communities. The exhibit did, in fact, tour nationally but was displayed at Iowa State University, the Philbrook Art Center in Tulsa, Oklahoma, the Heard Museum in Phoenix, the Pacific Arts Association conference in Seattle, and the American Institute of Decorators meeting in Chicago. At the latter venue three students were among the eight recipients of international awards for excellence in their textile work. In addition, UA's President Harvill had the school's Radio-TV Bureau produce a short film of the exhibition.[46]

The Rockefeller Foundation, meanwhile, touted the project as representative of their successful worldwide educational programs. A *New York Times* photo featured ceramics students in Tucson alongside pictures of Tibetan refugee religious leaders lecturing at the University of Washington, researchers at the University College of Rhodesia and Nyasaland collecting ticks for health studies, and graduate students in the Sudan training in the field of agriculture. The caption of the project photo explained that "in workshops at the University of Arizona, talented young Indian artists learn to seek new forms that will draw upon their cultural heritage without reflecting a way of life that no longer exists."[47]

Much of the planning for the project's third year centered around adjusting the workshops to developments in Santa Fe. Dean Little wrote to the Rockefeller Foundation's John Harrison in December 1961 regarding the changes the new BIA art school there might require:

> I am not sure that you are aware of the Santa Fe situation, but we have learned that there has been a very substantial government appropriation to reestablish the Santa Fe school along pretty much the same lines as we have been operating under your sponsorship at the University of Arizona—undoubtedly partly because of our project here. I gather that their intention is to do precisely what we are doing but on a larger scale and at the moment it would appear to me that our future

here would be to draw from that school those topnotch students who would be appropriate to put on a regular status with scholarship help to available Indian scholarships at the University of Arizona rather than to try to carry on a smaller repetitive program here. This might be the basis for our low-budget fourth year effort.[48]

Little added that Lloyd New had been approached to be the director (in fact, the art director) of the school and that if he accepted he would be moving to Santa Fe. The project's other codirector, Andreas Andersen, was expected to leave the University of Arizona for a position at the Otis Art Institute of Los Angeles. This created a considerable void in faculty continuity for the workshops. Harrison's friend Radakovich, meanwhile, had not worked well with the students and would not be asked to return for another season.

With all this in mind, Little suggested a revision of the program for the summer of 1962. He requested approval to invite only returning students to participate. Students in the area of ceramics and metalwork would join those in painting in being integrated into UA's regular summer session. Emphasis would be placed on production and marketing, as well as design. Individuals in a position to determine the commercial possibilities of the students' work would be brought in at the end of the workshops for consultation. Little had earlier proposed that representatives from fabric houses and craft outlets be present at the terminal exhibit, prepared to purchase student work. New had also recommended such a shift in focus in his 1961 evaluation. "More attention should be paid to the economics of the artist-craftsman," wrote New, with production costs, selling relationships, bookkeeping and finance, promotion and salesmanship, and the location of proper markets given more coverage than in previous years.[49]

By April, Little had learned that New, Otellie Loloma, and Charles Loloma had all accepted positions at the Institute of American Indian Arts in Santa Fe, although each had agreed to teach for the summer workshop already scheduled for 1962.[50] He felt compelled to reduce the program for 1963. Harrison responded by reassuring Little of his contribution to the burgeoning institute, which now seemed to jeopardize the Southwestern Indian Art Project, and suggested that foundation monies could be reprogrammed to suit these recent developments. "Certainly everyone realizes that the new school at Santa Fe is a tribute both to the University of Arizona's conceptualization and more particularly your careful and thoughtful administration of this Indian art program," Harrison soothed. "In fact, it seems fairly clear to all that the concept and success of your program were basic to the decision to open the Indian art school." Harrison added that, if after observing the school's progress Little decided that Arizona could more effectively aid the development of Indian artists by using the Rockefeller funds for fellowships to enable graduates of the Santa Fe school to take advanced work within UA's regular curriculum, the terms of the grant could probably be changed to accommodate such a request. Little began to work on these revisions, requesting that a portion of the Rockefeller funds be used to supplement a scholarship offered by the Rochester School for American Craftsmen to the outstanding student of the 1962 session.[51]

In December, Little spoke with Chadbourne Gilpatric, deputy director for the humanities and social sciences at the Rockefeller Foundation. He reiterated his frustrations regarding the latest developments in Santa Fe. He charged that Lloyd Kiva, "who has dropped the use of his last name (New) to emphasize his Indian status," had had some difficulty in building staff and students at the new school and in his efforts to do so had been drawing on both the faculty and students of the University of Arizona program. He pleaded for a restructuring of the project's last year and Gilpatric concurred.[52]

Little then drafted a written request to the foundation's board. He explained that had it not been for the unexpected turn of events of the past year, there would have been no question about fulfillment of the project as originally conceived. "We feel our efforts up to this point have been highly successful, noted Little, "and also that we have been able to establish teaching methods which have permitted us to approach the goals we sought when the project was initiated in 1959. A measure of this success lies in the fact that the curriculum and method established for the project has been adopted in its entirety for the new Santa Fe school—which also took our three Indian instructors and sixteen of our best students." As the 1963 session would face an entirely new faculty and new students, Little requested that the summer workshops for Indian students alone be eliminated and in their stead a few individuals "of particular abilities" be selected for full subsidy to study in regular university sessions—summer and academic. This would, according to Little, complete a third phase in Indian art education: "In the first year of our project, under a protected environment, this student has made an initial contact with contemporary art and practice from the view of his particular background. He has solidified this new knowledge with further familiarization and technical training after the first defenses were dissolved. (Second and third years of the project.)" Thus, the student's transition from "special education" to a regular university curriculum in art would be accomplished.[53]

Little's proposed budget for 1963 included $2,500 for student Michael Penrod's second year at the School for American Craftsmen at Rochester, $5,000 for two new students at Rochester, $1,750 to continue Fritz Scholder at the University of Arizona on full fellowship, $4,500 for two new students for summer and regular sessions at UA, and $3,600 in regular session scholarships for students to be selected from the group at Santa Fe. The remainder of the funds were to be used for "hardship" family allowances, faculty travel for recruitment, and the publication of a final report (the session report for 1962 was to be combined with the 1963 report). The request was approved by the foundation's executive committee on 4 February 1963.[54]

The Southwestern Indian Art Project thus formally ceded its Indian art education experiment to the Institute of American Indian Arts. In their final report, the university committee stated that their goal had been twofold. First, to determine if a translation from pure tribal art into a more modern expression could be made without sacrifice to the tradition that produced it. Second, if the first stage proved successful, "to train as many young artists as possible in this revived approach so that they could return to the tribal centers and the Indian schools and begin the long artistic reorientation of an even younger generation." They had been unusually successful and fruitful on both counts, they concluded. As evidence of this, they cited the accomplishments of their students. Two were attending the Rochester School for American Craftsmen on full scholarships. Three others were enrolled in the regular session at the University of Arizona. Fritz Scholder had just finished his graduate studies there and was teaching at the new school in Santa Fe. Students had been awarded national art prizes in painting, silverwork, and textiles. All these students produced "outstanding work and seemed to retain the philosophy of Indian Art that was developed during the first summer project sessions."[55]

The project represented the practical application of the tenets that emerged from the Rockefeller conference of 1959—modernist individualism as expressed in New's emphasis on the "personal creative approach," d'Harnoncourt's redirection of focus from the anthropological and historical to the aesthetic, and modern applications of traditional forms. The project's staff operated from the supposition that the way in which to best achieve these reforms within the realm of Indian art was through education of the young Indian artist and that the guidance that such youth required was not to be found in their own communities.

Indeed, the value of those communities and the student's Native culture seemed to be acknowledged only as a source of inspiration from which to depart—New's "springboard for personal creative ideas." The project was in sum, by its own description, "designed to offer the student-artist a means to use his own unique background in meeting the commercial and aesthetic demands of our modern society." And though the project organizers claimed that they had determined that "a translation from pure tribal art into a more modern expression could be made without sacrifice to the tradition which produced it," there is no evidence that anyone seriously examined those traditions nor the sacrifices that were indeed at issue. For the goal was always the fit with the dominant society rather than the Native. The challenge, as Dockstader had described it, was "to find out how to inculcate the artistic concepts of our contemporary world while at the same time not cause the artist to lose those very qualities of identification which are so highly prized." The study and analysis required to discover the "legitimate culturally different expression to be considered," mentioned by New, seems never to have commanded the project's attention.

The groundwork was clearly laid for the direction to be taken by the new school in Santa Fe. There the New and Rockefeller conference philosophy would marry the ideologies of BIA educational priorities and New Frontier politics. And the Institute of American Indian Arts would be born.

CHAPTER 3

THE INSTITUTE OF AMERICAN INDIAN ARTS
A Tumultuous Gestation, 1960 – 1962

Contrary to popular perception, the Institute of American Indian Arts was not a direct outgrowth of the Southwestern Indian Art Project, but rather a parallel and contemporary development that quickly superseded the Tucson workshops as a permanent manifestation of the University of Arizona experiment. While the Rockefeller Foundation was planning the Directions in Indian Art conference with Lloyd New, Charles Loloma, and UA faculty, Rene d'Harnoncourt was busily meeting with Commissioner of Indian Affairs Glenn Emmons, Director of Indian Education Hildegard Thompson, educator George Boyce of the Intermountain Indian School in Utah (see fig. 2), and Assistant Secretary of the Interior Roger C. Ernst regarding the Bureau of Indian Affairs' support, or lack thereof, for Indian arts and, more specifically, for Indian arts education. It was during the course of their discussions that the idea of the Institute of American Indian Arts was conceived and given its first official sanction. It is, therefore, critical to examine closely the key players at this meeting, as their philosophies regarding federal Indian policy and Indian education would in due course strongly influence the school's curriculum, pedagogy, and basic operations.[1]

FIG. 2. George Boyce.

D'Harnoncourt, who had requested the meeting, was at the time serving as director of the Rockefellers' Museum of Modern Art and vice president of Nelson Rockefeller's Museum of Primitive Art, as well as chair of the Indian Arts and Crafts Board. Emmons, Thompson, and Boyce's Indian Service careers had been intertwined and synergistic for the past six years, each working in a separate capacity during the terminationist 1950s to prepare Indian peoples for assimilation into mainstream society.

Glenn Emmons had been Bureau of Indian Affairs commissioner since 1953. A Gallup banker who had run unsuccessfully for governor of New Mexico on an anti–New Deal, probusiness platform, Emmons had been instrumental in Eisenhower's electoral victory in the state in 1952. Partially in recompense for that campaign work, and most assuredly because of his complete faith in the sanctity of private enterprise and industrial development, Emmons was rewarded with the top political position in Indian affairs, despite the fact that he had no previous experience in this realm.[2]

Ten days before Emmons took office Congress adopted House Concurrent Resolution 108, the legal impetus for termination. While not having the authority of law, the measure set a clearly defined course for Indian policy that had at its heart the abolition of the trust status of Indian lands, the legal status of Indian nations as sovereign, and with these, all special services to Indian peoples. This intent was succinctly and euphemistically stated in the resolution's introduction: "It is the policy of Congress, as rapidly as possible, to make the Indians within the territorial limits of the United States subject to the same laws and entitled to the same privileges and responsibilities as are applicable to other citizens of the United States, to end their status as wards of the United States, and to grant them all of the rights and prerogatives pertaining to American citizenship."[3]

The resolution targeted all Indian tribes located within the states of California, Florida, New York, and Texas, as well as the Flathead tribe of Montana, the Klamaths of Oregon, the Menominees of Wisconsin, the Potawatomis of Kansas and Nebraska, and the Turtle Mountain Chippewas of North Dakota for termination "from Federal supervision and control and from the disabilities and limitations specially applicable to Indians." This accomplished, all offices of the Bureau of Indian Affairs previously serving terminated tribes would be abolished. The resolution further directed the secretary of the interior to review all existing legislation and treaties dealing with those tribes and to report to Congress no later than 1 January 1954 his recommendations for "legislation as, in his judgment, may be necessary to accomplish the purposes of this resolution." The measure passed with minimal debate, the Eighty-third Congress being preoccupied with the more pressing matters of the Korean conflict and the posturings of the senator from Wisconsin, Joseph R. McCarthy.

Termination sentiments had been building for nearly ten years, World War II having served as a catalyst in a number of respects. An estimated twenty-five thousand American Indians served in the armed forces during that time, and up to three hundred Indian women were members of the nurses' corps, military auxiliaries, the Red Cross, and the American Women's Voluntary Service. An additional fifty thousand Native men and women worked in war industries and on the railroads. Most were assured of returning to dismal poverty on their home reservations at war's end. Popular support for Indian reform, characterized by a heightened nationalism that lauded the Indian's patriotic wartime service and a belief that Indian soldiers had demonstrated their ability to function and contribute in the non-Indian world, began to emerge.[4]

One of the earliest expressions of this view came in an article written by O. K. Armstrong and published in a 1945 *Reader's Digest* entitled "Set the American Indians Free!" Its lead page illustrated with a drawing of an Indian soldier in uniform silhouetted by the profile of a stereotypical Plains warrior in full war bonnet, the article recounted briefly the history of federal Indian policy, characterizing early reservations as "concentration camps" and criticizing trust relationships regarding land use and ownership as fostering a system of "perpetual guardianship." The Indians had never been "emancipated," the author charged, and continued to be restricted in property rights and to live under conditions of racial segregation.[5]

"More than 22,000 Indians are serving with our fighting forces," Armstrong declared. "Many have given their lives; many more have won decorations. There can be no doubt that all who return from the service will seek a greater share in America's freedom." The article called for legislation that would remove restrictions from "every Indian who is able to manage his affairs" (according to Armstrong this should include veterans, graduates of high school, and all Indians born henceforth) and a redirection of the Bureau of Indian Affairs toward assisting all Indians to be self-supporting. "We're tired of being treated like museum pieces," the author quoted Frank Beaver, a Winnebago sergeant in the Army Air Corps, "I'm a mechanic. I want a real job. They're not going to send me back to live in a shack and loaf around in a blanket!"[6]

Two months later Montana congressman Wesley D'Ewart introduced House Resolution 4196, which was to remove restrictions on the property of Indians who had served in the armed forces. At about the same time, Rep. Roy O. Woodruff of Michigan called for the cutting of the entire BIA budget as a way in which to reduce federal spending. "We have around 400,000 folks who have some trace of Indian blood," reported Woodruff. "Their care has become big business in Washington. It pays handsome dividends to the professional do-gooders to keep them as a 'guinea pig for experimentation,' as Senators Thomas of Oklahoma, Wheeler, Chavez, and Shipstead have put it. . . . Isn't it time to emancipate the Indians and let them look after themselves?" The congressman pointed out that if the Bureau of Indian Affairs' requested appropriation of $32 million were cut in half, the savings would be adequate to pay congressional salaries for three years. The bureau, he complained, was a "sewer-hole" through which taxpayers' money was being poured.[7]

That same year, Pres. Harry Truman called for the elimination of the Bureau of Indian Affairs within three years. Truman's report to Congress on aspects of Indian policy reveals the tenor of dissatisfaction with the agency that had come to dominate the rhetoric of those demanding reform:

> The original purpose of the Indian Bureau was to help the Indian become a citizen and it was intended as a service rather than as an administrative agency. Thus we see that although the original aim was to make the Indian a citizen the present aim appears to [be to] keep the Indian an Indian and to make him satisfied with the limitations of a primitive form of existence. . . . The Bureau . . . has segregated the Indian from the general citizenry, condemned him to an indefinite if not perpetual wardship, tied him to land in perpetuity, and forced a system of Bureau-controlled education and land use upon him.[8]

Congress quickly passed the Indian Claims Commission Act the following year in anticipation of settling all claims with Indian nations and wrapping up any pending Indian business that might prolong federal responsibility. This legislation created a special court wherein tribes could file for compensation for land cessions. Previously, any such claims had to be resolved by special acts of Congress.[9]

Changes were also made in the committees that held responsibility for Indian affairs. The 1946 Legislative Reorganization Act called for the House Committee on Indian Affairs to be merged with committees on public lands, territories, irrigation and reclamation mines, and insular affairs into the House Committee on Interior and Insular Affairs. A similar restructuring in the Senate consolidated the Committee on Indian Affairs and the committees on public lands and surveys, mines, territories, and insular affairs into a Senate Committee on Interior and Insular Affairs. These new committees were dominated by Western conservative congressmen preoccupied with the financial gains to be derived from their states' resources. The West being in the midst of an economic boom, there was considerable interest in opening up Indian lands for sale and taxation, particularly holdings with valuable natural resources. It is no coincidence that the Klamaths and Menominees, whose reservations were rich in timberlands, were singled out for early termination.[10]

The 1952 elections gave the Republican party control of both the Senate and the House, as well as the presidency. The former commander in chief of the Allied Forces, Dwight D. Eisenhower, was now commander in chief of the United States, and he believed the American middle class would demonstrate to the world the benefits of democracy with its television sets, vacuum cleaners, and gleaming kitchen appliances. Eisenhower's American Dream for the nation was one of modernization and patriotic homogenization. Donald Fixico trenchantly recounts what that meant for Indian peoples: "Anything or anyone who represented something different immediately became a target for criticism. 'Un-American' became a much-used phrase to describe anyone who was deemed to be disloyal to the United States. . . . Simultaneously, public indifference swept Native Americans toward the Eisenhower melting pot in which everyone would be just an American."[11]

The Eighty-third Congress was to introduce 288 public bills and resolutions on Indian affairs, 46 of which were enacted into law. Their terminationist campaign was led by Republican senator Arthur V. Watkins of Utah, who maintained that the Indian Citizenship Act of 1924 had ended all special federal relationships with Indian tribes and who, therefore, opposed both continued government assistance and the recognition of treaty obligations. As he stated to Elsie Gardner Ricklefs of the Hoopa Business Council during her testimony before a joint hearing of the subcommittees of the Committees on Interior and Insular Affairs, "we do not recognize now within the confines of the United States any foreign nations. You have now become citizens of the one nation. Ordinarily the United States does not enter into treaties . . . in an international sense, between any of its citizens and the Federal Government. . . . You cannot be both; you cannot be an American citizen and a foreigner at the same time." Watkins became chair of the Senate Indian Affairs Subcommittee in 1954.[12]

Watkins was supported by Montana senator George Malone, who introduced legislation each session to abolish the BIA. One such bill, which Malone promised would "emancipate a great race of people from the shackles of bureaucracy," proposed to dissolve the bureau, remove the trust relationships regulating Indian land, and repeal the Indian Reorganization Act of 1934. The latter, Malone contended, only served to encourage un-American "socialistic" tribal governments:

> The Indian Bureau, like some great tropical parasitical vine, entwists and entangles its way over the tree of liberty with ever increasing deadlines. It has become completely incompetent to accomplish the purpose for which it was originally set up, namely, to civilize and assimilate the Indian. Instead it has reversed the process of assimilation and civilization of the Indian and since 1933 it has been trying to disassociate the Indian from the main current of American free civic life, and to stimulate the Indian to readopt the ancient and uncivilized usages of a long distant past. . . .
>
> While we are spending billions of dollars fighting communism and Marxist socialism throughout the world, we are at the same time, through the Indian Bureau, perpetuating the systems of Indian reservations and tribal government, which are natural Socialist environments.[13]

In addition to the numerous bills submitted that proposed termination for individual tribal groups, Congress took other measures to absolve the federal government of responsibility for Indian tribes. These included the passage of Public Law 280, which transferred civil and criminal jurisdiction over Indian lands to the states and allowed states to supply government services to tribes, and Public Law 568, which placed health services for Indian peoples under the jurisdiction of the U.S. Public Health Service. In this same vein, the secretary of the interior cut the BIA's proposed budget for 1954, especially those funds designated for new construction, in the belief that services would be terminated before the projects were complete.[14]

Termination of individual tribes was, however, the most threatening and final of the actions. Glenn Emmons, who marshaled the Eisenhower administration's efforts on this front, described for Congress in 1954 the general procedure for termination. Tribal rolls were first closed and each member given an individual interest in tribal property. The tribe was then authorized to keep its property, divide the property among its members, or sell it. The tribe could organize a business corporation or put the property in the hands of a private trustee. If the tribe failed to act, the secretary of the interior was authorized to appoint a private trustee to handle the liquidation of assets and distribution of the proceeds among tribal members. Once all restrictions from the property had been removed, a proclamation would be published in the *Federal Register* declaring that the federal trust relationship to the tribe had ended, and tribal members would be subject to all federal and state laws like any other citizen.[15]

During Emmons's tenure with the BIA, sixty-one tribes, Indian groups, communities, rancherías, and allotments would be terminated by these methods, affecting some 1,362,155 acres of Indian land and 11,466 individuals. "I believe the Indian people, as a whole, are intelligent," Emmons told Congress. "And I think, given a chance to develop these talents and these adaptabilities that they certainly have, they can be a great asset to the country in which they live." Emmons explained that the bureau was in fact exploring additional options to this end. Economic development in areas adjacent to the reservation was one means of achieving this goal. Through loan programs and special incentives, Emmons hoped businesses would be attracted to reservations and provide the employment needed to make tribes economically self-sufficient. In this way special government services would no longer be necessary. Relocation was another alternative.[16]

Operation Relocation had been initiated by Emmons's predecessor, Dillon S. Myer, the former director of the War Relocation Authority in charge of Japanese internment camps. After the war, as the demand for factory production decreased, many Indian workers were laid off. They were joined in the ranks of unemployment by returning veterans, some of whom sought refuge in the cities from extreme conditions of poverty on their reservations. Under the relocation program, Native Americans, lured by an elaborate advertising campaign that promised "skilled, life time jobs" with full benefits and washing machines and television sets in every home, were given minimal federal assistance to relocate from the reservation to an urban area. Only the poorest 25 percent actually received financial support, and this covered solely the cost of moving the participant's family and subsistence until the first paycheck was received. The remainder were assisted in finding employment and housing.[17]

Most were unskilled; some were not fluent in English. They qualified for only the lowest wage jobs. Housing, often at a premium in urban areas such as Los Angeles after the war, was difficult to find, and because of scant salaries usually substandard. Health care was no longer provided. No funds were available to help families struggling financially after the initial period, nor was there any help for those who, homesick or dissatisfied with city life or having lost their job, simply wanted to return home. In fact, in an effort to discourage returnees, the bureau frequently assigned participants in the program to cities far away from their home reservations. The result was legions of stranded Indian peoples scraping a living together in the poorest neighborhoods of metropolises such as Denver, Oakland, Chicago, Dallas, and Cleveland.

Emmons was well aware of Indian disapproval of both his efforts at termination and the bureau's relocation policies. Indian leaders gathered at tribal area conferences and criticized the BIA's recruitment tactics and the living conditions to which participants in the relocation program were subjected. Blackfeet tribal secretary Iliff McKay charged in 1956 that welfare aid requests were withheld so as to force people into relocation. Paul Bernal of Taos Pueblo reported that the program was detrimental to communities' religious and social order, with tribal members living away from the pueblo in cities not being available for such communal obligations as ditch cleaning for irrigation. Moreover, relocation efforts served as brain drains on Indian communities, taking their youth and the most skilled. Yet Emmons was able to report Indian support of the bureau's policies by railroading tribal leaders at such conferences into adopting favorable resolutions written and distributed by BIA staff.[18]

The bureau's Office of Indian Education was not immune to this termination tide, and their pedagogical goals came to mirror and reinforce the larger policies and programs set in Washington. The impetus for cross-cultural education begun in the 1930s quickly fell by the wayside as BIA educators set about preparing Indian peoples for life off the reservations. Willard W. Beatty, Indian Education director from 1936 until 1952 and one of John Collier's Indian New Deal warriors, signaled the changes in his 1953 preface to a collection of Indian Education articles entitled *Education for Cultural Change*. Adherence to traditional patterns and resistance to change, wrote Beatty, had "given way to a recognition that the richest future for Indians of the United States lies in mastery of the material culture of the dominant race."[19] Mastery of the individual's own culture was now viewed as not only valueless but indeed detrimental:

> Children raised in an environment in which they are not exposed
> to certain types of training which are necessary for their later success,
> do not achieve that later success. If we are to expect Indian children to

know how to bathe, how to use sanitary toilets, how to dress, how to care for their hair, how to use the eating utensils which are part of the American culture, how to handle money, how to save money, how to drive an automobile . . . then it is essential that we create an opportunity for the Indian child to experience these same things. Experience, however, must take place in school, because the home from which the child comes does not practice any of them and whatever the child learns within the home is contrary to the thing he needs to know rather than helpful.[20]

"Homelike" experiences, where Indian youth could practice the "modern living" skills necessary if "succeeding generations of Indians are to pull themselves out of the hogans, tipis, wickiups and igloos of their ancestors," became essential components of BIA schools. Lessons in etiquette, money management, and personal grooming received equal time with English, math, and vocational education. The ultimate goal, of course, was to prepare the Indian to live as a non-Indian and to ready students for a post-termination world.[21]

The bureau's pilot effort in this realm was a project called the Navajo Special Education Program. Under its auspices some forty-three hundred Navajo students were given vocational training and taught assimilation survival skills from its inception in 1946 until the early 1960s. Other bureau vocational programs were modeled on the techniques and strategies developed for use with these students. Although the initial program site was Sherman Institute in California, during the 1950s the Intermountain Indian School in Brigham City, Utah, a converted army hospital, superseded all other BIA schools in its enrollment of Navajo special education students. As Margaret Szasz has aptly observed, it is significant that Intermountain was the "stepchild" of Sen. Arthur Watkins, one of termination's leading proponents. Before becoming Indian Education director in 1952, Hildegard Thompson directed the Navajo Special Education Program. George Boyce was the superintendent of the Intermountain School.[22]

The program was designed for overage (twelve years and older) Navajos who had not previously attended school with any regularity. The curriculum was five years in duration. The first-year students learned the proper care and use of hand tools and equipment and were to develop "good work habits and desirable attitudes toward work." The second- and third-year students gained sufficient vocational experience so as to supposedly be able to select a particular vocation for themselves, and the fourth year was spent in the acquisition of this "marketable vocational skill." The fifth year was devoted to "putting in an honest day's work" and mastering the "requisites of good living in any community."[23]

In point of fact, the "requisites of good living" were given particular attention throughout the curriculum, as Beatty admonished Indian Education teachers that they had to accept, "both superficially and intellectually, the fact that Navajo children start near zero." The Navajo Special Education Program students were thus instructed in such "essentials" as the use of eating utensils, the mechanics of dusting, how to run a vacuum cleaner, and proper decorum for the wardrobe: "They are taught what one wears at night and what one does with one's nightclothes in the daytime, when one puts on some other kind of clothing. They are taught exactly what kind of clothing to wear. They are taught exactly when to change it, how to wash it, how to dry it, how to iron or press it, and where to store it in a dresser drawer or in a closet." School banks were set up so as to instruct students in handling money and some students were placed in small practice apartments following intensive home economics courses.[24]

The acquisition of basic English was a particular focus for the first three years of the program. Instruction was bilingual, with Navajo-speaking aides being brought in to assist the teachers, but the Navajo language was used for three purposes only: as a basis for learning English, as a means of testing the understanding that pupils had gained through English, and as a medium through which new ideas could be accessed more rapidly.[25]

The Indian Education Office declared that the project was indeed a success at preparing Indian boys and girls for permanent employment in industrialized areas such as Los Angeles and speculated that with "proper effort" graduates could qualify for skilled positions "equivalent to those occupied by many middle class white mechanics."[26] The changes in the students, they marveled, had been very promising:

> Those who worked with these pupils have seen them develop from youngsters who would scarcely say their names loud enough to be heard, when they enrolled, to youths who greet and carry on a conversation with adults in accordance with the amount of English at their command. To have such shy pupils learn to ask adults to dance with them and then thank the adults courteously at the end of the dance, has been remarkable progress in socialization in a year's time. Some of them have developed this far.[27]

Although Hildegard Thompson oversaw several similar vocational programs for terminating tribes and prospective relocation participants, she was also a firm believer in post–high school education, convinced that students needed at least two years' training beyond the secondary level to successfully compete for jobs in an increasingly technologically complex world: "Ten years ago most of us knew little about earth satellites. Today we know that several are orbiting the earth, some orbiting the sun, and that the moon has been reached by a man-made missile. . . . No doubt, many of the students now in school will travel in space as a matter of course, just as we now think plane travel common place."[28]

The launching of Sputnik I in 1957 sent reverberations of self-doubt and inferiority through American education. Commenting on the Russians' claim to have looked at the moon's backside, Thompson quipped, "I'm sure [it] hasn't embarrassed the moon a bit—but how it embarrassed us—a people who pride ourselves on progress, on achievement, and on being first."[29] This Cold War national humiliation thrust the teachers of the country into the front lines of a new offensive that was not limited to new math and science curricula but included model lessons in democracy. Thompson understood this new charge well:

> Our world situation is tense. The cold war has not lessened. Vast numbers of down-trodden peoples the world over are awakening and struggling desperately to lift themselves out of their mass poverty and illiteracy. . . .
>
> Our Nation, in striving for its own freedom less than 200 years ago, mobilized its patriots and fired the shot heard around the world. If this country is to exercise its leadership in promoting freedom, it is up to us to set off a different kind of shot to be heard around the world. The manpower behind this modern shot will be the teachers of this country, and their arsenals are the classrooms of our schools.
>
> If we are to achieve leadership in promoting our beliefs concerning the dignity of the individual and his right to live out his life with the greatest possible measure of freedom, we must have quality instruction for our youth.[30]

Teachers had a twofold responsibility according to Thompson: to develop individuals and to strengthen the democratic way of life.[31] These were not viewed as mutually exclusive goals. Just as individualism in the guise of abstract expressionism could serve as a weapon against Communism, so also could the education of the individual in the classroom reap benefits for democracy and the Western world. Raising the educational standard of any group of American children, but particularly a minority group, was a victory in the fight against totalitarianism.[32] Individualism was even cited as the moral and political justification for termination: "This Administration holds that our government is built on the freedom of the individual, the right to develop one's capacities, to manage one's own affairs, to go and come as one chooses, and to own and pass on property to one's children. We believe segregation is wrong and that wardship for competent people is repugnant to our way of life." [33]

In order to motivate Indian students to aspire to continue their education after receiving their high school diploma, Thompson advocated a strengthening of academic skills and less emphasis on the industrial arts in all bureau high schools. Terminal vocational education that was geared to immediate employment at the end of high school training was to be discouraged in favor of college preparatory courses or classes that would prepare students for more advanced training in trades or technical fields. Moreover, vocational courses would not be offered until the tenth, preferably the eleventh grade. This served two purposes: insuring that students would be grounded academically before pursuing a vocation and that they would probably need to continue their training beyond graduation. To cut costs, Thompson felt that expensive terminal courses in special disciplines should be offered in designated schools, rather than be duplicated at several sites. In addition, home economics courses and dormitory living were to help the Indian student "bridge the gap between the living standards of a modern community and an impoverished Indian community of low standards." [34]

Emmons, Thompson, and Boyce brought these shared experiences and philosophies to the meeting with d'Harnoncourt in the late 1950s. They remained stalwarts of assimilation despite by then dwindling public support for their views. Foes of termination had begun an effective media campaign mid-decade to educate Americans about the devastating consequences of the policy. John Collier published an article in the *Christian Century* denouncing the break in the trust relationship and pleading for citizen action against a Congress that believed cultural diversity was un-American. "These men are blind . . . toward history," wrote Collier, "toward the shames, the sadnesses and de-populations, the vast legalized lootings which ensued in the past from governmental actions identical with those which they are pressing now." The *Christian Century*'s editor, Harold Fey, was a leading opponent of termination and began to pen his own critiques of Indian affairs, spurring further interest among Christian groups. [35]

In the popular press Dorothy Van de Mark condemned relocation as early as March 1954, declaring that it was "just another slick scheme to hand [the Indians'] last refuge over to the land-grabbers." From the beginnings of the nation, Van de Mark charged, the chief issue of federal Indian policy had been to determine how best to transfer Indian resources and land to non-Indians. Forced removal, such as that endured by the Cherokees, had been employed first. "Some 14,000 left their homeland; more than 4,000 died on the way," recounted Van de Mark. "The only comparable march in our history was the Death March of American prisoners on Bataan; we later described the Japanese responsible for that one as 'war criminals.'" Removal was followed by allotment, and allotment by termination. Only the tactics changed, she explained, the end results were the same.[36]

Ruth Mulvey Harmer published a damning account of relocation in the *Atlantic Monthly* that same month. "For every success story," wrote Harmer, "there are a hundred failures. For every former trapper-farmer now adjusted to assembly-line work and city life, there are ninety-nine adrift in a new and hostile environment." She warned that thousands of indigenous Americans were being "turned loose upon the asphalt jungles of metropolitan centers in one of the most extraordinary forced migrations in history." Carl Rowan followed with a fifteen-part series for the *Minneapolis Tribune* entitled "The First Are Last" on the problems of urban Indians, and radio commentator Paul Harvey did a piece on Indians in Arizona. Finally, in November 1958, the National Broadcasting Company aired a documentary entitled "The American Stranger" on its *Kaleidoscope* series. Depicting dire conditions on the Blackfeet, Flathead, Navajo, and Menominee reservations, the show attacked the Bureau of Indian Affairs and the policy of termination, as well as other policies that contributed to loss of Indian land.[37]

Moreover, the 1956 elections had given the Democratic party a decisive majority in Congress, and some of the terminationist leadership was being replaced by more liberal representatives. Secretary of the Interior Fred Seaton, seeing the large handwriting on the wall, was doing a backward dance on Indian policy. In September 1958 Seaton declared on a radio broadcast in the Southwest that "hereafter no group would lose federal services or supervision unless it clearly demonstrated that it was fully prepared and understood and supported the action."[38]

In reality, however, termination would remain a federal agenda into the 1960s, with the seniority system insuring that many old-line assimilationist congressmen continued to hold positions of influence. Withdrawal programs for the Menominees, Choctaws, Klamaths, and California rancherías were still pending as the Kennedy administration was moving into the White House, and the comptroller general issued a report that the Interior Department should proceed drafting bills terminating other tribes deemed ready with all due speed. Relocation was renamed Employment Assistance to divert attention away from the physical realities of the program, and the Democratic party even boasted in 1964 that the Kennedy and Johnson administrations had doubled its enrollment. Lakota scholar Philip Deloria recalls being told by

BIA functionaries throughout this period that termination was still the policy of the federal government and would remain so until House Concurrent Resolution 108 was repealed.[39]

Glenn Emmons was certainly such a functionary. He continued to prepare tribes for withdrawal from federal trust obligations well after Seaton's public retraction of termination. Even after his resignation in 1960, he began a book entitled "Freedom for the First Americans" that promoted a vision of all tribes terminated in time to celebrate their "emancipation" on 4 July 1976—the country's bicentennial.[40] Likewise, Hildegard Thompson did not make any concerted effort to return the Indian Education Office to a spirit of cross-cultural tolerance and respect after the heat of termination had passed. It is unlikely that any new appropriation for an Indian art school would win their approval and gain their support without its accommodating their own agendas to some degree. Indeed, as plans for the new Institute of American Indian Arts began to unfold, the influence of the termination years was readily apparent.

Under fire for the BIA's inaction in the field of art education, Emmons authorized Thompson to set up a school "of some sort" for Indian artists at the close of the meeting with d'Harnoncourt. An allocation of sixty-two thousand dollars was then made available for an arts and crafts instruction center at the Santa Fe Indian School (SFIS) in 1960.[41] In keeping with Thompson's emphasis on post–high school education, the program was not part of the regular curriculum; instead, the art courses were offered to high school graduates from across the country between the ages of eighteen and twenty-five. This also complied with Thompson's concern that specialty vocation programs be concentrated at certain schools, rather than offered at each BIA institution. Mary Mitchell, who had for years managed the Pueblo Market at the Santa Fe Indian School, was recommended by George Boyce to serve as director.[42]

Underfinanced and poorly publicized, the program suffered from very low enrollments. Charles Minton grumbled in his monthly report for the state of New Mexico's Commission on Indian Affairs that this was an unfortunate par for the BIA course. "It is typical," wrote Minton, "that after allowing the Arts and Crafts program to deteriorate to almost nothing, the Indian School was given $60,000 and told to set up an Arts and Crafts Department 'the day before yesterday.' It was also typical that almost no recruiting was done, so that the School opened with only one pupil."[43]

Dissatisfied with the situation, Hildegard Thompson began lobbying for funds to establish a full-fledged school. Meanwhile, Willard Beatty, now chair of the Indian Arts and Crafts Board, proposed that a senior high school and post high school technical institute be created with a vocational Indian arts and crafts program and a student body drawn from all of Indian country.[44] Santa Fe was considered the logical location because of its association with the Pueblo painting "revival" of the 1920s and the Studio art department. Moreover, the Santa Fe Indian School facility was expected to soon be available, as declining enrollments and administrative changes in recent years continued to contribute to its seemingly irrevocable decline. The school had originally enrolled students in grades seven through twelve. In 1958, however, the entire high school was moved to Albuquerque, while fifth- and sixth-grade students from San Felipe Pueblo were, in turn, transferred to Santa Fe. The arts and crafts department continued to function until the following year.[45]

George Boyce remembered Thompson submitting to the BIA a request of under a million dollars for new construction and remodeling of the Santa Fe Indian School in 1960. The Indian art school proposal was finally presented to the budget bureau and the appropriations committees of both houses of Congress in late 1960 and early 1961: $1,312,303 was obligated for the physical renovations, and $541,000 was allocated for operational funds.[46]

Boyce, still superintendent of Intermountain's Navajo Special Education Program, was invited to Washington to help plan basic policies for the school. It is logical to assume that Thompson was impressed with his work for the Navajo project, which she had formerly directed. Boyce was subsequently asked to travel to Santa Fe in the summer of 1961 for several weeks of consultation on the new school and was at that time offered the position of superintendent of the recently named Institute of American Indian Arts.[47]

Boyce was given considerable latitude in developing the blueprint of IAIA. He was charged not only with directing the new construction and remodeling but also with setting up the organization of the school, recruiting staff he deemed appropriate to the operation, and "working up . . . the many unsettled details as to 'what is an art school for Indians'"—details from targeted enrollment to basic philosophy.[48] For the latter Boyce drew on forty-five years of experience in education, twenty-eight of which had been spent with the Bureau of Indian Affairs. In addition to his tenure at Intermountain, Boyce had served for eight years as director of the Navajo and Hopi schools at Window Rock, Arizona, and had worked at Haskell Institute as a BIA curriculum specialist and textbook writer.

Boyce's time with the Navajo Special Education Program in particular had led him to develop a pedagogical ideology that he called "environmentalism." Simply stated, Boyce believed that "people desire only what experience proves to be advantageous to them." In a manuscript entitled "The Indian Tribal Mind: A Study of Social Concepts for Indian Rehabilitation," which Boyce wrote as a "primer of data governing the collective Indian mind or

Indian cultures" and "guide to social engineering," Boyce expounded at length upon this principle. "Our society, based on the unique concept of the 'American Dream,'" Boyce declared, "is designed to meet the needs of the common man and the downtrodden better than any nation yet evolved on this earth. Our culture has many advantages to offer the Indian—if he can be led to see the advantages."[49]

The challenge for the white man, Boyce concluded, was to determine how best to bring to the Indian a "forward-moving kind of dissatisfaction." Too many Indians were unaware of the satisfactions that could be gained from greater comfort, better shelter, improved diet and health, and increased income. The substandard buildings and equipment characteristic of BIA schools, hospitals, and other facilities serving Indian peoples did not, however, provide environments conducive to this goal. Indian children who attended dismal, run-down boarding schools where sixty or more children slept in one room, for example, would not be shown the "advantage" of owning a multiple-room house after graduation. If, on the other hand, a child came to a school that offered first-rate equipment, pleasant buildings, a friendly staff, and enticing amenities, the stage was set for a successful education program and mutual respect. Mutual respect, Boyce explained, facilitated acculturation.[50]

Boyce noted that acculturation represented a unique and difficult objective for educators, one foreign to most societies' pedagogies:

> No society . . . operates an educational system to destroy itself. The educational system of a nation may aim to transmit improvements ac- cepted by the society, such as knowledge of vitamins, for example, to improve health through diet. But no nation sets out to do all teaching in a new language, while discontinuing teaching of the traditional lan- guage. It normally does not set out to change the native costume of the people, to change the manner of housing, the social customs, the voca- tional aims, the values of living. This is a revolutionary process. It is a very different process from what our public schools are designed to un- dertake. Yet, this is the task of education for acculturation of Indians.[51]

Although his tactics would undergo various revisions, the "acculturation of Indians"—a revolution designed to "destroy" Indian societies—remained at the core of Boyce's educational agenda.

His third day on the job at the Institute of American Indian Arts, Boyce appeared on the front page of the *Santa Fe New Mexican*, cigar in hand, hunched over plans for the new Pueblo-style campus. "There is no reason why there shouldn't be Indian influence in architecture, furniture design," Boyce told the paper's reporter. "The Indian School's buildings are a demon-

FIG. 3. *The Institute of American Indian Arts campus. (National Park Service Photo, Fred Mang, photographer)*

stration of this." Estimating that one in every one hundred Indian children had artistic aptitude, Boyce envisioned the school as a place where Indian poets, dancers, and musicians, as well as visual artists, could nurture their talents. Vocational studies at the institute would be arts related—with offerings in fields such as furniture design, window decorating, textile design, and architectural drafting. The school would also be accredited and geared to accommodate those estimated 35 percent of students who were potential college candidates. "We'll turn them all out employable," Boyce promised.[52]

Getting students better adjusted socially would be as critical to the success of the operation as additional classes in English and mathematics, according to Boyce. He reported that institute staff would "apply considerable effort to get the students out into the community and into white men's homes until the students feel comfortable in such an atmosphere and desire it for themselves." Boyce explained that, "the Indians have so few wants they work only to satisfy those wants. If they develop wants they will work for them." In accordance with this philosophy, Boyce was in the process of ordering nonstandard BIA furnishings for the dormitories (including new shampoo bowls and hair dryers for the girls' "good grooming room" and single, rather than bunk beds), to provide students with living and dining arrangements that he hoped would create American consumerist habits that would far outlive their school days.

A month into his new position Boyce announced that the old Santa Fe Indian School was to receive quite a face-lift in other respects as well. Three buildings were to be constructed on the campus before the opening of the institute in the fall of 1962. A new academic building would house fourteen classrooms, language arts laboratories, and an academic library with a conference room. The old one was being remodeled into studios with skylights on the second stories and droplights on the ground floor for bench work. A new administration center would provide office space, while a student union with twenty-five-hundred square feet of floor space for dancing and a snack bar was also on the drawing board.[53]

Boyce acknowledged in the announcement that he hoped the school would attract international as well as national attention, commenting that foreign visitors had shown particular interest in what the institute "is doing for this country's oldest minority." Boyce saw in this an opportunity to somehow globally market the benefits of the American Dream. The rest of the world, like the Indians, Boyce noted, was not sold on materialism. Our industrial system depended on developing "wants," calculated Boyce, and the institute would attempt to cultivate these wants in its students. It is not clear if this was to then translate into a worldwide conversion to American consumerism.

Boyce was ever mindful of the school's political value, both domestically and abroad. In a report to the commissioner of Indian Affairs during the institute's early planning stages, Boyce asserted that the school's purpose, together with its popularity among Indian peoples, made it "easy to visualize the hand of the Government in setting up the Institute as a great force in international relations and in moving many Indian groups off the dead-center on which many have been stagnating."[54]

Boyce frequently emphasized that the school enjoyed enthusiastic support in Indian country. "This is the finest thing the Government has ever undertaken for our people. This is what we have waited a long time for," was the widespread response among Indians of all tribes, reported Boyce. He attributed this supposed popularity to an overdue acknowledgment of Native cultural values. "For a long time the white man has been trying to sell various forms of materialism," Boyce noted. "On the other side, the Indian people have had only meagre recognition in what they have to sell to the white man. What Indians have to offer is rooted primarily in the aesthetic, the dramatic and the spiritual side of human relations." Boyce's personal notes, however, reveal that honoring Indian cultures was not his ultimate goal. "Building pride and security in one's own cultural aspects is itself a measure of security to contemplating 'borrowing' from other cultures," he observed. "The tendency to reject and withdraw becomes softened!" Conversely, if the dominant culture made the minority person feel inferior, he or she would defensively reject the "superior" cultural practice. Respecting cultural difference for Boyce became yet another useful strategy to effect acculturation.[55]

With the physical plant taking shape, Boyce turned his attention to questions of staffing. He solicited advice from Rene d'Harnoncourt and Frederick Dockstader, both members of the Indian Arts and Crafts Board, as well as from art departments across the country regarding potential candidates for the position of director of the Arts and Crafts Division.[56] "The Director should be a capable leader in assisting a staff to acquire knowledgeable regard for many diverse Indian traditions, while also exposing students to new media and new applications to modern living from various Indian backgrounds," Boyce wrote in one inquiry. The encouragement of "creative applications to modern living" and broadening of insight into traditional Indian techniques and concepts were listed by Boyce in a separate informational sheet as general objectives of the Institute of American Indian Arts. "This is a new door for expression of a unique American Indian message in aesthetics and things of the human spirit," promised Boyce to prospective applicants.[57]

By December 1961 temporary arrangements had been made for Lloyd New to serve as acting director of arts. Boyce brought New on as a consultant to the planning process, and the two met at the school that month to work up notes regarding staffing and recruiting that were then forwarded to Hildegard Thompson. The recommendations strongly reflected the organizational and personnel patterns of the Rockefeller workshops in Tucson. For example, design and history were blocked together into one section or department, a combination utilized in the Southwestern Indian Art Project but not commonly practiced. The studio disciplines to be offered were ceramics, metals, sculpture, painting, graphic arts, weaving, and modern textiles. Music, drama, and dance rounded out the arts curriculum. Otellie Loloma was recommended to teach ceramics and Charles Loloma, metal work. Roy Sieber was the first choice for design and history.

Prominent Indian artists' names punctuated the remaining roster of possible faculty. Richard West of Bacone College was suggested as assistant art director. Oscar Howe was a favored candidate for painting instructor, Woody

FIG. 4. *IAIA students in traditional techniques class.*
(Kay Wiest, photographer)

Crumbo for graphics arts. Allan Houser was thought to be the best choice for sculpture and painting. For the textiles and fibers sections, however, it was recommended that a nationally recognized non-Indian be recruited so as to bring "contemporary sophistication" to the program. Lloyd New made it clear he did not want to inherit in his department any of the current Santa Fe Indian School arts and crafts faculty, including Mary Mitchell. New had visited classes and was "very disturbed" about the manner in which the students were taught and the resulting products. After consulting with New, Boyce determined that "we need more diverse skills and demonstrated commercial success than is the case for any of the present staff of four art teachers."[58]

Offers were sent out over the ensuing four months to prospective faculty and staff considered to be more in tune with the school's goals. Boyce first contacted Allan Houser, inquiring as to his willingness to accept a position divided between painting and sculpture. He had known Houser from their days together at the Intermountain Indian School, where the noted Apache artist was still teaching. Throughout January, Boyce negotiated with James McGrath, arts and crafts director for American Dependent Schools in Europe and North Africa, regarding the assistant director of arts post. Louis Ballard, a Quapaw-Cherokee musician and composer, who had come to Boyce's attention "for his excellence in the field of concert music, Indian dancing, and his experimental work in musical composition based upon Indian things," was invited to join the faculty in March. That same month, Boyce nominated Charles Loloma as department head of Plastic Arts.[59]

Boyce now drafted a memorandum, "For the Record," that outlined the fundamental concepts that were guiding the institute's decision makers in developing the school's program. He listed three areas of responsibility that were essential to the accomplishment of the "goals" set for students:

> (a) Academic strength aimed at reduction of dropouts at the high school or college level, and academic competence adequate for competing and succeeding in the more selective universities and colleges than has been the case for very many Indian students
>
> (b) Creative talents in the Arts which grow out of an objective and detailed understanding and feeling for traditional arts. At the same time, exposure to new materials and new functions and new economic demands for the contemporary scene
>
> (c) Personality development through the home living activities which will enable the graduate to be a person of the world and able to live in the midst of diverse cultures successfully. This would be at every economic and social level in our own society.[60]

The keys to success in these three areas were a conducive environment, a "clinical" approach to determining student needs, a problem-solving oriented pedagogy, and an outstanding staff. Everyone at the institute was, according to Boyce, an "environmentalist" and carried the responsibility "of modifying and controlling the environment so as to condition students automatically to the goals." The clinical approach, Boyce explained, would allow the supervisory and instructional staff to ascertain to what extent the resources of the institute could be brought to bear on the special needs of each individual student. The school's curriculum would grow out of the awareness of these needs. Finally, a problem-solving teaching strategy, whereby a student learned through an "awareness of tensions or problems of some sort, developing of hypotheses or experimental approaches to solutions, the experience of satisfaction in the creative activities involved, evaluation of the results and the placement of value on progress accomplished," would shift the fundamental aim of the educational process away from acquisition of specific information.

None of this was possible without the right faculty. "In the recruitment of personnel," Boyce concluded, "effort shall be directed toward obtaining persons as employees who have achieved some degree of eminence in their field of endeavor, and encouragement shall be given toward their continuing to develop professionally in a total contemporary scene rather than being restricted to their obligations to activities centered here at the Institute."

Boyce expounded further upon his "goals" for art students in letters to BIA area directors. He listed economic objectives first. "My way of saying it," wrote Boyce, is "We hope to aid many Indian youths toward becoming $15,000 and $20,000 and $25,000 a year Indians. This may sound fantastic. But why not some future Indian Frank Lloyd Wrights in architecture? Why not some future Indian Hemingways as creative writers? Wouldn't some Westerns written by Indian authors be interesting for a change?" Academic goals focused on preparation for college or specialized technical training. "We feel that great artists today must be well-educated," Boyce admonished, and accordingly they aimed to reenergize students' ambitions for advanced education, as well as to strengthen their prospects for success at the best schools. Economic and academic success, as well as social acceptance anywhere in the country, were contingent upon the student developing a "secure personality." The school would thus stress student participation in the life of the off-campus community in Santa Fe.[61]

As for the art goals, Boyce noted that courses such as business methods and salesmanship, which emphasized the "practical side of making a living through employment or management of private business," would be part of the curricular offerings. Moreover, the plastic arts section would include the practical fields of architecture, furniture, clay products, and jewelry, while in textiles and fabrics students would consider various media and techniques for floor coverings, drapes, apparel and accessories. Book illustration and commercial art were to be taught in the fine and graphic arts section, together with painting and other graphic media. And in the Music and Dramatic Arts Program, Boyce hoped that an approach utilizing the students' Indian backgrounds would yield "exciting new contributions." "The big aim," stressed Boyce, was to "train each student as an INDIVIDUAL, creative in his own right."[62]

In March, Boyce began notifying some Santa Fe Indian School personnel that they did not qualify for positions at the institute. Scarcely more than half of the staff appointments open were to be filled by former SFIS employees. Of the twenty-six veteran teachers at the school, only two were to be retained. Boyce explained his faculty selections as being based on "our desire to recruit arts instructors of a demonstrated contemporary commercial success." The exclusion of SFIS faculty and staff, however, was the first falling domino in a burgeoning public relations crisis that at times threatened to close the new art school before it ever opened.[63]

As early as April 1962 Charles Minton of the New Mexico Commission on Indian Affairs complained in a confidential report to Gov. Edwin Mechem of New Mexico that at the Santa Fe Indian School "experienced teachers are being let out and transferred elsewhere, their places being taken by 'long hairs.'" He further advised Mechem that appeals were being made to the president of the National Federation of Federal Employees. At the March meeting of the commission a press release detailing aims and objectives of the new Institute of American Indian Arts had been distributed to members, and Minton was asked to look into the brewing controversy over the impending changes on the SFIS campus.[64]

The press release described an Indian "center of arts and culture" that would "open new doors of opportunity for self-expression . . . in the whole rainbow of the arts." Designed for Indian youth of "high artistic talent," the institute would offer a comprehensive academic program of studies for selected students in grades 10, 11, and 12. The high school would serve those students preparing for fine arts work in college and technical schools. In addition, an advanced program would allow students who had graduated from high school to strengthen their general education while gaining training in some area of art specialization. Art talent as an "economic resource," which, when developed, could result in excellent "make-a-living" careers, was to be stressed. Related academic courses, such as business training, salesmanship, Indian history and anthropology, English, mathematics, applied science, history of art, art appreciation, and typing, would complement the vocational curriculum. Student support services were to include guidance programs, recreational activities, and job placement, all in an atmosphere of "wholesome campus living."

The program promised to be "unique and important in the world of arts"; indeed, the promotion proclaimed that "it may become an important instrument in our country's program of international relationships." Since one way to create friendship in the family of man was to know and understand the "so-called 'stranger' ethnic groups," read the release, the institute represented a very important resource in the telling of the story of American Indians to the world. At the very least, the trained Indian artist would be a "responsible citizen with an income adequate to maintain a good standard of living for himself and his family."

The Indian employees of the Santa Fe Indian School, meanwhile, drafted a letter to Martin Vigil, chairman of the All-Pueblo Council. They were outraged that children attending the school were to be pushed out "to go to strange surroundings among strange teachers while millions of tax dollars are being spent to bring only a few other Indians from all parts of the country to replace those who have every right to their education in this school." Santa Fe schools were already overcrowded, they maintained, and could not absorb an additional influx of Indian students. Moreover, some Indian families would not be able to furnish the necessary food and clothing for children attending public or day schools. What was needed in the present location of the Santa Fe Indian School, they charged, was a vocational high school. "We are concerned about our young people, particularly our high school graduates," the letter stated, "who are now unemployed for want of vocation skills. We are aware of . . . young people idle in our pueblos who would greatly benefit from a vocational high school to meet their needs and overcome their handicaps. . . . We all know that not all pueblo children are college material." [65]

The letter also addressed the treatment of the Santa Fe Indian School staff. The employees contended that the changes being implemented had taken place without their being properly informed. Assignments had not been carried through as promised by the Gallup Personnel Office and the seniority rights of the Civil Service had been ignored. To add further insult to already grievous injury, some employees had been asked to agree to a furlough without pay because there were no funds for their salaries, while outsiders were compensated handsomely for their work as consultants:

> We now call your attention to money spent this year for highly paid personnel, some of whom have been on this campus since September and other [sic] since Christmas and early spring. The only work these people appear to do is that of planning for the Institute. Will these people who are drawing such exorbitant salaries continue on these salaries through the summer? . . . Are not funds appropriated for the Institute rightfully to be used in payment of these salaries [of SFIS employees] and not to be used for other purposes such as for high salaried personnel who are being brought in from Intermountain, Scotsdale [sic], Arizona, Germany and other places unknown to us. We believe many of our employees are equally as well or better qualified as those being brought in.[66]

The group asked Vigil to use the influence of the All-Pueblo Council to save the school for "our own children whose right it is to have it."

This letter was forwarded by Vigil to Charles Minton, in order that Minton might draft a complaint to the president of the National Federation of Federal Employees, Vaux Owen. Minton then prepared a report on the institute, which was approved by both the New Mexico Commission on Indian Affairs and the All-Pueblo Council and was issued as a supplement to the commission's newsletter for June. The information presented, Minton contended, was not available elsewhere and he deemed it advisable that members of the commission and the legislature, as well as state, bureau, and tribal officials, had it. "I wasn't 'mad' at anybody when I wrote it," Minton explained to Governor Mechem later, "all I was doing was trying to strike another blow for Indian education, hoping to get the Bureau to see the primary importance of basic education, instead of going in for the 'artistic elite,' as they call it, while Indian children are without classrooms and teachers."[67]

In the report Minton reviewed the history of the Santa Fe Indian School's art programs briefly and summarized the information presented in the institute's press release. He noted that the Pueblos had consistently advocated a senior high school and more vocational training at the site. "They had heard that there were from three to five thousand Indian children for whom there were no classroom seats and no teachers, no opportunity for an education," Minton related. They also regarded the Santa Fe Indian School as their own, as their grandfathers had been told that it was built specifically for the Pueblos. Now they felt betrayed and feared that their objections to the new school were being raised too late, some of the original buildings on the campus having already been torn down.

Minton went on to write that the former SFIS teachers had been snubbed by an autocratic George Boyce, who failed to treat them with common courtesy and consideration. Letters to Vaux Owen from employees and Chairman Vigil thoroughly outlined the grievances. Faculty demanded that Owen investigate the school, which, they claimed, had been started "at the whim of an outgoing Secretary of the Interior" and had a budget of $3.5 million. Why, they asked, were proven, qualified teachers being replaced by "'artists' with no training whatever in the teaching field, and in most cases . . . very little education?" They also questioned the salary levels of the new faculty, pointing out that there seemed to be one department head to each teacher and that all positions, excepting those for the academic subjects, had been raised from the normal civil service rating of 7 to 9, 11, and 13. Washington had ignored the Indians' wishes for a vocational school in favor of a program in the arts, they charged, even though this type of program had proven over the past two years to be a failure. Vigil succinctly summarized this position: "Indians are born with a gift for arts and crafts, and those who wish to make a livelihood of it can pursue the study in a number of places, preferably at home in their spare time. But very few will be able to support themselves at it, while an education will enable them to earn a living and be of use to their people."[68]

The report prompted New Mexico state senator Albert Amador Jr. to ask U.S. senator Dennis Chavez for a thorough investigation "all the way from Hildegard Thompson . . . down to Mr. Autocrat, himself, Dr. Boyce, concerning employment practices, and covering everything pertaining to the so-called Institute of American Indian Arts." Boyce responded that he was not consulted by Minton during the course of his investigation and that the report was riddled with errors. The institute's budget was not even close to the $3.5 million cited by Minton, and, in fact, several advertised positions would not be filled because of budget constraints. Not a mere "whim of an outgoing Secretary of Interior," the school had been created by the actions of the central office of the Bureau of Indian Affairs and Congress. And while it was regrettable that children who had formerly attended the Santa Fe Indian School would be displaced, that decision had been made before Boyce joined the institute's staff. Boyce suggested that the SFIS faculty view their impending transfers to other schools in light of what was best for the students involved. Bureau policy, he reminded them, maintained that boarding schools such as the one in Santa Fe were only to be utilized when there was no alternative closer to the student's home. New facilities were being opened at Crown Point and Grants that would better serve many of the SFIS children. As for Indian peoples not being able to earn a living as artists, Boyce replied that the institute hoped to upgrade the value of Indian art. He noted that his staff would comprise producing Indian craftsmen of recognized eminence.[69]

Despite Boyce's efforts to quell the institute's critics, the debate over the school had only just begun. On June fifteenth Gov. Joe Trujillo of Cochiti Pueblo penned a letter to Sen. Clinton P. Anderson, chair of the Senate Committee on Interior and Insular Affairs, with copies sent to Sen. Dennis Chavez and U.S. Representatives Joseph M. Montoya and Thomas Morris. The governor requested the congressmen's help in returning the Santa Fe Indian School to the Pueblos. "The plan for this change to the institute was never clearly explained by the officials," wrote Trujillo. "The community, the employees of the Santa Fe Indian School as well as my pueblo people were kept in the dark. We were led to think that the change would give us a vocational high school. This was the kind of school we Indians have been asking for for many years." Three days later Geronima Montoya, former director of the arts and crafts program at the Santa Fe Indian School, took the SFIS employees' grievances to President Kennedy. Montoya wrote that their school had been made a "political toy" by the BIA and that help was needed immediately to check the bureau's "run-away" actions.[70]

The complaints prompted Commissioner of Indian Affairs Philleo Nash to fly to New Mexico and meet with the interested parties the last week of June. He was accompanied by Hildegard Thompson and Asst. Commissioner Robert Vaughn. After the first day, when it appeared that Nash's support for the institute was faltering, a breakfast meeting with the commissioner was requested by Lloyd New, Wilma Victor, and Oleta Merry. Victor had been appointed academic director for the institute, and Merry was to head the Guidance and Home-Living Department. Boyce arranged the conference, which was held up an hour while Nash swam in the hotel pool with BIA area director Wade Head. The institute staff (including Boyce, who, by his own description "called the shot[s] with Philleo") were all irritated by this apparent show of disregard. They told Nash they had come to Santa Fe with high expectations, and if they were not going to be afforded the opportunity to realize their goals they wanted to know immediately so they could all seek work elsewhere. Nash offered a compromise of a joint operation—180 SFIS elementary and junior high students from the Gallup area sharing the campus for the first year with the new art school. The institute's enrollment was not expected to reach full capacity for two years anyway and the arrangement, which would delay termination of the entire SFIS program and most of its academic staff for another year, might help to soften the impact of the inevitable change.[71]

The compromise did not placate the institute's opponents. Within days Martin Vigil sent a volley of letters to congressmen and other individuals, to which he attached copies of a press release from the All-Pueblo Council. The press release reported on a meeting attended by Nash, Wade Head, Hildegard Thompson, Boyce, IAIA publicity director Alvin Warren, Vigil, and Joe Herrera, who was serving as executive secretary of the council. It was noted that of the one hundred applications for enrollment in the institute, only eight were from the local area. Vigil made the council's opposition clear, citing a June sixth vote to condemn the program set up for an "arts elite": "The Pueblos don't want it. We don't need it. Our greatest need is education. Indian children should be learning to read, write and speak English. Indian men and women should be learning skills so they can get jobs. This is the real need. If Indians want to learn music and ballet and those things, there are hundreds of schools that teach them."[72]

Some Pueblo youth wanted to go to college; some wanted to learn a trade. There was a demand for both levels of training but not for those with no advanced education at all. "The average of Indian education is the fifth grade, while the average for non-Indians is the tenth," the press release reported. "Who thinks a fifth grade education is good enough for the Space Age?" Vigil went on to solicit his readers' help in establishing a first-rate college preparatory high school with vocational training at the Santa Fe Indian School and putting an end to the Institute of American Indian Arts.

The responsibility for answering many of the congressmen's subsequent inquiries fell to Asst. Secretary of the Interior John A. Carver Jr. Carver responded that the Bureau of Indian Affairs had long recognized the need for an art school that would provide Indian students with both traditional courses in a variety of media, as well as "exploratory" courses in art and an academic core. It was only now made possible, as the Santa Fe Indian School was no longer needed by younger Indian students. Construction programs initiated under Public Law 815 and the bureau's own building efforts had provided places in schools nearer the children's homes. The Santa Fe facility was judged to be ideal for this new cultural center.

Indian art students would at last have the opportunity to familiarize themselves with new materials and contemporary functions of objects, while becoming aware of the best in Indian art traditions. "In most cases," Carver added, "neither their parents nor their home communities can provide the necessary guidance or exploratory experiences." The institute, on the other hand, would seek to develop in each student "an awareness and understanding of commercial avenues through which his cultural heritage and his unique talents and interests can be used to insure a good future for himself, his family, and his community." Those students who wished to pursue traditional vocational study could attend Haskell Institute, Chilocco School, or public high schools. Scholarship assistance was available for students who wanted to attend colleges and universities. Carver, therefore, saw no immediate need for a vocational school or college preparatory program in Santa Fe. While the cost per student of the institute was higher than the average boarding school program, it was reasonable considering the specialization of the training to be offered. Carver further noted that the institute had received "only interest and support" from Indian groups other than the Pueblos.[73]

Indeed, the Window Rock (Ariz.) *Navajo Times*, which had published the All-Pueblo Council's news release on 11 July, included in that same edition three additional articles, all of which were optimistically favorable toward the new school. One profiled a Crownpoint student, Charlie Chee Long, who hoped to be among the first class attending the new Indian art school. Long explained that he felt the institute would be his only opportunity to advance in the field of art. "I know there are relocation and trade schools," Long told the reporter, "but by all means, I do not intend to become a factory worker, because I think I can use my art talent to be among the leaders instead of being led."[74]

A second article was drawn from student application letters the institute had enthusiastically supplied. "After reading the bulletin about the Art Institute," read Roger Tsabetsaye's letter, "I was very pleased and overwhelmed. I said to myself that, 'this is the school I dreamed of attending.'" Tsabetsaye, from Zuni Pueblo, had attended the Southwestern Indian Art Project and was one of two students to receive a scholarship from the School for American Craftsmen at Rochester. Boyce frequently quoted from his letter in promotional materials for the institute. Another prospective student, Navajo Harry Walters, wrote that he had never been taught anything about painting and had never seen a "real artist" at work but had learned from reading and studying other artists, especially Indian painters. "I hope some day to be a well-known artist," concluded Walters. Mary Jane Blue Spruce of Laguna Pueblo claimed that she would be very happy and work to the best of her ability if given the chance to pursue her interest in the fine arts, particularly ballet. Sharon Kay Lente, from Isleta Pueblo, wrote that the institute would offer specialized training that would allow her to realize her dream and goal to be the best in the field of architecture.[75]

The third feature recounted the impressions of a *Navajo Times* reporter who had been asked by tribal leaders to survey the institute for the purpose of "determining the goals of this new school . . . and to reach conclusions as to the potential value to Navajo and other Indian students." He had been preceded in his visit to the institute by the Navajo Relocation Committee, the members of which, he stated, were in basic agreement with his report. "I'm not an educator and I'll probably be put in my place by some who insist vocation is the entire answer," the reporter ventured in his folksy writing style, "but it does look like these people have come up with a new approach. They are going to open a new can of peas, so to speak."[76]

The school was not designed for the masses, he cautioned, but rather to "recognize the latent talent in the various arts which most Indians seem to have and intends to obtain the cream of the crop, with the hope that just a few great Indian artists, Indian composers, Indian writers, Indian architects or even Indian playwrights, may emerge on the national or world scene." The institute intended to take the natural creativity of students and channel it into "making the unique Indian cultural and artistic heritage a strong and moving force in the business life of America."

The reporter found Boyce to be an "enthusiastic man" who believed that the institute would open a "new era in cultural education." The article also seemed pleased with the "social training" that would be made available to students, including guidance in eating habits, manners, decorum, consideration of others, dress, conversational ease, and self-confidence—all in a "college atmosphere." "I saw lots of old decrepit buildings being remodeled and modernized," the reporter recounted. "I saw new buildings under construction. I heard about new concepts in dormitory living, a student's canteen, like home family-style dining, a student's organization building and campus type life." The article also noted brightly that Boyce promised the school would encourage students to participate in civic affairs and prepare in every way to "be at home away from home, on the golf course, or at a great man's table."

Boyce further explained that the school's objective was "to turn out individualists—non-conformists, if you will—who will perhaps drive on to paths which have not previously been explored and which stem from their rich ancestral inheritance." The article observed that the gap in instruction and overall social experience that the Institute hoped to fill had never been dealt with on these terms—alongside the development of traditional Indian originality. The writer genuinely hoped the concept would prevail:

> Will it work? Gosh, I don't know, but it sounds good to a reporter. . . .
> If enthusiasm, a staff comprised of producing artists of national reputation, a sincere attempt to achieve a new depth of rapport between students and teacher; if such factors count for anything, we should see some remarkably interesting developments.
> We'll take a good long look after the program gets well underway, and in the meantime, wish it every success.

A postscript suggested that the Navajo tribal chairman might ask "Uncle" to bring the school to the Navajo reservation, noting that "there's some sparks flying in Santa Fe!"

The chairman, however, had some serious reservations about the new school in Santa Fe. Paul Jones, chair of the Navajo Tribal Council, drafted a letter to Commissioner Philleo Nash on 20 July expressing concern over the apparent disregard for Indian views and wishes that seemed to characterize the school's establishment. "Since all of the Indian tribes affected by this decision vigorously opposed the conversion of the Santa Fe school into an art institute, I should like to be informed of the considerations which prompted your determination," demanded Jones. The bureau had not progressed far enough with the basics of education to "warrant the installation of such a costly program which will serve so few." Those with talent for the fine arts should be given the opportunity to develop that talent, but not at the expense of the many who had a more pressing need for elementary education, he reasoned.[77]

Nash responded that practically all Indian children, with the exception of Navajo and Alaskan children, had school opportunities. "If the Santa Fe plant were in a location where young Navajo and Alaska children could use it, we would have made it available to them," the commissioner assured Jones. Moreover, Nash made it clear that the institute would not teach art at the expense of basic subjects such as English, science, mathematics, and history. He complimented the *Navajo Times* article on the school, remarking that though written in a somewhat humorous vein, "it presents very well the philosophy of the Institute." In closing, Nash noted that he had received protests regarding the school only from the Pueblos; other areas had shown interest and support.[78]

Meanwhile, the institute media war in and around Santa Fe had intensified. John O. Crow, deputy commissioner of Indian Affairs, found himself fielding questions about excessive expenditures at the school, costs that supposedly included linen sheets for student beds and silver table service in the dining hall. While Crow didn't know about the sheets, he admitted that he hoped the utensils were at least silver plated. "We want some experience of gracious living included for students at the Institute," Crow replied. "I spent four years in an Indian Boarding School, and if I had any table manners when I went there, I lost them or else went hungry." There were more rumors of a silver stamping machine to be used in the manufacture of Indian jewelry and recessed tubs in the dormitories.[79]

In an article entitled "Boyce Shoots Back," the IAIA superintendent raged against such critics. He knew nothing about any silver stamping machine. The accusations regarding the sheets had probably been inferred from the bureau's use of the term "linen closet," and students would not be enjoying bathtubs at all, much less recessed ones. Communication of the aims of the school had become difficult, complained Boyce, because people with no background in, or appreciation of, the arts were resentful of the special considerations being given those with talent. Boyce said that one person out of a thousand saw the world in a different way. "Instead of the other 999 yakking 'Why aren't you like the rest of us?' we need encouragement in the other direction," he chided. "Let's have some support in turning out creative Indians."[80]

Boyce charged that traditional vocational training was no longer an ethical educational program. "We have enough unemployed wheelbarrow pushers around," Boyce exclaimed. "Automation is providing more and more of them. The real economic opportunities of the future lie not in the vocational fields, but in architecture, music, art and writing." As for the option of Indian students attending other art schools, he warned that students' work would then only be an imitation of the white man's cultural expression, hastening the destruction of "the thing for which the Indian can make a unique contribution to our culture."

Santa Fe was being given an opportunity for "greatness" by virtue of being chosen as the site for this "unique experiment in human affairs on the world scene." Boyce urged the paper's readers to consider the school's larger ramifications:

> We are the first government in this wide world that I know of that is in the process of going out of its way to put new life in the expression of a minority culture. This is more than just putting up with it in the hope it will die. This is to nurture it.
>
> This is the fundamental war of freedom. It's opening up the doors of maximum freedom for the individual—Doors that have been closed in the past.
>
> We've learned that the people of Africa don't want to grow more spinach, they want to express themselves. This is the issue of our times.

Any idea as new as this was bound to be controversial, Boyce added. Art was controversial. But shouldn't they be given time to show what could be done?

The very next day Martin Vigil vowed that the fight against the school would continue. "Indians care a lot more about their culture and tradition than the white man does," admonished Vigil, "and arts and crafts are a part of it." But Indians made paintings, pottery, jewelry, and other things precisely because they were a part of their culture, not because they could sell them. Potter's wheels, electric kilns, commercial glazes, and other things to be used at the Institute of American Indian Arts were not part of Indian culture and tradition, and arts of that nature were not made in the spirit of Indian religion, according to Vigil. "This is not freedom; this is slavery to modern machinery. This is in imitation of the white man's culture. This is no opportunity for greatness." As for art forms such as ballet, Vigil noted that high school was too late to begin such studies. "You must start young. That is why our Indian children begin to learn traditional dancing when they are four years old." [81]

The public exchange between Boyce and Vigil triggered a weeklong media battle in the strongly polarized Santa Fe community. It began with the *Santa Fe New Mexican's* own editorial in support of the institute. Calling the school's critics "Don Quixotes," who, like the literary character, were breaking their lance on the wrong target, the newspaper maintained that they kept their eyes shut to the facts. The arguments used against the institute—unemployment among Indians, lack of educational opportunities, Indian interest in tradition and culture, and inability of Indians to earn a decent income in the field of art—could be better used as reasons to support the school. Through misrepresentation these knights fighting windmills had managed to undermine the confidence of some area Indians in the project. "With friends like these," concluded the editorial, "the Indians don't need any enemies." [82]

John Collier entered the fray three days later with a letter that attempted to allay the critics' fears by recalling the successes of the institute's predecessor. "I would remind Martin [Vigil], and the Santa Fe public, that an Indian Arts Institute was conducted at the Santa Fe boarding school, starting more than 30 years ago," wrote Collier. "That Institute did not corrupt the Indian arts; instead, it helped them to a more beautiful flowering, which became famous all over the world." The former Indian commissioner saw the institute as the reestablishment and enlargement of Dunn's disparaged Studio, which he ironically claimed had never "been adversely criticized by Indians or by those white people who love the Indian arts." George Boyce had worked with distinction for more than twenty years in Indian education, noted Collier. There was no reason to believe he had lost his bearings now. He suggested that the school's detractors take a wait-and-see attitude.[83]

Collier was quickly taken to task by Dorothy Dunn's old friend Olive Rush, who responded that the Santa Fe Indian School Studio that he so richly praised had been brought to its end "by ambitious people who were eager to tear it down and to build up this Institute of American Indian Art [sic]." She bristled at Collier's statement that Martin Vigil was "unwise" in his opposition to the new school, retorting that Vigil and the All-Pueblo Council realized, "as do many of us who understand not only Indians, but Art and the danger of using wrong methods of teaching, that Indian Art suffers when directed along the usual art school courses." She insisted that the institute's critics were not a "vocal few," as Collier had maintained, but many who were "proud to join hands with [the Indians] on finding them awake to the danger threatening them."[84]

Surprisingly, Dorothy Dunn herself, claiming that she had been misquoted during the controversy and wanted to set the record straight, contacted the *Santa Fe New Mexican* from her California home to make public her support of the institute. Dunn wrote that she had long been an advocate of reestablishing the Santa Fe Indian School as an art center. "Often before his death Mr. Chester E. Faris, superintendent of the first arts and crafts school at Santa Fe, expressed his heartfelt wishes for such a school," remembered Dunn. "We knew of no finer way than through development of their own arts for Indians to gain livelihood for themselves while also gaining understanding and respect for Indian thought and works."[85]

Quoting from her presentation at the Rockefeller conference in 1959, Dunn again outlined her own ideas for such a center. The basic tenets of the Studio could be expanded to offer supporting subjects, such as business training for exhibiting and marketing, experimentation in adaptations of crafts, and liberal arts courses sufficient to meet college entrance requirements.

However, she warned against allowing commercial and outside interests to dictate pedagogy and curriculum: "The real and rich resources are in the Indian arts and in the potential artists. Within the school it would be a vast mistake to manipulate these resources to conform to popular non-Indian modes rather than to aid their extension within Indian traditions. Major adaptations have their place beyond the school and at the hand of any designer any time, but the Institute would be a wellspring of timeless Indian art." The safeguard to this would be the choice of personnel, noted Dunn, for the "perceptiveness, knowledge and creative spirit of the staff, and the student response to these will determine outcomes of the Institute." [86]

Meanwhile, others joined the debate. John Rainer, a Taos Pueblo businessman and the immediate past chairman of the All-Pueblo Council, drafted a letter that characterized the institute's opposition as being led by disgruntled former Santa Fe Indian School employees who did not want to transfer to other jobs out of Santa Fe. "In any educational program a student is the most important," stated Rainer. "And it seems to me the Indian should be concerned with a real education for their children instead of fighting against a plan which would enrich further the gift of the Indian people through their art." Rainer was joined in his support of the school by Oliver LaFarge, president of the Association on American Indian Affairs. "It appears to me that they (opponents of the institute) are protesting about being given what they want." [87]

With less than two months until the school's opening, Indian Commissioner Philleo Nash submitted an eight-page report to Sen. Clinton P. Anderson, hoping to quell the tenacious opposition. Nash made it clear that the decision to convert the Santa Fe Indian School to the Institute of American Indian Arts had been made before he took office. Nevertheless, he felt that the new project would satisfy a heretofore unmet need and would grow into a "major element in the life of Santa Fe." Despite two days of meetings with all parties in June, Nash wrote that there were still deep-seated misunderstandings that required clarification. The report primarily addressed the issues of Pueblo demands for vocational education, the need for additional school spaces for children not in school, and the excessive cost of the new art program. "I hasten to assure you," the commissioner concluded, "that if we felt that the allegations about the school were correct we would accept them and change course. However, I am satisfied that the real educational needs of the Gallup Area are being met by the current and foreseeable programs and that the proposed change-over of the Santa Fe School represents, in fact, the highest and best use of the facility." [88]

By month's end, Boyce proffered an olive branch of rhetoric designed to mend enough fences to go on with the school's 1 October opening. "We need the help of the people in Santa Fe to succeed," announced the superintendent to a party of thirty invited guests touring the institute. "We are willing to listen and to seek advice on this new adventure." Among the visitors were Santa Fe mayor Pat Hollis; the president of the Chamber of Commerce, Dale Bullock; and the president of the New Mexico Parent-Teachers Association, Mrs. Jack Sturgeon. Boyce told the community leaders that the institute was a "kind of salvage operation of our unusual Indian youth and of the Indian approach to aesthetics."[89]

The tour was part of a two-week-long orientation for all institute employees, and the school's administrative staff was on hand to discuss plans for their respective programs. Oleta Merry, an Oklahoma Choctaw who was to later marry Boyce, explained that her approach to guidance through the dormitories, dining room, recreation and community would turn out poised and confident students who could look forward to a higher economic level. Merry had developed her "home living program" while head of the Home Economics department at Intermountain Indian School.

Principal Wilma Victor, also Choctaw, said she was operating the academic program on the assumption that Indian students were able to absorb a well-rounded education and would continue that education beyond the institute. Lloyd New spoke of his plans to develop a dance troupe that would travel the world interpreting Indian culture and of training musicians who could write Indian themes in modern music. A tour similar to this one had been conducted for religious leaders two days earlier.[90]

A week before the staff gathered at the institute for their first official introduction to the new school, a newsletter had been sent out to students accepted to the program. "Each day, if you were here," read the enthusiastic update, "you would see progressive changes in form and shape of our new academic building. The interior work has begun. The latest in modern building construction is being employed. Modern equipment and the most recent editions in textbooks and instructional materials are now arriving daily." Work on the Home Economics Building, where the emphasis would be placed on "gracious modern living," was proceeding nicely as well. Walls were being repainted in the dormitories with more "attractive and cheerful color," and the laundries, baths, and girl's "good grooming" rooms were being tiled to give them a new look.[91]

As the time was drawing "excitingly nearer" for the students to join the staff in Santa Fe, the newsletter proposed to offer a brief word on what they and their parents could expect with regards to student behavior and responsibility. "The Institute of American Indian Arts aims to turn out graduates who are earnest, sincere and trustworthy," the letter stated. "We assume that all our students are young adults or nearly so. We want to treat them as adults. We want them to be able to assume the same responsibility as they would have in a good home or in college."

The school would be offering training in family relations, home management and consumer buying, child care, foods and nutrition, and health and personal grooming to assist students in achieving these standards of responsibility. In addition, two complete apartments were being constructed and furnished for "practical experience in Apartment Living." Oleta Merry, the institute's director of Guidance and Home-Living, was, of course, a veteran of Intermountain's Navajo Special Education Program, where this type of curriculum had been developed.

"Remember that to be a great artist today one must have a very good education," admonished the letter. Students were expected to discuss their interests and future plans with the curriculum counselor upon their arrival in order to best select their academic courses. Certain classes were required for a high school diploma, and in the arts areas there were two additional requirements—design survey and vocational arts survey. The first was devoted to developing certain understandings, skills, and attitudes in the arts through American Indian sources. The second exposed students to a variety of vocational arts such as mechanical drawing, interior design, photography, illustration, advertising art, film, theater art, and others. The school would offer a wide selection of electives in both the arts and academic subjects, and postgraduate students were allowed to take any of these high school courses.

All supplies in each area would be furnished by the school, but students were encouraged to bring favorite tools, brushes, stones for jewelry, and so on. Students were also invited to bring decorative items for the residence hall, as well as dance costumes and drums. "Just tuck them away in your suitcase at the last minute!" A special museum-gallery was being developed to house traveling and student exhibitions, and the newsletter also solicited student suggestions for the first show, which was described as being "created around dramatic, old Indian art pieces from every tribe that is to be represented at the Institute."

Students were advised that few part-time jobs were available in the Santa Fe area and that they should not plan on this source of income. Since books, paper, and art materials were being furnished, however, they would only require money for items such as toiletries, stamps, movies, and special events. The school had been receiving numerous inquiries as to the type of clothing students should bring and the newsletter gave them a casual list:

> Some suggested items of clothing for both boys and girls might be
> a wool coat for cold winter days, flat shoes for everyday school wear, a

pair of dress shoes for church and other activities requiring dress wear, simple tailored clothes for school, one or two outfits for dress-up occasions, clothes for lounging such as bathrobes and dusters, etc. Don't forget sleeping clothes for night time! These are only suggestions. Plan your wardrobe with regard to your finances. And don't overlook informal sports clothing for golfing, skiing, bowling, picnicking, etc.

Transportation schedules were being arranged so that students could arrive the last week in September. All that was left for the student to do was to mail back an enclosed medical affidavit promptly.

The period of gestation now drawing to a close, the original concept of an Indian arts school had been cultivated in such a way that it seemed palatable to Bureau of Indian Affairs hard-liners and a largely terminationist Congress. The institute fit nicely with Hildegard Thompson's educational agenda of strengthening academic skills, deemphasizing traditional terminal vocational programs, and preparing students for college or advanced technical training. And IAIA was being ably marshaled by George Boyce, a man whose name was synonymous with the Navajo Special Education Program, one of the bureau's most successful attempts at preparing Indian students to "master the material culture of the dominant race" and live off the reservation.

The same conservative, nationalistic furor that spawned termination, however, had also given rise to the government's abdication of its cultural Cold War battle duty to the Rockefellers and the latter's interest in "safe" and authenticating Indian modernists. It remained to be seen how the BIA version of an Indian art school would mesh with the Rockefeller-New variety, how the resulting configuration would be packaged and marketed, and how it would be received by the public and media.

CHAPTER 4

A CONVERGENCE OF IDEOLOGIES, 1962–1968

When students began arriving on the Institute of American Indian Arts campus the last week of September 1962, the cool rainy weather that greeted them seemed to match the gray mood of the staff. Dormitories were still being painted; the home economics building was full of workmen; and basic equipment for the kitchen, dining room, and dormitories had not yet arrived. Teachers and other employees were scrambling to clean up and haul old equipment back into place and were readying temporary quarters for art studios and student sleeping rooms. It was to be another month before the academic building (which housed not only classrooms and laboratories but also the library), arts and crafts facility, and dining hall were expected to be operational.

Despite the disarray, Boyce reported that this first class of IAIA students was a positive group. "They strike us as being earnest, mannerly and at the same time lively and forward-moving youngsters," Boyce confided to a BIA area director. With a student body of 130, representing sixty-nine tribes and nineteen states, Boyce felt confident that "whatever happens here may very well symbolize what our Government and the American people . . . render as special cultural services to Indian youths." This sentiment had indeed been formally incorporated into the school's basic statement of purpose, which stressed that "by providing adequate tools, professional leadership, freedom for exploration in various art fields, and encouragement of each student toward maximum freedom of artistic expression, our Government makes a unique contribution to greater freedom and economic betterment of young peoples of all tribes."[1]

The staff was in the process of completing their orientation and was endeavoring to "reach quickly a tone of maximum student responsibility and cooperation." A "responsibility code" was distributed to students so as to clarify the school's expectations in this area. "Responsibility is the path to maximum freedom," the memorandum began. "Therefore, it is the policy of the Institute of American Indian Arts to incorporate into its educational program relationships among students, and between staff and students, which will foster student responsibility for strong adult citizenship." The code dealt with a variety of topics, from smoking, drinking, and dating, to school work details, dining procedures, and class attendance. Students were reminded that their behavior off campus during the summer vacation and on job sites was of concern to the institute and that they would be expected to "exercise personal influence for good and to help prevent undesirable conduct by other students." In matters of dating and smoking, the "practice of discreet adults" was to serve as the appropriate standard. "Socially acceptable customs" were to be observed by both girls and boys at all times. The use of intoxicating beverages was considered "definitely contrary to the purposes of the Institute." Attendance in class and promptness in meeting work details were expected from all students.[2]

The work details, Boyce insisted, were a part of the curriculum and not an "economic measure, wherein students help 'to pay back' for the cost of the program." He explained that these assignments were educationally desirable for all people and were a commonly accepted practice in many of the most select preparatory schools. Such tasks as cleaning and care of the dormitories, food preparation, cleanup of dining and kitchen facilities, and disposal of trash were intended to develop a "sound American attitude toward any kind of work that is of community benefit." This attitude included a willingness to accept criticism and suggestions where standards of work performance could be improved, promptness and efficiency, courtesy and consideration, cooperation in group endeavor, proper use and care of tools and equipment, and a familiarity with good performance standards.[3]

Boyce noted that the kitchen and dining facilities at the school had been reequipped and refurnished to achieve other "important educational goals." One of these was to "develop methods whereby Indian youths enter the modern world with social poise and confidence." An orientation session in the dining hall served to introduce students to the complexities of table service, and a mimeographed sheet, "Introduction to Gracious Eating," was provided as a guide to appropriate dining practices. "Your table manners at . . . meals reveal your background and breeding so quickly and have such an influence on other people at the table that their importance cannot be over emphasized," the sheet warned. "It is therefore essential that we learn to eat graciously and to adhere to the fundamental of good table manners. When we stop to think that strangers judge us by the way we look and act, we realize that good manners are important."[4]

The dining guide came complete with illustrations covering the correct placement of a spoon with a cup, the proper way to hold a fork, and the acceptable manner in which bread was to be buttered. "Before coming to the table you should have smoothed your hair and washed your hands," the instructions began. "Unfold the napkin halfway and lay it across your lap. Use your napkin to wipe your lips lightly when necessary. Always keep it smoothed on your lap while it is not being used whether it is of paper or cloth." There followed eight pages of explicit "dos" and "don'ts" for everything from posture to placing jelly on a plate. "It is considered bad form to play with the silver at the table or to seem otherwise nervous, uncomfortable, or in a hurry," the guide admonished. "Good manners demand that we chew quietly with our lips closed and that we refrain from laughing or talking when we have food in our mouths. Do not fill your mouth so full that you cannot answer if you are spoken to. Take mouthfuls that can be managed easily. Eat slowly, quietly, gracefully." If students practiced every day, they were told, their good manners would come naturally.

The students would have ample opportunity to practice. At each meal they were assigned the role of host or hostess, server (wearing aprons and jackets) or guest, and were expected to abide by the etiquette outlined in an additional instructional sheet, "Family Style Dinner." Another handout, "Dining Hall and Dish Room Detail," listed the rules for those assigned to be "toast and coffee girls" or "trash boys," as well as the lucky students who would be cleaning bathrooms, sweeping the cafeteria, or washing dishes.

Students' performance on these work details and in other matters of conduct was measured by a "list of personality traits to be used in a rating scale." The sixty-nine-point checklist was divided into eight sections covering personal appearance, social adaptability, courtesy, emotional stability, trustworthiness and honesty, dependability and self-reliance, industry and effort, and civic responsibility and cooperation. Students were thereby judged on cleanliness, good posture, and taste in makeup and clothes. They were expected to

FIG. 5. *IAIA students at mealtime in the dining hall.*
(National Park Service Photo, Fred Mang,
photographer)

demonstrate certain social skills deemed desirable, such as being "a good
mixer" and not shy, speaking in a well-modulated voice and using good English, and being "a good sport and democratic." High marks were earned for
showing consideration for others, having good manners, and being "poised
emotionally." Lying, cheating, procrastinating, or being sensitive to criticism
were not admirable qualities. A good student was one who was ambitious,
worked well with others, cheerfully obeyed rules and regulations, and was
"loyal to ideals of school."

Clearly, not every recruit had the same ideas as Boyce about what constituted a student's responsibilities. A month into the school year Boyce wrote
to express concern to the BIA Area Office about conditions on the campus.
"The student body, coming from such varied backgrounds, poses many problems of restlessness and teen-age irresponsibility," complained the superintendent. Tardiness and absence among students had been very high. A great

deal of time had been devoted to these types of problems. Moreover, tensions were mounting over the lack of access to facilities, books, equipment, and tools. The Guidance Department, which normally would help diffuse and mitigate such difficulties, was suffering from its own morale crisis. New employees were at odds with staff inherited from the Santa Fe Indian School, and two members of the guidance program, as well as a physical education teacher, resigned in the midst of the melee.[5]

The three employees had apparently been popular with students and their resignations caused a great deal of dissatisfaction on campus. A student petition was drafted immediately and a letter of protest submitted to Boyce. The letter stated that the students were aware of the reasons for the resignations and that they did not want to see these faculty leave. "Without them life at this Institute would be very dull and very disappointing," they continued. "Without them also you will be without many of your most promising students." While the students insisted that this was not a threat, but rather an attempt to inform Boyce of their wish to see the faculty reinstated "in conditions agreeable to them and everyone," the letter ended on an ominous note: "If these resignations should go through, we cannot gurantee [sic] that we students will be able to restrain ourselves. Drastic measures are on the verge of being taken. Matters are very strained now and we stand united in our cause!"[6]

The petition, which was signed by sixty-five students, read:

> Students of I.A.I.A.; this petition is being cirulated [sic] throughout the student body in the behalf of [sic] several members of the teaching and advisory staff. Miss Irving, girls advisor, Mr. Black, boys advisor, and a person very dear and important to all of us—Mr. Fulgenci, recreation director. All persons wishing them to remain in the preasent [sic] stations please sign below. This paper will go directly to Dr. Boyce's office.
>
> The reason for their leaving is quite evident, their difficulty in reaching agreement with the immediate head.[7]

Additional sheets were attached to the petition for student comments. One student added the following:

> Mr. Black and Mr. Fulgenci means [sic] a lot to all the boys. They feel that they can take their problems to them. Our problems are theirs, I think they understand us more than anybody. They're someone we really feel we can trust, if they leave your [sic] going to start something you won't be able to stop. About the only way you could stop it is by closing the school, and everything you worked for will go down the drain. I feel I speak for the whole dorm.[8]

Although Boyce had encouraged students in the "Responsibility Code" to make suggestions for improvement at all times—both individually and through the formally organized student council—it soon became evident that the invitation did not extend to real student involvement at this level. He acted quickly to squelch the smoldering rebellion, threatening students with expulsion and refusing to rehire one teacher.

The retributions were, of course, explained on other grounds. For example, Nell Irving, the faculty member in question, was accused of being "immature" and "less than responsive in assuming a responsibility for the essential details in the physical aspects of dormitory living." Boyce claimed that Irving had been involved in the preparation of the petition and that she had not taken any steps to clarify her role in the students' actions nor to express any concern for issues of professional ethics. She tendered her resignation when Boyce demanded a personal conference wherein he expected to take administrative action. "Our own view," Boyce reported to the Area Office, "is that we would not want to offer re-employment to Miss Irving in view of the attitude she showed during the several months employed here on a probationary basis."[9]

In a letter to the Colville Indian Agency, the student who organized the petition drive was accused of being uncooperative in his art classes, having a critical attitude, and harboring strong resentments against adults, white persons, and the world in general, "growing out of his background in not having had a stable family life." Boyce alleged that the young man was unwilling to take the required high school courses and that his "manner of necking and petting with the girls here constantly has been extreme beyond acceptance of either the staff or other members of the student body." The student's role in soliciting student signatures for the petition and his written statement "threatening to close up and destroy the Institute and all that we had worked for unless we could come to terms that suited him" were cited only as additional examples of his rebelliousness. Boyce related that the staff had unanimously decided this student "did not belong here" but had since agreed to give him a chance to show that he could do better and "exercise some leadership in support of, rather than an attack of, the Institute."[10]

The parents of another student participant in the petition drive received both a telegram and a letter regarding their daughter's conduct. Boyce wrote that the school was impressed with the student's "capable skill in expressing herself clearly and persuasively" and with her potential for strong leadership. However, she had chosen to exercise her powers of leadership to incite a large group of students to create a general disturbance. Moreover, Boyce charged that she was not settling down to her studies and had "not been pursuing an attitude to take advantage of what the Institute is designed to offer." The staff had, thus, unanimously reached a decision to return the student to her home. Once informed of this, however, the student had expressed a desire to be given another chance, and the school was happy to report that they would do "everything possible to assist her in furthering her education and preparing her for successful adulthood." [11]

These were not the only students who would be threatened with dismissal. Others, for a variety of reasons, were actually sent home or left of their own accord during the first semester. One young man had been described in a psychiatric report as a "basically schizoid person with homosexual problems of a critical nature." He was given a ticket home the second week of the semester, Boyce explaining that the school was not staffed or otherwise prepared to offer the special services required for such a student. Another youth left for a ranch job that same week. Yet a third was dismissed because the staff felt he had not made every effort to adjust to the program, which Boyce described as "based upon very high standards of conduct and work performance." [12]

A fourth student became the subject of some controversy when she insisted on returning home so as to take her ailing father to a medicine man in Montana. Boyce drafted a memo to Lloyd New, Oleta Merry, and Wilma Victor, stating that the student's welfare worker at home reported her to have a "long record that he characterized as being a quitter and withdrawing from various programs laid out for her." The father was being cared for adequately in town, and it was the welfare worker's hope, and apparently Boyce's also, that the staff could persuade her to stay at the school and "reverse that record." The girl persisted, using her own per capita payment to purchase the ticket home (a trip Boyce called a "vacation"), and promised to take her books and work on the road. Boyce relented, noting that the student was "very strongly imbued with the native Indian attitude regarding the importance she attaches to her father going to a medicineman [sic]" and that in his judgment any attempt to dissuade her "would only incur rebellion or evasiveness." [13]

Boyce referred some students to the Public Health Service for behavior he felt might require psychiatric diagnosis. One such youth, who was characterized as "brooding" and "unstable," had been involved in several drinking episodes. Two other "moody" students were asked to transfer to Concho School in Oklahoma, which according to Boyce "had been established to help children adjust to school routines." [14]

Boyce had been acutely aware of the special needs many of the school's students presented from interviews conducted during the first weeks of the semester. "Our student body has a tremendous range of backgrounds," reported the superintendent to the area director. "Many of them have come from stable homes. And everyone comments what a fine group of young Indian youths have come here. On the other hand, it is astonishing . . . how many are orphaned, in many cases their parental ancestry actually unknown, many years of shifting for themselves and other tragic backgrounds." [15] One young man, tall, athletic, and "a real extrovert," had startled the school administrator with the following exchange:

"Is your father living?" I ask, seeking some basic information.
"Nobody knows," he says, staring me down.
Changing tack, I ask, "Do you have any brothers?"
"I did have two. My stepfather poisoned them," he says. "This upset my mother. They all started picking on her. Now she is in an institution. Permanently. I stopped on my way down here to see her." [16]

Despite the obvious seriousness of problems among the student body and the delays in moving into campus buildings, the school's acclaim was not slow in coming. Their first national showing of student work was miraculously launched as early as the spring of 1964. This first exhibition's venue, like several yet to come, was a government-orchestrated one in the offices of the Department of the Interior in Washington. Secretary of the Interior Stewart Udall, and to an even greater extent his wife, Lee, were ardent supporters of and frequent visitors to the school, and they remained instrumental in providing political backing throughout Udall's tenure. [17]

Indian Commissioner Philleo Nash, delivering the commencement address at the institute's graduation ceremonies in May 1964, spoke enthusiastically of the exhibit and its impact upon the art world, confiding to the young graduates that sophisticated art patrons had been astonished that student work could be of such high quality. Prominent among the thousand visitors who had seen the exhibit thus far were Rene d'Harnoncourt, Frederick Dockstader, and actor Vincent Price, all members of the Indian Arts and Crafts Board. "Because some of you have already attained national attention," Nash told the students, "the country will be watching with eager interest the progress of every graduate of this school from now on. . . . This school must be a pacemaker in Indian education." [18]

This initial success was followed in the fall by participation in the *First Annual Invitational Exhibition of American Indian Paintings*, held in the Department of the Interior's newly refurbished art gallery from 2 November 1964 to 29 January 1965. The show was composed of two sections—eighty-eight works solicited through direct invitation and a companion selection of forty-four paintings dating from 1930 to 1958 on loan from the Philbrook Art Center, which according to the accompanying catalog was to function as "introduction and background" to the body of more recent work. It was an exhibition technique that would find favor with the institute in the near future—a visual juxtapositioning of source and departure, which served at the same time to legitimate through association and appreciate through disassociation.[19]

The show highlighted IAIA faculty and students, and presented a sampling of the breadth of expression that characterized the school at the time. The expressionist energy of Larry Littlebird's *Bird Man* was countered by the serene dignity of Jennie Trujillo's *Zuni* (see figs. 6 and 7). The haunting *Faces of Mankind* by George Burdeau presented a vivid contrast to Ernest Whitehead's Studio-reminiscent *Crown Dancer* (see figs. 8 and 9).[20] Yet it was here for the first time in the school's exhibition history that emphasis was placed on the experimental new forms, with which the institute was now being directly credited.

> Beginning in the late 50's, and more especially during the past several years, Native American art has experience [sic] considerable revitalization through a wide-spread renaissance of interest in experimentation with both media and new forms of expression. This has resulted in part through the work of such individual artists as Joe Herrera, Pablita Velarde, Theodore Suina, Yeffe Kimball and George Morrison, but more generally through the founding in 1962 of the Institute of American Indian Art [sic] in Santa Fe, New Mexico.... The invitational section of the exhibition which includes the work of several recent Institute students, vividly reflects the new experimentation and invention now at the command of Native American artists.[21]

Three months later the institute was invited to send a dance group to perform at the White House for President and Mrs. Maurice Yameogo of Upper Volta (see fig. 10). The school frequently served as host to foreign dignitaries, but its intended role as an international model of minority education was now to take a more visible turn. Although the dances performed were traditional, as were the gifts presented the Yameogos, the institute's emerging new focus was clearly stated. These art forms were not merely a means to their own end. Rather, as the printed program for *An Evening of American Indian Art* announced, the institute had been "conceived on the idea that living Indian art forms were to be esteemed and encouraged on the premise that exciting new art forms should evolve from the traditional Indian arts."[22]

Fig. 6. Bird Man, *Larry Littlebird, 1963, magic marker, 12¾″ × 10¾″.*

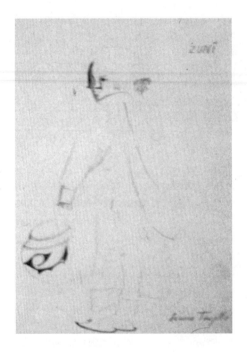

Fig. 7. Zuni, *Jennie Trujillo, 1963, pencil, 9½″ × 7″.*

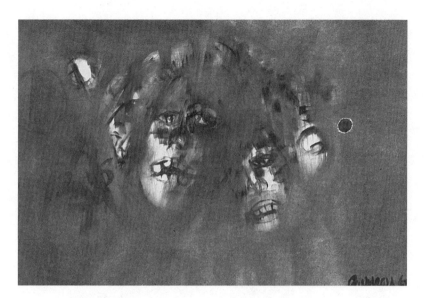

FIG. 8. Faces of Mankind, *George Burdeau, 1964, oil,* 22" × 28½".

The student performers joined the reception afterward, freshly changed into dinner jackets and formals. The hometown press declared this to be in and of itself a major historical triumph, noting that it marked "the first time Indians had mingled at a state dinner and reception in the White House so freely." Cabinet members, congressmen, State Department officials, social-ites, and people who had been identified with "the development of interest in African affairs" were all part of the large audience. Prominent among the guests were the Udalls, who were said to have skipped out early on a compet-ing performance at the State Department, with Mrs. Udall explaining, "I can't wait to see the Indians dance."[23]

Residents of Indian Country were by now accustomed to an almost steady stream of State Department–orchestrated publicity and photo oppor-tunities designed to showcase their accomplishments to the world. As early as 1959, for example, a young Cochiti Pueblo student, Clarence Weahkee, was sent to Soviet-bloc countries as a goodwill ambassador able to "carry a great deal of influence in putting young people in the Iron Curtain nations straight about life in America." Weahkee attended an anti-Communist youth rally in Vienna that had been organized as counterpropaganda to the concurrent "communist-engineered" World Youth Rally there.[24]

FIG. 9. Crown Dancer, *Ernest Whitehead, 1964, casein, 16" × 12".*

FIG. 10. IAIA dancers perform at the White House, 1965.

The following year the U.S. State Department arranged for a young East African from Tanganyika to attend the National Indian Youth Council's annual meeting held in Albuquerque, with the hope that he would "take home with him ideas that would be helpful in planning programs for African youth." Marcel Ibalico, president of the National Assembly, Republic of the Congo, similarly toured the Southwest under the U.S. State Department's foreign leaders program in 1961, stopping off to view the Navajo craftsman exhibit at the Museum of Northern Arizona.[25]

Meanwhile, Navajo tribal chairman Paul Jones, Annie Wauneka, chair of the Navajo Health Committee, and three Navajo medicine men appeared on the Voice of America in 1962 to refute Communist accusations that government medicine was being forced upon Indian people. That same year *America Illustrated*, an upscale magazine distributed in the Soviet Union by the U.S. Information Agency, included a twenty-eight-page insert on "the first Americans—their cultural heritage, their contributions to the United States and their life today." The same issue contained an article by Albert Roland entitled "Many Cultures in a Wide Country," which emphasized that while "the Indians' traditional ways of life were shaken and sometimes disrupted by the impact of the European settlers," much had been preserved and today each group and individual had a choice of living "in a shielded enclave on the reservation or moving toward assimilation into the American society." Another article, "The Navajos—A Case History of Progress," by Veslet Wood, emphasized the growing economic benefits of the Navajos' oil, uranium, and coal interests and concluded that "thoughtfully, with dignity and with the dedicated eagerness of a free people, the Navajos have taken the road that leads them into the mainstream of American life." The Navajo tribe subsequently served as host to Tass News Agency bureau chief Gennadi A. Shishkin (a visit arranged by the Department of State's Bureau of Education and Cultural Affairs), as well as to a young field coordinator for the Nigerian Unitarian Service Committee, Dr. Ben Uzoukwu Nzeribe.[26]

Amid the ferment of the Civil Rights movement and increased Native American activism, however, the institute's political value was not limited to U.S. interests abroad. Only a week before the school's scheduled White House visit, the nation's headlines were awash with the news of President Johnson ordering federal troops to Alabama to protect Martin Luther King Jr. and his fellow marchers on their famous trek from Selma to Montgomery.[27]

The White House appearance was followed less than a month later by another Washington event, the first American Indian Performing Arts Festival, held April twenty-second through the twenty-seventh. The festival, for which Lee Udall was credited, consisted of two components—an Indian arts and crafts exhibition and a performing arts program. The latter was written, staged, and directed by Lloyd New, assisted by Rolland Meinholtz, dramatic arts instructor at the institute, and Louis Ballard, chair of IAIA's Music and Drama Department. The presentation featured Ballard's IAIA chorus, Pueblo and Mescalero Apache dancers from the school, and parts of Meinholtz's original play of the Pacific Northwest, *Moqwina*. The first performance was a private affair for government officials, but public showings were held each evening thereafter.[28]

The exhibit, held at the Department of the Interior's art gallery, was designed by James McGrath, who escorted students to Washington to hang the show. McGrath took this opportunity to further explore exhibition techniques. As before, older objects, on loan from museums and collections across the United States—among them Hopi leggings, a Tlingit dance cane, a Seminole turtle shell rattle, and a Sioux flute—were shown with recent IAIA student work. Display stands were crafted from traditional Indian forms, such as drum stands, and were secured with sinew and beads. Two model kiva structures were built to house Awatovi kiva murals and Pueblo woven dance sashes, while the entrance walls and ceiling of basalt black were embellished with ancient pictographs of the Rio Grande Valley and masks from different tribes.

An array of dignitaries was on hand for the opening, including Senators Frank Church and Frank Moss, Associate Justice Tom Clark of the U.S. Supreme Court, and Indian Commissioner Nash. Also present was the family of Oklahoma senator Fred Harris—representing four generations of Comanches—including his young daughter Kathryn, who some twenty-four years later would become president of the school. President Johnson purchased two pieces of jewelry from the items on display—a necklace by Charles Loloma that was to be given to Queen Juliana of the Netherlands and a silver necklace by student Roger Tsabetsaye intended as a present for Queen Ingrid of Denmark.[29]

The show was the forerunner of the European festivals traveling exhibit, and in the catalog McGrath began to outline the philosophy that would guide IAIA exhibition theory and practice for the next three years:

> This Exhibition of the Performing Arts of the American Indian . . .
> is the first time that the newest experimental directions of contemporary Indian artists and craftsmen from throughout the United States . . .
> are being exposed along with the traditional American forms of past cultural achievements out of which the experimental developments are growing. For example, the ceramic forms of a young Comanche artisan growing out of her tribal buffalo hide, feather bonnet carrying cases; the Snohomish weaving experiments of cedar bark, shell, horse hair coming from traditional Snohomish weaving materials; new paintings from the Sioux and the Crow artists growing out of the three-dimensional shield cultural pattern where actual objects are suspended from the shield; the Eskimo jewelry designer who is building his experiments around the dance rattles that have movable parts; and the hard-edge Colville painter basing his expressions on the plateau parfleche and corn husk bags. . . .
> These are important developments in American art: new, deep, natural rooted directions extending from the ancient native roots. All the contemporary pieces in this exhibition—poetry, song, dance rhythms, legends, the crafts and fine arts—are being conceived by Indian artists who, some for the first time, are discovering their Indian sources reflecting and casting shadows on the new worlds of arts everywhere.[30]

Clearly, for McGrath the implications of the new forms were not limited to the realm of Native American arts alone.

McGrath's sentiments were echoed by Vincent Price, who also contributed to the catalog. "In recent times primitive art has been the inspiration for many of the world's great artists," noted Price. "In America we are always reaching back to find our cultural roots in our early peoples, and there is a growing awareness that from these roots we can draw our own artistic identity." Price's words were reminiscent of the artists of the 1940s who were eager to assert the Indian role in the evolution of their own modern American art forms. McGrath hoped in a like manner to win a legitimacy and acceptance for the new Indian art by exhibiting it with its indigenous origins. Not surprisingly, his criteria for inclusion of student work in the show was that it be "new directional" but also that its "traditional source" be readily apparent.[31]

Included among the catalog essays were student statements that reinforced McGrath's theme for the exhibition. "I paint a picture from what I know from my Indian culture," wrote Kevin Red Star. "I visit museums whenever possible and am very proud of the work of the best contemporary artists.... I believe in painting with both the contemporary and my Indian culture has given me a bigger and a broader insight in my art life." Earl Eder described a similar melding of cross-cultural inspiration for his work. "I find myself in two cultures," Eder explained, "in this I find my art. I try to incorporate different old Sioux artifacts and things that the Indian valued, into new modern ideas." Eder added that he drew from a range of sources, including poetry, myths, and Indian folklore. "Now being exposed to new modern concepts, I can express myself. As a contemporary painter I feel this is a new moving type of Indian Art."[32]

The month following the arts festival in Washington, Lloyd New published "Using Cultural Difference as a Basis for Creative Expression" in the *Journal of American Indian Education.* In this seminal statement of his pedagogical philosophy, he portrayed the new forms as part of a necessary and natural process of development for any vital, living culture:

> Given the opportunity to draw on his own tradition, the Indian artist evolves art forms which are new to the cultural scene, thereby contributing uniquely to the society in general. He learns to live up to the best of himself in his role of the creative artist, evolving personal criteria for his conduct in the realm of the art world. He learns to stand on his own feet, avoiding stultifying cliches applied to Indian art by the purist who sometimes unwittingly resents evolution in Indian art forms, techniques and technology.
>
> It should be made clear that the Institute does not ram anyone's culture down his own throat; but it does acquaint its young Indian students with an appreciation of his own traditions, to be used as a springboard for personal creative action. The Institute does not believe it pos-

sible for anyone to live realistically in outmoded tradition, but does believe it to be the business of the artist, especially, to create new and worthy actions leading to new traditions. The Institute assumes that the future of Indian art lies in the Indian's ability to evolve, adjust, and adapt to the demands of the present, and not upon the ability to remanipulate the past.[33]

New's trepidations regarding the "purists" were certainly not unfounded. Despite the institute's best efforts to break free of "stultifying clichés," many bastions of formal conservatism remained resolute. For example, the previous year's entry form for the Philbrook's annual *American Indian Artists Exhibition* specified under Classification I–Regional Painting that works "should be documentary representational painting depicting an Indian theme. Flat two-dimensional coloring should be employed. No wash shading; only line modeling, or no shading at all." The rules sheet further dictated that the subject matter of all sculpture "MUST relate to the Indian culture and/or have an American Indian theme." By way of clarification, the form stated: "If an animal is the subject shown it must be one which is familiar to the American Indian and natural to this country." Even in the Special Category, which was "designed to recognize new trends in American Indian art," where "abstractions, symbolic designs having little or no specific or recognizable subject matter, and methods of painting which use European-derived shading and perspective" were allowed, the entry form declared that all work "MUST be based on an Indian theme."[34]

By the end of 1965 the school was mounting its first national exhibition held in a private venue, the Riverside Museum in New York—albeit still in cooperation with the U.S. Department of the Interior. Among the sponsors were Indian Commissioner Nash and the Indian Arts and Crafts Board (which included at this time d'Harnoncourt, Dockstader, and New). "Though its roots go deep into the past," wrote Stewart Udall in the introduction, "Indian art today, as exemplified in this collection, is fresh and stimulating. While preserving ancient symbols and traditional designs, it employs new mediums and modes of expression that are in keeping with life in space-age America."[35]

Although the title was *Young American Indian Artists*, it was a painting and sculpture show dominated by abstraction. A perusal of the institute's Honors Collection from this period reveals that the exhibition was definitely not indicative of the wide range of styles, media, and subject matter the students were exploring. For instance, it is evident that some students were concerned with depicting the ceremonial life of their tribe. Arden Hosetosavit's *Night Dancers* and Melvin Olanna's *Animal Dance* are two examples of this

FIG. 11. Night Dancers, *Arden Hosetosavit, 1964,
oil, 20½″ × 19″.*

interest (see figs. 11 and 12). For others, such as Alfred Clah and Betty
Nilchee, landscape was a central theme. Content and form ranged from Angelo John's *Sing after the Hunt* to Alfred Youngman's *Bird, Rabbit, and Man,*
Nathan Jackson's *Kooshta,* and Kingsley Kuka's *Sun Bird* (see figs. 13, 14, 15
and 16). Yet none of these fit into the exhibition's unstated theme. In instances
wherein a student was investigating a number of different avenues of expres-
sion, as was, for example, Paiute student Carol Frazier in *Girl with Doll, Paiute
Land Nevada Landscape, Girl Waving* (see fig. 17), *The Crow, Face,* and *A
Woman Portrait,* only a certain genre of work was chosen for the exhibition
(*Basket Design* [see fig. 18] and *Fish in the Sun Spot in the Water*).[36]

FIG. 12. Animal Dance, *Melvin Olanna, 1964, oil,*
24" × 36".

FIG. 13. Sing after the Hunt, *Angelo John, 1964,*
acrylic, 26" × 39".

FIG. 14. Bird, Rabbit, and Man, *Alfred Youngman, 1965, mixed media, 72″ × 60″.*

Response to the show hints at the reason for the selectivity. In an *Arts Magazine* review that McGrath quotes extensively in subsequent exhibition catalogs, "coincidence of form" became the prevailing leitmotif:

> That two artists without knowledge of each other and sharing not even a similar culture or geography could work in the same style, perhaps with the same intention or meaning strikes our wonder both in

FIG. 15. Kooshta, *Nathan Jackson, 1963, woodblock, 16¼″*
× 9½″.

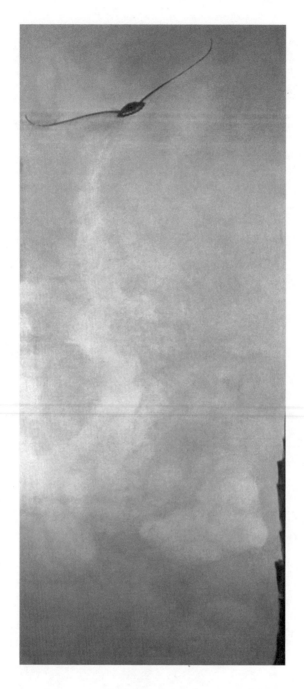

FIG. 16. Sun Bird, *Kingsley Kuka*, 1964, oil,
84" × 36".

FIG. 17. Girl Waving, *Carol Frazier, 1963, oil,*
22″ × 16¼″.

FIG. 18. Basket Design, *Carol Frazier, 1964, oil,*
75" × 52".

anthropology and aesthetics. This quality of marvel makes the River-side Museum show one of the most provocative. . . . The students are sixteen to twenty years old and have had no exposure to modern art. Whereas our artists have consciously explored new expressive modes in the exotic arts of Africa and the Orient, the young American Indian, us-ing elements of his own heritage and found objects from the reserva-tion, creates with but an introduction to oil painting works immediately suggestive of our most modern art. It is difficult to dissociate the works of Kirby Feathers from Jackson Pollock, or Kevin Red Star from Mother-well, or Zachary Toahty from Georgia O'Keeffe, or Tommy Montoya from Leger or current Pop artists [see figs. 19, 20, 21, and 22].[37]

For the modern audience these works had an organic quality—the natural flowering of McGrath's "ancient native roots of the Americas," a sentiment paraphrased in the catalog by Oriole Farb, who explained that although the "work looks as if it could be associated with such modern schools as Assem-blage, Pop, or Op," the styles "blossom naturally out of the roots of their an-cient heritage."[38]

The students had, of course, been exposed to modern art. For example, the IAIA advanced design class featured slides and films provided by the Mu-seum of Modern Art and an accompanying textbook that included essays by Henry Moore and Susan Sontag, and an interview with Pablo Picasso. Fritz Scholder taught a contemporary art history course. In aesthetics class students heard much about abstraction and distilling the "essence" of their Indian cul-tures. And as already suggested by Earl Eder and Kevin Red Star, students en-gaged in their own private exploration and study in museums and journals.[39]

An ahistorical, static concept of these young Indian artists' intellectual and artistic development was essential, however, to the myth of the linear progress of Western art, which was seen as being affirmed by its newfound "affinities" with the primitive. The formal similarities had to be parallel, not derivative or appropriated, if the "universality" of modernist form was to be validated.

Joseph Michaels, reporter for an NBC news affiliate in New York, also found natural origins for the student work at the Riverside Museum: "Ab-straction and symbolism are an important part of Indian life and it shows in this exhibit," noted Michaels. "Touch and feel are also vital to people who still cling to nature and as far as they can to simpler ways and this is probably why so many actual material things are used in these paintings."[40] Significantly, while this "natural life" was viewed as an ideal inspiration for creative ex-pression, Michaels revealed a distinct disdain for it as a viable alternative to

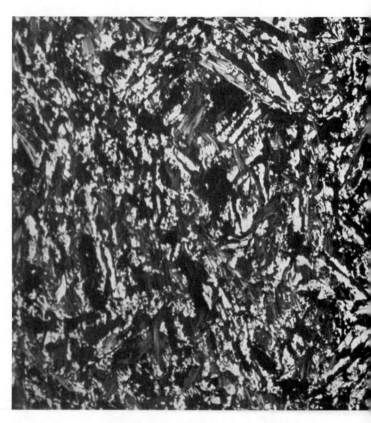

FIG. 19. Blue Feathers, *Kirby Feathers*, 1966, oil, 19″ × 36″.

the dominant modern society in his characterization of students George Burdeau and Alberta Nofchissey:

> George finds reservation life binding. He's restless and certainly this junk painting which he calls *Train across the Reservation* reveals it [see fig. 23]. Burdeau is one of those who would not forswear his own people, but he must move on. Only, a stranger in his ancestral soil, he does not know where. Alberta Nofchissey does. For her the immediate answer was to marry an Indian, go back to the reservation and to surround herself with Indian life like a cloak. Her painting reveals this [see fig. 24]. The owl for her tribe is a symbol of wisdom and power. It holds in one claw all animal life, in the other, plant life, and if you could see the small pieces of the mirror on its face you would find something else in its

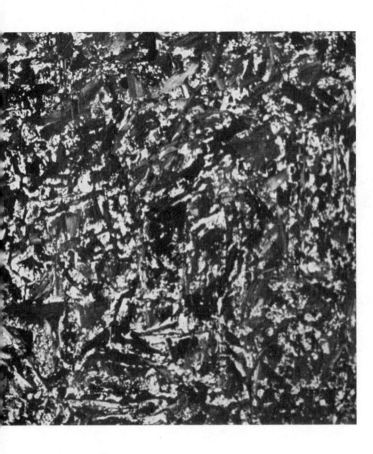

power you—yourself. This girl was a brilliant student, but she chose withdrawal.[41]

One cannot escape Michael's implication that "withdrawal" was the equivalent of regression and failure. Thus drawing on tradition in some limited respect—keeping that which was useful and appropriate to "life in space-age America"—was to be encouraged. To participate in that tradition in its totality, that is, to return to the Native community as did Nofchissey, was not.

In a subsequent statement for a student exhibition at the Museum of New Mexico, New defended the students' right to borrow selectively from Native traditions: "Each is expected, in the name of personal freedom, to determine the meaning to himself of this unique background. . . . He is charged

FIG. 20. Black Bird, *Kevin Red Star, 1966, mixed media, 60" × 48".*

with the responsibility of evolving from his traditions a way of life which fits him, however far it may vary from the cliche expectations of the purists and the traditionalists." New explained the preponderance of abstractions by noting that "Indian artists have never been primarily pictorial or realistic in their approach to art, leaning toward the symbolic and abstracted meanings manifested in their daily lives." As Indian life was dynamic, so also was the Indian artist's art. While acknowledging that "traditionally the configuration of art forms was determined by the group both in subject matter and style of treatment," New proclaimed that "today's young Indian artist incorporates the tribal motif only as it relates to the realism of his life, which inevitably is a dualism of Indian and non-Indian concepts." In this way, concluded New, the young Indian artist was still symbolizing, still abstracting from his world.[42]

Similarly, student statements included in the printed program for a panel entitled "An Evening with the Young Indian Painters from the Institute of American Indian Arts" focused on the individual and personal aspect of their work, rather than the cultural or communal. "Painting is a very personal ex-

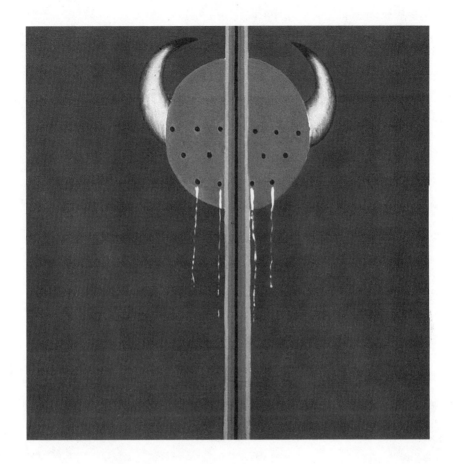

Fig. 21. Buffalo Shield, *Zachary Toahty, 1966, oil,*
30" X 30".

perience to me," commented Agnes Pratt. "When I paint, nothing exists except the canvas, paints, brushes and my feelings. . . . I would say most of my
paintings are 'mood' paintings (there is no evidence of indentifiable *[sic]* subject matter,) it is all feelings or emotions that work their way out in color." "I
am alone," echoed Earl Eder, "and in this way I find meaning."

T. C. Cannon warned against outside intrusion in a painter's work. "I believe that an artist, regardless of the influence he obtains from others, cannot
afford to be influenced by that which is told to him by others who wish to
form him or it will cause the destruction of his idiom as a painter," wrote the
young Caddo-Kiowa student. "Painting would no longer be personal, but a

FIG. 22. San Juan No. 2, *Tommy Montoya, 1963, oil,*
62" × 78".

FIG. 23. Train across the Reservation, *George*
Burdeau, 1964, mixed media, 48" × 96".

132

FIG. 24. The Circle of Life, *Alberta Nofchissey,*
1963, mixed media, 62" × 37½".

group discussion that not only speaks the painting but paints it," he concluded. Earl Biss explained that despite the absence of "traditional" subject matter, style, or medium, the essential aesthetic of his painting remained Indian: "I feel that the inborn flair for art is due to my Indian background. I believe that my sense of balance and color was passed down by my ancestors and this sense cannot be lost even though tradition is not portrayed in my work. . . . And, therefore, though my painting is not materially related to Indian tradition, it is still basically Indian art."[43]

James McGrath, who served as narrator for the evening, was candid about the selection of students to appear on the panel at the museum: "These seven students represent only the cross section of the total Institute student body that is viewing Indian culture as a source for new vistas in Indian Art. They do not represent the strongly traditional student. We should like you to meet this other group at a future date."[44]

McGrath expounded further on the subject of tribal versus individual art in the introduction to a southwestern exhibit held at the same museum three months later. "The young Indian artist of today and most certainly of tomorrow remains free to perform as artist, rather than to function as tribal symbolist, or historical apologist for a native order that exists freely in a few places in our country," wrote McGrath. "He is free, therefore, to create those new symbols from his ancient or recent past, however disturbing and strange they may appear on first glance, that will bring both him and us emotionally and intellectually to terms with our own times."[45]

A promotional flyer issued by the school conveyed a similar philosophy:

> The Indian tradition is not a material tradition based upon material wealth. Because its values are of the human spirit, it needs help in a Space Age of automatic, impersonal machinery.
>
> The purpose of the program being developed at the Institute of American Indian Arts is not to embalm old Indian ways of grandparents who worked creatively with deerskin, reed, clay and stone. For today's young Indian asks, what is my role to be?
>
> At the Institute he is helped to gain knowledge of old Indian esthetic feelings and to rearrange such knowledge through the freshness of approach that characterizes creative youth. Through study of new functions, experimentation with new materials and new arrangements with young Indian eyes and feelings he learns to create new Indian solutions for the contemporary scene out of his own cultural roots. The true artist can only be himself, not an imitator of elements utterly foreign to his own insights.[46]

The school's public notoriety began to escalate with a visit from Lady Bird Johnson in September. Accompanied by the Udalls (Lee Udall having been instrumental in the inclusion of IAIA on the travel agenda), the First Lady stopped off at the Cerrillos Road campus en route to her brother's home in Santa Fe. There she chatted with faculty and students, toured classrooms, and watched an "interpretation" of a Plains Indian Sun Dance.

Addressing a large crowd assembled on the school lawn, Johnson characterized the institute's success as one indicative of American principles. "This Institute—already soared to high rank for its artistic accomplishments—isn't just talking about freedom, it is showing the rest of the world what free expression is." The school demonstrated both the nation's respect for its cultural diversity, as well as the superiority of the democratic system that engendered such a pedagogical experiment. "America is a country that puts high value on education," proclaimed Johnson. "We invest our money and our faith in it. . . . Talents are not frustrated here. They unfold in an environment that nurtures the spark of genius that lies in every man. America's Indian people have a shared wisdom and a symbolism that are admired the world over. Here . . . they find living expression in the finest of traditional works, and the most imaginative of contemporary ventures." [47]

The following week the school hosted Pres. Leopold Sedar Senghor, chief executive of the six-year-old Republic of Senegal and a moving force behind the First World Festival of Negro Arts held in the capital city of Dakar the previous year. The African president was said to share an interest in developing contemporary art forms based on traditional sources. Senghor toured the campus, viewed an exhibit in the institute's gallery, had lunch with students in the cafeteria, and watched a dance performance. He was accompanied by New Mexico governor Jack Campbell, Santa Fe mayor Pat Hollis, the chief of protocol of the United States, other State Department officials, and several ambassadors. [48]

That fall the school launched its largest exhibition, one that toured four continents between 1966 and 1968. The *European Festivals* exhibit officially represented the United States in a number of foreign venues, including the Berlin Festival and the controversial 1968 International Olympics in Mexico City. [49] McGrath's extensive connections abroad were to prove invaluable in orchestrating the traveling show and related activities.

Sponsors of the tour were the Department of the Interior, the Department of State, the U.S. Information Agency, and the Center for Arts of Indian America. McGrath received an "American Specialist" grant from the State Department, which provided his airline ticket and a travel allowance with per

FIG. 25. Main room of Edinburgh Festival Exhibition,
1966. From left: Sioux War Shield and High Flying
Feathers by Earl Eder; Plains pipe bag and shield on loan
from Philbrook Museum, Tulsa, Oklahoma; and Kevin
Red Star's Crow Breast Plate. Douglas Hyde's Man of
Time and Kingsley Kuka's Porcupine are on the table.
On the floor is a woven rug by Joe Menta. (Alan Daiches,
photographer)

diem, while transportation within Europe was provided by military aircraft.[50]
He met with members of the State Department's Bureau of Educational and
Cultural Affairs, as well as representatives from the U.S. Information Agency,
before departing for the first stop on the tour, the Edinburgh Festival in Scotland.[51] The U.S. Information Agency, conceived in 1953 as an integral part of
the "cultural Cold War," had withdrawn from the public eye in the early
1960s following a tumultuous decade of canceled exhibitions and congressional attack for its sponsorship of artists suspected of Communist sympathies (see chap. 1). The Center for Arts of Indian America was a nonprofit organization headed by Lee Udall, with board members that included Rene
d'Harnoncourt and Lloyd New.

The nucleus of the exhibition was gathered once again from the institute's
Honors Collection of student and faculty work, while "traditional" Indian
forms were represented by sixty-seven pieces borrowed from American and
European collections. McGrath's installations were clearly designed to com-

pare "new directions" and "traditional source objects." In the main room at the Edinburgh Festival, Earl Eder's *Sioux War Shield* and *High Flying Feathers*, and Kevin Red Star's *Crow Breast Plate* were juxtaposed with a Sioux shield and a pipe bag on loan from the Philbrook (see fig. 25). Likewise, Earl Biss's *Crow Beads* was hung adjacent to a beaded shoulder bag, and an Acoma coiled pot was displayed with Lucille Hyeoma's *Sacred Bird* (see figs. 26 and 27).

Like its predecessors, this exhibition was largely representative of one aspect of art being produced at the school. For example, students were still making the "source objects" of sinew, hide, beads, and shell in Josephine Wapp's traditional-techniques course (see fig. 4), but these works were not prominently displayed. If McGrath's intent was to gain acceptance for the "new directional" forms from a European audience that might have rejected them as not authentically Indian, he may have felt that student work did not lend the same authority as the older museum pieces. But it could also be argued that the "traditional" student work did not fit the image the school was attempting to project of being on the cutting edge of the new Indian art.

The exhibit was supplemented with a number of educational activities. A Navajo couple, Fred and Bertha Stevens, toured with McGrath and demonstrated weaving and sandpainting techniques (see figs. 28 and 29). They also participated in Tuesday evening programs wherein they told "legends and myths" and McGrath read traditional and contemporary Indian poetry, prose, and songs. In addition, McGrath had assembled a slide lecture and albums of Native music, including one by the institute's Yah-Pah-Hah Singers. A promotional film on the school was also available for viewing.[52] Other evenings the Stevenses and McGrath spent at concerts and performances held in conjunction with the Festival, such as the Moscow Radio Symphony Orchestra and the Polish Mime Theater. They also attended official events, including an evening party with the American consul and a luncheon where they were guests of Nancy Kefauver who, representing the Department of Defense, had opened the exhibition.

Some forty-five hundred Edinburgh Festival visitors viewed the exhibition, while Scottish television and the British Broadcasting Company provided frequent coverage. McGrath, meanwhile, hired his own photographer, at the U.S. Information Service's expense.[53] Local newspapers carried reviews and photographs almost daily. The response was uncritically favorable to both the work and the installation. "Although much of the work is by contemporary Indian and Eskimo artists and craftsmen," noted the *Glasgow Herald*, "the fact that it is often shown side by side with the traditional craftwork which has been its inspiration lends not only extra interest but in a sense, another dimension to the exhibition."[54]

FIG. 26. *Edinburgh Festival Exhibition, 1966.*
From left: *Earl Biss's* Crow Beads; *Plains beadwork
on loan from the U.S. Department of the Interior.
(Alan Daiches, photographer)*

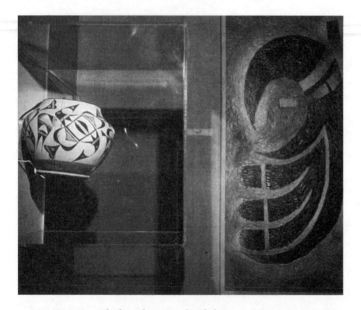

FIG. 27. *Edinburgh Festival Exhibition, 1966.*
From left: *Acoma pot and* The Sacred Bird *by Lucille
Hyeoma.*

FIG. 28. *Fred Stevens demonstrates sandpainting for viewers in Edinburgh, Scotland, 1966.*

Significantly, although more than two-thirds of the student and faculty pieces shown consisted of textiles, jewelry, and pottery, these received little attention in the popular press, which seemed preoccupied with the paintings and sculpture that comprised a small portion of the total exhibit. "The success of an educational policy in the arts which encourages the Indian to respect and perpetuate his spiritual heritage while adopting modern techniques and integrating with a modern society is not yet established," commented Edinburgh's *Evening News and Dispatch,* "but works such as Kevin Red Star's 'Plains Breast Plate' (atavism and old tube tops), Earl Eder's 'High Flying Feathers' (bent twigs, polymers, and plumes), or the eerie welded metal 'Man Spirit in the Wind' by Ted Palanteer [sic] are favourable pointers."[55]

When the exhibit moved on to the Berlin Festival, thirteen hundred attended its Amerika Haus showing within the first three days. The exhibition was so popular that it was extended an extra week. German reviewers were especially enthusiastic about the independent forms consistent with modernism: "The European observer sees much that he knows well: constructionism, tachism, hard edge and monochrome painting," noted a critic for *Der Tagesspiegel.* "But the Indian artists do not exhaust themselves in imitating cur-

FIG. 29. *Bertha Stevens, Navajo weaver, with Mrs. Udall, mother of Secretary of the Interior Stewart Udall, Indian Arts and Crafts Exhibition, Amerika Haus, West Berlin, 1966.*

FIG. 30. *Poster for the Indian Arts and Crafts
Exhibition, Amerika Haus, West Berlin, 1966.*

rently popular practiced art forms but blend them with their own traditional
artistic means." The sentiment was affirmed by an addition to the German
language version of the catalog (the remaining text closely followed the catalog introduction to the First American Indian Performing Arts Festival),
which read: "Together all of these creative efforts of modern Indian artists are
not without meaning for world arts, for here is a question of new directions
rooted deep in an independent cultural tradition. . . . It should be easy in view
of this exhibition to imagine others: from the developing African countries,
from the reach of the South American culture circle or from other forming
cultures in the entire world." Meanwhile, the embassy in Ankara, Turkey,
wanted to host only the weaving and sandpainting demonstrations and slide
lecture portion of the project as part of its Community Relations Program but
declined to include the exhibit itself. This arrangement had also been con-
ceded to the Horniman Museum in London.[56]

When the exhibition traveled to Buenos Aires, Santiago, and Mexico
City in 1968, McGrath drew on the earlier *Arts Magazine* review to embellish
the catalog. "The Institute students mentioned are from sixteen to twenty-
three years old and have not had contact with modern art," he paraphrased,
implying that the assertion was correct, even though he must have been
aware of the school's curriculum and the overt and frequent opportunities for

FIG. 31. *James McGrath* (left) *and Ernest Ramsaur, director of the U. S. Information Service, U. S. Mission in Berlin, view Ted Palmenteer's* Man Spirit in the Wind *at the Indian Arts and Crafts Exhibition, Amerika Haus, West Berlin, 1966.*

FIG. 32. *Poster for Latin American exhibition tour, 1968.*

exposure to modern art contained therein. "Their work . . . raises the question," he now went on to directly quote, "of the sophistication or naïveté of modern art, and it suggests that perhaps, regardless of conscious intention or lack of it, Pop and Op might please us for some definite and quite simple reason after all." [57]

Between international showings the exhibit was put on display in the school's gallery and at the Alaskan Centennial. "In general, this exhibition is what thousands of Europeans saw as representing the new directions in American Indian arts and crafts," wrote McGrath in the mimeographed sheet that served as an introduction. "It is timely, as much of this work was not being created ten years ago in 1957, and for all we know of the Indian artist in the evolving world of art, in 1977 there will be most likely another story to show the world about traditional and contemporary American Indian Arts and Crafts." [58]

Then, in a transparent twist of logic, McGrath implied that the proportion of IAIA student and faculty representation in the show was somehow directly related to their stature in the "new directions" Indian art: "It is interesting to note that 80 of the artists in this exhibition are either former or present students or faculty of the Institute of American Indian Arts, indicating the importance of this Institution in the formation of American artists and craftsmen." What the percentage indicated was that the exhibit was an institute-organized show of student and faculty work—in no way was it an open invitational. Those few contemporary pieces that did not have their origins at the school had been selected by McGrath. Yet McGrath was correct in assuming that by virtue of the sheer magnitude of their exposure, the school was destined to wield influence and command authority as the new contemporary Indian arts pundit.[59]

This role was already being played out as the school received its first round of national press coverage, with articles in the *New Yorker*, the *New York Times*, *Life*, and *Time*. Robert Coates of the *New Yorker* applauded the school's efforts "to unloose the artistically inclined young Indian from his ancestral tribal practices and at least expose him to modern international techniques," pleased that their emphasis was "on the arts, and for once . . . not wholly, or even mainly, on the dreary round of basketry, ceramics, rug- and blanket-weaving, and all the other small skills that have been for so long set aside . . . as the traditional provinces of the Indian." [60]

Like others before him, Coates maintained that the preponderance of non-representational student art was the instinctive working of "natural-born abstractionists." Moreover, he went on to argue that the cultural isolation of the students had served to insulate them from contaminating representational imagery they would have been forced to suppress in order to "progress" in the abstract field, the most "sophisticated" of the art techniques: "Growing up, pinned down as they are on their isolated reservations, they see almost nothing of the magazine illustrations, posters, parlor prints, and other examples of naturalistic art, mostly of extremely poor quality, that our young people are brought up on and that they have to break away from before they can progress to freer methods." [61]

Coates had high praise for the "ingenuity" of Earl Eder and Ted Palmenteer in combining traditional materials with modern designs. He was likewise impressed with their classmate Tommy Montoya's "hard-edge abstraction that demonstrates the linkage between Pueblo Indian design and Kandinsky." But Coates suggested that students who elected representational courses did relatively poorly, having "found themselves cast adrift, uneasily, from their traditional procedures." [62]

By December 1967, when Robin Richman introduced IAIA to the audience of *Life* magazine in a special issue entitled "Return of the Redman," the modernist myth of the school's young Indian artists had been neatly codified. "Students who have been scarcely exposed to the Western tradition of realistic representation turn out to be naturally gifted abstractionists," Richman noted dutifully. "This is hardly surprising, considering that Indians have a centuries-old tradition of geometric art," the author explained. Referencing Earl Eder's *War Shield* and an abstraction by Carl Tubby, both reproduced in the article, Richman marveled that what was surprising was how rapidly Indian students applied their hereditary talents for abstraction to "advanced" hard-edge styles. [63]

The institute's attempts to prepare its graduates for modern life in the dominant society also received high marks from the popular press. Robert Coates especially commended an extracurricular course he called "social indoctrination," asking, "What was the use of teaching the young people the skills of applied and other arts if, because of their elementary behavioral educations, they might only make fools of themselves in the world their training would lead them into?" Included in the course content was instruction in table setting, how to accept or turn down a date, and how to behave in a movie theater or restaurant. Since the fall of 1965 all thirteenth-grade students had been required to participate in an "apartment living" course, where they received instruction in personal grooming, food purchasing, meal preparation, and responsible citizenship. Coates also took note of another school function he described as "designed to accustom the students to appearing in public and to bolster their poise and self-confidence"—a rally in the gymnasium, "where a bevy of lively little drum majorettes in fringed buckskin skirts and short jackets were leading a crew of students in pep talks and cheering as a send off for the basketball team." [64]

In this same vein an earlier article in *New Mexico Magazine* had enthusiastically highlighted the recently opened student sales outlet, later called Hookstone, observing that the first day's receipts totaled more than a thousand dollars. The outlet was complemented by a class in sales technique taught by Charles Loloma. Any student "in good standing" was eligible to submit works for public purchase. Requirements with regards to design, craftsmanship, and salability were set by the head of the department from which the work originated. The department head was also responsible for determining the costs of production. If a work met the given criteria, it went before a selection committee comprising the sales and production faculty sponsor, all members of the art faculty, and six student members selected by that same art faculty. This committee was charged with final approval and pricing the item for sale. From the sales revenue were deducted reimbursement to the government for materials and "incidental costs" and a predetermined commission that went into the student council treasury. The remainder would go to the student artist. All works for sale, whether to government agencies, art dealers, or individuals, even if produced with the student's own materials and on his or her own time, had to be handled through the student council as a sales agency for the institute. No piece could be sold directly from studio to buyer. [65]

Student work that did not sell became part of the school's private collection. The manner in which this Honors Collection was acquired and justified has remained controversial. James McGrath remembers that when he started the collection in 1962 students were required to donate two works per year. The IAIA policy statement on acquisition and sales of student artwork did indeed state that "the Institute of American Indian Arts may acquire, without remuneration, no more than two art products from any particular student during the course of a school year. When such an item is selected by the Institute, the student will receive an Honors Certificate in recognition thereof. . . . Such items acquired by the Institute shall then be taken up as Government property and handled thereafter as such." McGrath had two criteria for their selection: (1) that they be the student's best work and (2) that they be "new directional," bridging the gap between the traditional and realistic and the modern. [66]

Some former students have charged, however, that all their work was confiscated and they were not allowed to freely retain any pieces. A few tell of hiding work in suitcases and spiriting it off campus. [67] In fact, the IAIA acquisitions policy specified that students who wished to acquire "an occasional piece" of their production could do so only by paying a sum designated as reimbursement to the government for the cost of materials and incidental expenses. Students who elected to buy back their own artwork from the government were required to sign an affidavit stating that the item was not intended for resale but for their own personal use.

The alumni's charges of IAIA's total control over their creative property would seem to be confirmed by a memorandum from Administrative Manager W. W. Larson in 1967 outlining a new procedure by which students could acquire their own artwork after reimbursing the government for the cost of materials. The protocol was as follows:

1. The student should request permission from the instructor to obtain the art work he desires.
2. The instructor should determine if the work is to be retained for the honors collection, or if it can be released for sale. If it can be released, the instructor should prepare a sales card indicating the cost of the material. In addition to the cost of material, please include the 10% overhead charge.
3. The student should bring the card to this office for payment and to obtain a receipt.
4. Dormitory personnel will not release a student taking art work off campus unless he can produce a receipt showing payment.[68]

In addition, students who left artwork to be sold over the summer would receive a portion of the price upon their return. If the student did not return, the entire proceeds of the sale went into the Student Senate General Fund. McGrath maintains that when numerous works by a single student appear in the institute's collection it was because a student had work that didn't sell, and the school took the work so it would not be damaged, lost, or destroyed.

Since the stated intent of the Hookstone enterprise was "to provide opportunities for realistic and practical experience in business practices," "select students" from the sales class were chosen to manage the operations of the shop on a rotating basis. Student responsibilities included arranging and displaying merchandise, maintaining necessary records and accounts, acting as sales representatives and organizing promotional activities, advertising, keeping tax records, handling correspondence and shipping and handling, and observing proper banking procedures.[69] The following were among the school's additional stated goals for the sales outlet:

1. Through recognition and potential economic incentive, to encourage exercise of creative talents and craftsmanship to the fullest at all times in the learning process. In this manner, experimentation with new

media and ideas may, in their initial results, produce highly saleable items.

2. Continuously to give students firsthand experience with what kinds of art treatments are most pleasing to the public, and realistic knowledge as to the price structure which art pieces command on the market, both wholesale and retail.

3. To encourage students to devote out-of-school hours, on evenings and weekends, in production of art items for sale as being both a desirable application of effort and as a source of income in view of the limited employment opportunities for students.[70]

The revenues from the operation (after expenses) were to be used for loans to students for special art supplies not otherwise available, to purchase student works, and to maintain the sales center. Any remaining profits reverted to the Student Senate General Fund. The enterprise was so financially successful that by 1968 James McGrath was making a request that a part-time professional manager for Hookstone be hired and paid from Student Senate funds. He reported that the profits from student sales were estimated at thirteen thousand dollars.[71]

The sales center was frequently mentioned by journalists, including Howard Taubman, who produced a two-part series on the school for the *New York Times*, as well as an article in IBM's *Think* magazine. Taubman concluded that while the school represented only a "beginning to the demanding task of fitting an almost forgotten minority into a place in the bustling world," it clearly demonstrated the nation's eagerness to bring "the descendants of America's earliest inhabitants" into the "mainstream of American life." Like Michaels of NBC, Taubman had praise for what he considered the institute's success stories—students working on advanced degrees or those who had found jobs—but only scorn for those who were "totally defeated and drifted away, probably to their old lives, though no one is sure."[72]

In an article entitled "Cultural Difference as the Basis for Creative Education" published in the Indian Arts and Crafts Board's *Native American Arts* in 1968, New assured readers of the institute's promising record for keeping Indian students in school. Citing figures for the previous three years, New related that 86.2 percent of the students in the graduating classes (twelfth, thirteenth, and fourteenth years) had continued their education beyond the high school level. Of these, 27 percent enrolled in college or college-level arts schools and roughly 73 percent returned to the institute or chose to attend formal vocational training.[73] New repeated these statistics in testimony before the Kennedy Senate hearings on Indian education the following year, prefacing the progress report with a profile of the student body:

More than not, they are beset by misunderstandings regarding race, color and their general place in today's world. They are sorrily stung by discriminatory experiences. They are unmotivated and often negatively directed in many ways.

A great many, all too many, reflect unusual records of disorder in their previous life, ranging from mild deliquency [sic] situations to severe conditions verging on various kinds of virtual psychosis. Some are brilliant but extremely frustrated. Seventy-five percent by test—we have a whole battery of tests—75 percent are severely handicapped in terms of normal academic achievement. The majority have difficulty with the English language in any form—speech, writing, or in reading. . . .

Our group includes the revolutionists, the nonconformists, and the unacademically minded who find no satisfaction in the common goals set by typical school programs. Holding standards which are at odds with the majority, they reject and are rejected by the traditional American school systems.[74]

New went on to warn that without the opportunity for special education relevant to their needs, these students were likely candidates for "failure in life as well as in school, and will live only to perpetuate all the aforementioned negative aspects of contemporary Indian life."[75]

New acknowledged that the school's accomplishments—providing an environment wherein students were able to build personal security and confidence, offering a curriculum rich in the arts and cultural studies, mounting international exhibits of student work, presenting student theatrical and dance performances in Washington and abroad—had been made possible in large part through the preferential support received from the Bureau of Indian Affairs and the Department of the Interior. "We enjoy unusual autonomy, funding, and freedom that allows for innovation, without which we could not function successfully," noted New. The cost of the special education the institute provided was high—twenty-six hundred dollars per student. New reminded the senators that the cost was far less in the long run than not providing it, in terms of the support programs that would be required if these students were not afforded effective education. "While billions of American tax dollars have been spent for the purpose of solving the Indian problem," New observed, "perhaps not so much as a single million has been especially earmarked to further public recognition of the cultural wealth of the American Indian and to show him how to use these assets as a means of gaining financial independence and the dignity of self-sufficiency."[76]

The preferential treatment of which New spoke was, however, fast evaporating. Even as the school was enjoying its greatest round of press and public attention, fiscal cutbacks had begun. George Boyce, realizing the impact that reduced funding and favor would have, had taken an early retirement in 1966. He had become increasingly frustrated by the circus atmosphere he perceived the school to be assuming.[77] High-profile performances and exhibitions took precedence over students' class work. Disputes erupted over how many and which invitations would be accepted. The political coup Boyce had originally envisioned had turned into a political football. Howard Mackey, director of the institute's Academic Program, had been appointed acting superintendent but had asked to be transferred a year after assuming the office. Lloyd New was then chosen by Indian Commissioner Robert L. Bennett to head the school in the summer of 1967.

The ten years following New's testimony before the Kennedy hearings saw a steady decline in enrollment, an exodus of prominent faculty, a reduction in both academic and arts programs, and increasingly lax admissions requirements that resulted in higher numbers of at-risk students. Problems with alcohol, drugs, and even interstudent violence became endemic. Public interest and the attention of the press waned. Adding further strain to the school's already threadbare resources, the institute abandoned its high school program in favor of a two-year associate of fine arts college curriculum.

By 1981 the institute's old battle with the All-Pueblo Council (now the All-Indian Pueblo Council [AIPC]) resurfaced as the AIPC chairman, Delfin Lovato, lobbied for the IAIA campus to house a Pueblo junior and senior high boarding school. With the school's enrollment at an all-time low of eighty-nine and its political mentors no longer able or willing to withstand the local pressure, the institute was forced to hastily negotiate temporary quarters with the College of Santa Fe, where the school remains located. The era of privilege having profoundly ended, the school would now begin the difficult task of redefining its identity and future.

In 1986 the school's ties with the Bureau of Indian Affairs were severed by passage of the American Indian, Alaskan Native, and Native Hawaiian Culture and Development Act, which granted the new Institute of American Indian and Alaskan Native Culture and Development a nonprofit, congressionally chartered status. The institute would be governed by an independent board of trustees appointed by the president of the United States and funded through direct, line-item appropriation in the federal budget. Its survival far from assured, this experiment in Indian arts education had turned a distant corner from the public and private interests that had brought it into being.

Conclusions

The need to co-opt difference into one's own dream of order, in which one reigns supreme, is a tragic failing. Only fear of the Other forces one to deny its Otherness. What we are talking about is a tribal superstition of Western civilization: the Hegel-based conviction that one's own culture is riding the crucial time-line of history's self-realization.
Thomas McEvilley, "Doctor Lawyer Indian Chief"

From its very inception the Institute of American Indian Arts was, and remains, a curious and tense mix of ideological agendas. Federal Indian policy has traditionally been determined by concerns which are, at best, tangential to Native American welfare. Duplicity of intentions does not lend itself to coherent or holistic planning. It should, thus, come as no surprise that the school has been characterized by paradox.

The physical placement of the institute on the grounds of Dorothy Dunn's Studio, as well as adoption of the tenets of the Rockefeller Arizona conference, signaled a directional shift in Native arts production. As Anne LaRiviere has indicated, the move was analogous to the building of Catholic mission altars over Pueblo kivas, which symbolized for the invaders a triumph of church over paganism. Now modernist individualism, as institutionalized at the Museum of Modern Art, was raising its flag over newly conquered territory.[1]

The emerging "new directional" Indian art's canon formation relied on a process of "legitimation via referencing," which invoked MoMA's mythic modernist family of art as well as the cultural heritage of Native communities.[2] The genealogy was tightly woven with the rich and purposeful origin stories still recounted in college art history surveys. Stories that begin with Maurice de Vlaminck's mystical conversion on that hot day in Argenteuil when, imbibing of refreshment, he spied three objects from the Dark Continent behind the bistro bar and instinctively "knew" their value for the first time.

Its real concern the "tribal superstition" of the linear progress of Western art and, by extension, the Western world, the modernist myth does not deal in trifles—in the means and motives whereby African, pre-Columbian, Native American, and Oceanic objects came to rest in European museums, curio shops, and drinking establishments. It does not dwell on the original value and meanings the objects held for their creators nor the co-optation of those meanings into a Western value of self-redemption. The objects, like the cultures that produced them, were, after all, "more witnesses than models."[3]

Contemporary apologists to the contrary, however, twentieth-century vanguard artists' conceptions of the art of "primitive" cultures were not rooted in the cultural relativism of a Montaigne or the "scientific" spirit of a Boas. The collections they admired in the Trocadero, the British Museum, or Berlin's Museum für Völkerkunde were the spoils of colonialism. The ethnographic display cases and the burgeoning discipline of cultural anthropology that supplied them were designed to stimulate interest in, and provide understanding of, peoples in distant lands who held fragile reins over indigenous resources of both a human and material sort. Within two decades of Vlaminck's "discovery," cultural anthropology blossomed into the more fruitful social anthropology of Malinowski, Radcliffe-Brown, and Evans-Pritchard, which, under the watchful eyes and dollars of the Rockefeller Foundation, labored to produce a functionalist social science capable of giving "assistance to those engaged in the administration and education of Native peoples."[4]

If the value the new directional Indian art held for the non-Native art world is to be fully acknowledged, the primitivism that characterized modernists' interest in things Indian must be recognized both for its roots as well as the fruit it was intended to bear. The decontextualization and appropriation of non-Western arts and fragments of "primitive" peoples' ways of life were essentially an extension of Euro-American political and economic imperialism. Both harvests were intended to revitalize and nourish the colonizers. The intellectual and cultural could now sweeten an already rich colonial pot. Modern man was thus sustained by an illusion of the "primitive" that was wholly self-serving.

The very nature of the modernists' victory over their newly discovered territory of the "primitive" required that the latter be painted in ahistorical, impotent hues. Thus the young IAIA artists' sophisticated ability to appropriate modernist form and techniques to their own artistic agendas had to remain clouded.[5] At the same time that they were encouraged to produce modern art, their legitimacy rested with their being "natural" people existing in mythic time, untainted by contact with the modern world. Placed in a surreal void, the students were asked to be at once the "primitive" and the "primitivist" in a Western discourse wherein form took precedence over meaning, product over process, and "universal" aesthetic (and market) value replaced cultural context.[6]

The real meanings that informed the students' lives and work were ignored. It was not possible within this scheme to introduce any objective sense of a contemporary Native America—a reality of perseverance and despair, of proud hand-built adobe homes and federal housing projects, of fervent dancing and devastating alcoholism, of ritual calendars and workless days of boredom, of loving families and absent mothers and fathers. History was condensed into politically neutral "ancient native roots" and their bright modern flowerings, obscuring the years of starvation, disease, land theft, war, poverty, racism, and culture loss that scarred the tenacious indigenous vine. Barthes could have been reviewing a work in an IAIA exhibition rather than a French tour guide when he wrote: "All that is left for one to do is to enjoy this beautiful object without wondering where it comes from. Or even better: it can only come from eternity . . . objects from which all soiling trace of origin or choice has been removed."[7]

Inherent in the school's preoccupation with the new forms was the unstated implication that traditional values and beliefs were—in their totality, at least—somehow dysfunctional and inimical to success in the modern world, certainly in the modern art world. With "outmoded tradition" relegated to the role of "springboard for personal creative action," the viability of intact Native philosophies, religions, and political systems to insure the continued survival and well-being of Native peoples was called into question. Within such a framework the recognition of the equality of divergent aesthetic systems, values, and beliefs was precluded.

A true spirit of multiculturalism was, of course, never the goal. In the world according to MoMA, American-style democracy and capitalism—read Western individualism and modernism—were the sole roads to salvation in the "cultural Cold War's" self-styled intellectual apocalypses. The primitive could only be "preserved, redeemed, and represented" by Rockefeller grace.[8]

Paradoxically, the Rockefeller agenda, as manifested at the institute, managed to find willing bedfellows from the Indian New Dealers to the Terminationists. For the school offered an innovative approach to an old theme. Under the guise of cross-cultural education, students would be taught their tribal histories and cultures and, at the same time, would be encouraged to leave them behind for modern conveniences, more acceptable "manners," and an enlightened and more promising artistic milieu. Boyce's "environmentalism"— social engineering from a pedagogical perspective—conflicted in no real way with the aesthetic engineering of a Rene d'Harnoncourt, Lloyd New, or James McGrath. The superintendent's twenty-five-thousand-dollar-a-year Indians were reminiscent of d'Harnoncourt's furniture made in Indian schools but not in Indian style: both "consciously designed in the white style, to show how well Indian articles [or young Indian artists?] fit into modern homes." The point of reference always returned to the real benefactors. The Southwest Indian Art Project planners perhaps characterized the intent best when they described the project as a "program designed to offer the student-artist a means to use his own unique background in meeting the commercial and aesthetic demands of our modern society." Philip Deloria has insightfully pointed out the underlying premise of such tactics: "The transition of recent federal policy from termination to self-determination reflects only a tactical shift in the fundamental commitment of the society to bring Indians into the mainstream, not a movement toward a true recognition of a permanent tribal right to exist."[9]

Indeed, the institute's educational model conformed in most respects to that of a colonial system, in that it addressed foremost the needs of the dominant society. As Philip Altbach and Gail Kelly have suggested, "education" within such a system represents an alien institution designed to "fit people into a world different from the one in which their parents lived and work," regardless of whether indigenous languages are employed in instruction, indigenous culture is emphasized in the curriculum, or other adaptations are made to the culturally distinct student body. Such education has little, if any, relevance to life and work within the indigenous community, does not allow for the direct involvement of parents, and is conducted in isolation from the students' home.[10]

In the institute's purposeful effort to "liberate" students' behavior and artistic endeavors from cultural restraints, much was lost. Traditional art education imparted not only knowledge of the group's designs, techniques, and media but also the meanings embodied in each. Artistic proficiency included the intellectual, ethical, and philosophical, as well as the visual and tactile. For within a culturally and pedagogically autonomous society, all education functions as a socialization process that serves to transmit the knowledge, skills, values, and beliefs of a culture from one generation to the next.

Greg Cajete, Santa Clara Pueblo artist and educator, writes that a true exploration of indigenous education is a creative dialogue that liberates both learner and educator and is based on equality and mutual reciprocity:

> It allows both the learner and educator to co-create a learning experience and mutually undertake a pilgrimage to a new level of self-knowledge. The educator enters the cultural universe of the learner and no longer remains an outside authority. By co-creating a learning experience, everyone involved generates a critical consciousness and enters into a process of empowering one another. With such empowerment . . . Indian people may truly take control of their history by becoming the transforming agents of their own social reality.[11]

The Institute of American Indian Arts did not begin its tenure as a place of true exploration of indigenous arts education. And those now entrusted with the present and future art education of generations of Indian students cannot begin to plan effectively for the future without objectively assessing this school's past.

The dynamics of the institute's previous patronage lends insight into the crises of funding and political support the institute has experienced since the 1960s. It is, of course, no accident that the school's golden age coincided with modernism's slide into popular disfavor. Moreover, with American cultural hegemony assured, attention turned from the supposed shared ancient American roots to the diversity of the fruit. The postmodern predisposition for content thrust the new directional Indian art into a much different arena than the familiar coincidence of form. And the content of student work in the days of AIM (American Indian Movement) and Alcatrez was not as palatable to some as that of the golden days of yore. The social commentary of a Bill Soza, Richard Ray Whitman, or T. C. Cannon was not the stuff of State Department showcases and embassy soirees.

More important, however, the calling into question of the sources of the school's political and financial sponsorship opens the way for that creative and liberating dialogue of just what cultural and pedagogical autonomy should mean. It is not a dialogue centered in purism nor of mourning the ebb and flow of change in living cultures. It is not a discourse designed to defame the new directional Indian art or the artists who created it. And it is certainly not about attributing their work to non-Native patrons or sponsors. It is a dialogue that can restore the real past and future of the many talented students who have walked through the school's doors and of those Native peoples who continue to seek out this institute that promises to honor the traditions of their grandfathers and grandmothers.

The institute now stands at a critical crossroads in its history. If there can at last be a turning away from that "need to co-opt difference into one's own dream of order" toward true indigenous education, then perhaps the real narratives of the Institute of American Indian Arts—of its students and their work—can be told and the school benefit from the telling.

NOTES

INTRODUCTION

1. New, "Cultural Difference as the Basis for Creative Education," 8; Brody, *Indian Painters and White Patrons*, 198.

2. *Institute of American Indian Arts: A Basic Statement of Purpose.*

3. Brophy and Aberle, *The Indian: America's Unfinished Business*, 115.

4. Mathews, "Art and Politics in Cold War America," 786.

CHAPTER 1

1. "Grant in Aid to the University of Arizona toward the cost of a joint exhibit and conference on contemporary Indian art in Southwestern United States," 12 December 1958, Rockefeller Foundation Archives, RF 1.2, Series 200 R, Box 430, Folder 3708. The Rockefeller Foundation frequently sought ways in which to network its funding recipients and thereby consolidate and strengthen its interests. For example, the University of Arizona (UA) administered a Rockefeller exchange program with the University of Sonora in Hermosillo, Mexico, at the same time that it hosted the Southwestern Indian Art Project, and a Nigerian Rockefeller Foundation fellowship recipient, Onuora Nzekwu, was sent by the foundation to UA as an observer of the Indian art workshops. Associate director of the Rockefeller's Humanities Division, John P. Harrison, wrote Lloyd New, codirector of the project, that Nzekwu was a young writer and editor on the staff of *Nigeria* magazine who was particularly interested in the "problems of transition between a traditional tribal society and the formation of a modern westernised nation in Africa." Harrison concluded that he could have no better guide than New in

"the way in which his particular concerns are being handled in the field of art in the Southwest and other areas of our society" (John P. Harrison to Lloyd New, 3 October 1961, Rockefeller Foundation Archives, RF 1.2, Series 200 R, Box 431, Folder 3709); Rockefeller international interests are discussed more fully later in this chapter.

2. "Grant in Aid to the University of Arizona."

3. "Trip to Southwest, 13–18 January 1958, Tucson and Phoenix, Interviews: Clarence B. Fahs, 14 January 1958," pp. 2–5, Rockefeller Foundation Archives, RF 1.2, Series 200 R, Box 430, Folder 3708; hereafter cited as "Trip to Southwest, Interviews."

4. New cited in *Shared Visions*, 74; "Trip to Southwest, Interviews," 8.

5. "Trip to Southwest, Interviews," 8.

6. Charles B. Fahs to Richard A. Harvill, 10 March 1958, Rockefeller Foundation Archives, RF 1.2, Series 200 R, Box 430, Folder 3708.

7. "Southwestern Indian Art Project," Draft Proposal, 14 July 1958, p. 1, Rockefeller Foundation Archives, RF 1.2, Series 200 R, Box 430, Folder 3708. This focus on the aesthetic (or art) value as opposed to cultural context (or anthropological) was the tack of Rene d'Harnoncourt, then chairman of the Indian Arts and Crafts Board.

8. "Southwestern Indian Art Project," Draft Proposal, 2–4.

9. John Harrison to Charles Fahs, Inter-Office Correspondence, July 30, 1958, Rockefeller Foundation Archives, RF 1.2, Series 200 R, Box 430, Folder 3708; Oliver LaFarge to Charles Fahs, August 22, 1958. Rockefeller Foundation Archives. RF 1.2 Series 200 R. Box 430. Folder 3708.

10. *Shared Visions*, 75.

11. Rene d'Harnoncourt, Museum of Modern Art, 24 September 1958, Interviews: John P. Harrison, pp. 1–2, Rockefeller Foundation Archives, RF 1.2, Series 200 R, Box 430, Folder 3708.

12. On Fahs's request, see Charles B. Fahs to David L. Patrick, 14 August 1958, and Patrick to Fahs, 28 August 1958, Rockefeller Foundation Archives, RF 1.2, Series 200 R, Box 430, Folder 3708.

"A Conference on Southwest Indian Art entitled 'New Directions for Southwest Indian Art,'" Supplemental Proposal Submitted to the Rockefeller Foundation by the University of Arizona, Tucson, 20 October 1959, pp. 8–13, Rockefeller Foundation Archives, RF 1.2, Series 200 R, Box 430, Folder 3708.

13. "New Directions for Southwest Indian Art," Supplemental Proposal, 4.

14. Charles B. Fahs with the Indian Arts and Crafts Board, excerpt from interview, 15 November 1958, Rockefeller Foundation Archives, RF 1.2, Series 200 R, Box 430, Folder 3708; Charles Fahs to David Patrick, 20 November 1958, Rockefeller Foundation Archives, RF 1.2, Series 200 R, Box 430, Folder 3708.

15. The show was held over for a six-week period following the conference. The university also had a seven-minute color-sound film prepared of the exhibit, which was shown over television stations in the Southwest. The music background for the film was "based on an Indian theme" and written by Robert Baksa, a student in UA's School of Music; Frederick J. Dockstader, "Directions in Indian Art," 25.

16. For further discussion of the origins and development of the Indian ethnic art market see Holm, "The Discovery of Indian Art," 67–74; Schrader, *The Indian Arts and Crafts Board;* and Wade, "The Ethnic Art Market and the Dilemma of Innovative Indian Artists," 9–17.

A thorough discussion of these Indian rights groups and their political agendas and activities may be found in Kelly, *The Assault on Assimilation*, 213–54, and Philp, *John Collier's Crusade for Indian Reform*, 26–54. Meriam et al., *The Problem of Indian Administration*, 651–52.

17. Dockstader, "Directions in Indian Art," 19.

18. Ibid., 28, 26.

19. Ibid., 7.

20. It should be noted here that d'Harnoncourt's influence was not limited to the Directions in Indian Art Conference. He was cited by George A. Boyce, superintendent of IAIA from its opening in 1962 until 1966, as having initiated the request for funding for the school with then Commissioner of Indian Affairs Glenn Emmons in a meeting held sometime in the late 1950s. This revelation is found in a letter from Boyce to Lynne Waugh of the *Santa Fe New Mexican*, reprinted in Garmhausen, *History of Indian Arts Education in Santa Fe*, 62–67. Boyce mentions that d'Harnoncourt, Boyce, Director of Indian Education Hildegard Thompson, and a "top official from the office of the Interior Secretary" were among the small group present at this meeting. For further discussion of the early planning of IAIA, see chapter 3.

21. Hellman, "Imperturbable Noble," 62–64. For additional biographical information on d'Harnoncourt, see also Museum of Modern Art, *Rene d'Harnoncourt, 1901–1968*; Schrader, *The Indian Arts and Crafts Board*, 124–28; and Rushing, "Marketing the Affinity of the Primitive and the Modern," 196–97.

22. Rushing, "Marketing the Affinity of the Primitive and the Modern," 197.

23. Schrader, *The Indian Arts and Crafts Board*, 127–28.

24. *Indian Art in the United States and Alaska.*

25. Ibid.

26. Ibid.

27. *Shared Visions*, 75.

28. It should also be noted that the year before the San Francisco exhibit opened, Robert Goldwater published his seminal classic *Primitivism in Modern Art*, the first major attempt to document this particular aspect of modernist evolution.

29. *Indian Art in the United States and Alaska.*

30. For discussion of the surrealists' interest in, and appropriation of, indigenous cultures, see Braun's "Art from the Land of the Savages," 18–19, and *Pre-Columbian Art and the Post-Columbian World*; Cowling, "The Eskimos, the American Indians, and the Surrealists," 484–500; Jonaitis, "Creations of Mystics and Philosophers," 1–45; and Mauer, "Dada and Surrealism," 541–84.

31. Cowling, "The Eskimos, the American Indians, and the Surrealists," 486.

Ratton apparently obtained more than one hundred objects from the museum from its founder and director, George Heye, who was eager to increase the museum's collection in pre-Columbian art. Financially strapped by the depression, Heye traded the works to Ratton for cash and Peruvian goldwork. Upon their immigration to the United States, the surrealists continued to purchase works from the museum through the intermediary of Julius Carlebach. See Cowling, "The Eskimos, the American Indians, and the Surrealists," 488, 492.

32. Cowling, "The Eskimos, the American Indians, and the Surrealists," 487; Berlo, "Introduction: The Formative Years of Native American Art History," 14.

33. On surrealists' immigration see Lynes, *Good Old Modern*, 231–32.

Paalen, *Dyn*. In 1943 Claude Levi-Strauss, a close associate of the surrealists, told the art world that "the time is not far distant when the collections of the North West Coast will move from anthropological museums to take their place in art museums among the arts of Egypt, Persia and the Middle Ages" (Levi-Strauss, "The Art of the North West Coast," 175). For further discussion of Paalen and his relationship to Native American art, see Rushing, *Native American Art and the New York Avant-Garde*, 125–26.

34. For further discussion of the *Exposition of Indian Tribal Arts*, see Rushing, *Native American Art and the New York Avant-Garde*, 97–103.

The work of three of the contributing painters to Sloan's New York shows—Fred

Kabotie, Awa Tsireh, and Velino Shiji—was profiled by Edgar Lee Hewett in *Art and Archaeology* the final year of their participation (1922). The monthly periodical *Art and Archaeology*, published from 1915 until 1934, regularly juxtaposed articles featuring modern art and artists with those on Native American art (see Berlo, "Introduction: The Formative Years of Native American Art History," 13–14). Claiming that they were "absolutely free from white influence" (although each of them was at the time employed by the School of American Research, of which Hewett was director), Hewett admonished that these "splendid people, one hundred per cent American in ancestry and culture" were "certainly capable of being about the finest element in the American race that is in the making from so many diverse sources" (Hewett, "Native American Artists," 109). For another view, see Pach's two commentaries, "The Art of the American Indian," 57–65, and "Notes on the Indian Water-Colours," 343–45.

The Indian Arts Fund had been established in 1923 to conserve Native American arts for research and study purposes. It was closely associated with the Rockefeller-funded School of American Research, and in 1927 John D. Rockefeller Jr. contributed a "generous" donation to the fund. Two years later he financed the building of the Laboratory of Anthropology in Santa Fe to house the Indian Arts Fund's collection. See Stocking, "The Santa Fe Style in American Anthropology," 3–19. White had arranged for a Bureau of Indian Affairs booth of Indian arts and crafts at the International Antiques Exposition in New York in 1931 and had donated a number of objects previously exhibited in Paris in order that the Indian Office be able to establish a permanent collection. In addition, she had operated a gallery in New York that carried Native American arts.

35. Sloan and LaFarge, *Introduction to American Indian Art*, 56.

36. Ibid., 5–6, 56, 53.

37. "Indian Tribal Arts Exhibition Starts on Long Tour of Nation," 6; Pach, "The Indian Tribal Arts."

38. Jewell, "The American Indian Exhibition," sec. 9, 18.

39. Sloan and LaFarge, *Introduction to American Indian Art*, 6.

40. Jewell, "The American Indian Exhibition," sec. 9, 18.

41. Rushing, "Marketing the Affinity of the Primitive and the Modern," 227. Nelson Rockefeller was an avid collector of Latin American folk art and pre-Columbian art and quickly pressed d'Harnoncourt's expertise in these areas into his own personal service. After the nationalization of Standard Oil property in Bolivia in 1937 (followed by the expropriation of foreign oil interests in Mexico the following year), Rockefeller launched an extensive and multidimensional public relations campaign in Latin America (with a particularly strong focus in Venezuela and Brazil, where Rockefeller investments were heaviest). This operation took both public and private forms, spanning Rockefeller's tenure as coordinator of the Office of Inter-American Affairs (which employed d'Harnoncourt) and assistant secretary of state for Latin American Affairs during World War II, as well as his founding of the American International Association for Economic and Social Development (AIA) and the International Basic Economy Corporation in the postwar years. Exchanges in the arts and sports, together with technical, educational, and health assistance, were employed in these efforts to weaken opposition to U.S. investments and exploitation, inculcate U.S. political thought and consumerist values, and thereby ensure future U.S. presence and control. For further discussion of Rockefeller activities in Latin America see Collier and Horowitz, *The Rockefellers*, and Cobbs, *The Rich Neighbor Policy*.

42. Harold Ickes, "Department of the Interior Press Release, 13 January 1941," Indian Rights Association Papers, microfilm, reel 120, plate 92, cited in Schrader, *The Indian Arts and Crafts Board*, 231; Douglas and d'Harnoncourt, *Indian Art of the United States*, 9.

43. Schrader, *The Indian Arts and Crafts Board,* 79, 122–23. Under the Indian branch of the Public Works of Art Project, formed in 1934 and directed by Jesse Nusbaum of the Rockefellers' Laboratory of Anthropology in Santa Fe, forty-five Indian artists from the Albuquerque and Santa Fe Indian Schools created murals, rugs, pottery, and assorted other items for new Indian schools, hospitals, and community centers then under construction.

44. Roosevelt, "Radio Speech," 29.

45. Douglas and d'Harnoncourt, *Indian Art of the United States,* 8. Rushing notes that Eleanor Roosevelt signed the introduction but that it was written by d'Harnoncourt. See d'Harnoncourt to Eleanor Roosevelt, 19 December 1940, Records of the Indian Arts and Crafts Board, National Archives Record Group 435, box 34, file 300.36, cited in Rushing, "Marketing the Affinity of the Primitive and the Modern," 207, 229.

Charlot, "All-American," 165. For further discussion of the show's critical reception in relationship to American political sentiment of the time, see Rushing, "Marketing the Affinity of the Primitive and the Modern," 217–18.

46. "All-American Art," 17; Charlot, "All-American," 165.

47. Douglas and d'Harnoncourt, *Indian Art of the United States,* 199–200.

48. Ibid., 10.

49. Sloan and LaFarge, *Introduction to American Indian Art,* 11.

50. Adolph Gottlieb and Mark Rothko, "The Portrait and the Modern Artist," mimeographed script of a broadcast on art in New York, 13 October 1943, cited in Sandler, *The Triumph of American Painting,* 64.

51. *Pre-Columbian Stone Sculpture,* Wakefield Gallery, New York, 16 May-5 June 1944, cited in Sandler, *The Triumph of American Painting,* 69; Newman, *Northwest Coast Indian Painting.*

52. Newman, *The Ideographic Picture.* Newman contended in this catalog that the "ideographic painters," as he called the artists included in the show, were "abstract symbolists" like the Northwest Coast Indian artists. "The Kwakiutl artist painting on a hide did not concern himself with the inconsequentials that made up the opulent social rivalries of the Northwest Coast Indian scene," wrote Newman, in a blatant show of his ignorance of the fabric of Kwakiutl art, "nor did he, in the name of a higher purity, renounce the living world for the meaningless materialism of design. The abstract shape he used, his entire plastic language, was directed by a ritualistic will towards metaphysical understanding. The everyday realities he left to the toymakers; the pleasant play of non-objective pattern to the women basket weavers."

53. For further discussion of Jackson Pollock's interest in Native art and cultures, see Rushing, "Ritual and Myth," 281–93, and *Native American Art and the New York Avant-Garde,* 169–90.

Pollock said of his technique that, "On the floor I am more at ease. I feel nearer, more a part of the painting, since this way I can walk around it, work from the four sides and literally be in the painting. This is akin to the method of the Indian sand painters of the West" (Pollock, "My Painting," 79).

54. D'Harnoncourt himself had resigned his position as general manager of the Indian Arts and Crafts Board (IACB) to become vice president in charge of foreign activities and director of the Department of Manual Industries at MoMA in 1944 (where he was paid not by the museum, but by Nelson Rockefeller personally; see Lynes, *Good Old Modern,* 272). He became the director of MoMA four years later. He remained, however, as a member of the IACB and later became its chair.

55. Dockstader, "Directions in Indian Art," 13.

56. Ibid., 28.

57. Ibid., 12.

58. Ibid., 16.

59. Robert Motherwell, "The Modern Painter's World," *Dyn* 6 (1944), cited in Rose, *Readings in American Art since 1900*, 131.

The Museum of Modern Art forum was held on 5 March 1948 and was called "The Modern Artist Speaks." Five papers (now located in the Archive of American Art, no. 69/112, folder 59–66) were presented by Paul Burlin, Stuart Davis, Adolph Gottlieb, George L. K. Morris, and James Johnson Sweeney. See Guilbaut, *How New York Stole the Idea of Modern Art*, 181.

60. D'Harnoncourt, "Challenge and Promise," 252.

61. *Congressional Record*, 83d Congress, 2d sess., 1954, p. 5375.

62. "Ike Likes the Arts," 68. This fund was made permanent by the International Cultural Exchange and Trade Fair Participation Act of 1956, which authorized the president to use American art, as well as creative and performing artists, to "strengthen the ties which unite us with other nations by demonstrating the cultural interests, developments, and achievements of the people of the United States, and the contributions of the United States' economic and social system toward a peaceful and more fruitful life for its own people and other people throughout the world" (House Committee on Education and Labor, *Report on the Relationship of the Federal Government to the Arts: Hearings on H.R. 3541*, 85th Cong., 1st sess., 1958, 74).

63. "A Statement on Artistic Freedom," 95.

64. Whitney, foreword to *Masters of Modern Art*, 7.

65. *Congressional Record*, 84th Cong. 1st sess., 1955, p. 6844. For discussion of the impact of this policy see Larson, *The Reluctant Patron*, 98–99.

66. Thompson, "Are the Communists Right in Calling Us Cultural Barbarians?" 5; House Committee on Education and Labor, *Hearings on Various Bills Relating to Awards of Medal for Distinguished Civilian Achievement, and Cultural Interchange and Development*. 84th Cong., 1955–56, 3–12.

67. House Committee on Education and Labor, *Statement of Lloyd Goodrich, Chairman, the Committee on Government and Art, New York City: Hearings on H.R. 3541*, 85th Cong. 1st sess., 142. The Committee on Government and Art, established in 1948, was composed of twelve national art organizations: the American Association of Museums, the American Federation of the Arts, the American Institute of Architects, the American Institute of Decorators, Artists Equity Association, the Association of Art Museum Directors, the College Art Association of America, the National Academy of Design, the National Association of Women Artists, the National Institute of Arts and Letters, the National Society of Mural Painters, and the Sculptors Guild.

Larson, *The Reluctant Patron*, 111.

68. For further discussion of the various controversies that characterized federal patronage of the arts in the 1940s and 1950s, see Larson, *The Reluctant Patron*, 13–62, 115–42; Lasch, "The Cultural Cold War," 63–113; Kozloff, "American Painting during the Cold War," 43–54; and Mathews, "Art and Politics in Cold War America," 762–87.

69. *Congressional Record*, 81st Cong., 1st sess., 1949, p. 11584.

70. Barr, "Is Modern Art Communistic?," 22.

71. Barr, "Letters to the Editor," 184–85.

72. The relationship between individualism, abstract expressionism, the Museum of Modern Art, and U.S. foreign policy is explored extensively by Cockcroft in "Abstract Expressionism, Weapon of the Cold War," 39–41, and "Mexico, MoMA, and Cultural Imperialism," 12–15; see also Lasch, "The Cultural Cold War"; Kozloff, "American Painting during the Cold War"; and Mathews, "Art and Politics in Cold War America."

Braden, "I'm Glad the CIA is 'Immoral,'" 10. For more on the CIA's cultural Cold War operations, see Lasch, "The Cultural Cold War," 72–74, 99–113.

73. Lynes, *Good Old Modern*, 384–85.

74. Collier and Horowitz, *The Rockefellers*, 229–31.

75. D'Harnoncourt was still officially employed by the Department of the Interior, and in fact, Nelson Rockefeller repaid part of his salary at the Indian Arts and Crafts Board in order to have the privilege of borrowing him for the OIAA. Hellman, "Imperturbable Noble," 90.

This exhibit, prepared by d'Harnoncourt and Miguel Covarrubias, was called *El Arte Indígena de Norteamérica* and was sponsored by the Instituto Nacional de Antropología e Historia de México, the National Gallery of Art, and the Instituto Mexicano-Norteamericano de Relaciones Culturales. The catalog of the same name was co-authored by Covarrubias and Daniel F. Rubin de la Borbolla, with an introduction by d'Harnoncourt.

76. Larson, *The Reluctant Patron*, 59.

77. Mrs. Rockefeller cited in Preston, "To Help Our Art," sec. 2, p. 15; Lynes, *Good Old Modern*, 386–87.

78. Barr, introduction to *The New American Painting*, 15.

79. D'Harnoncourt, foreword to *The New American Painting*, 5; McCray, "As the Critics Saw It," 7.

80. Lynes, *Good Old Modern*, 383–84; see also Kozloff, "American Painting during the Cold War," 49. Indeed, the University of Arizona was at this time at the very least utilizing educational films developed by MoMA, and they relied on these for the core of their film program for the Southwestern Indian Art Project of 1960–63 (see chap. 2).

81. The sessions offered several presentations on the topic of education, with titles including "Guidance and Evaluation of the Indian Artist" (Dorothy Dunn, former director of the Santa Fe Indian School Studio); "New Education Directions in Southwest Indian Art" (Edward B. Danson, director, Museum of Northern Arizona, Flagstaff); "Education on the Pre-College Level" (Margaret Handlong, art teacher in Phoenix Public Schools); "Guilds and Special Schools for Indian Artists and Craftsmen" (Russell Lingruen, manager, Navajo Arts and Crafts Board, Window Rock, Arizona); and the banquet keynote address by Lloyd "Kiva" New entitled "Projections in Indian Art Education" ("Directions in Indian Art: A Conference on Arizona's Position on Southwest Indian Art Education," University of Arizona, 20–21 March, 1959, photocopied program, Charles Minton Papers, Box 1.)
Dockstader, "Directions in Indian Art," 27, 21, 25.

82. Dockstader, 21, 24.

83. Ibid., 10.

84. For further discussion of the Studio, see Dunn, *American Indian Painting;* and Rushing and Bernstein, *Modern by Tradition.*

85. Szasz, *Education and the American Indian*, 32–33.

86. It should be noted that this was not the first arts program in an Indian school. Dorothy Dunn seemed to deliberately perpetuate this misconception in her early published accounts of the Studio's history (see Dunn's "Development of Modern American Painting," 331–53, and "Studio of Painting," 16–27). In fact, extensive arts programs were developed at Hampton Normal and Agricultural Institute in Hampton, Virginia, from 1878 to 1923, and from 1906 until 1915 at Carlisle Indian School by Winnebago artist Angel DeCora-Dietz, perhaps Hampton's best-known student (Mary Lou Hultgren, "Native American Art at Hampton: An Early Boarding School Experiment," paper presented at the Sixth Annual Native American Art Studies Association Conference, Denver, 23–26 September 1987).

87. The adult artists who worked on the murals were Julian Martinez, Tse-Ye-Mu, Richard Martinez, and Oqwa Pi from San Ildefonso Pueblo, and Jack Hokeah, a Kiowa from Oklahoma. The students who participated were Miguel Martinez and Juan Diego Martinez of San Ildefonso; Riley Quoyavema, a Hopi; Tom Weahkee from Zuni; and Edward Lee, Alex Lee, Paul Tsosie, and Albert Hardy Begay, all Navajo. For contemporary accounts of the work, see Rush, "Indian Murals at Santa Fe, New Mexico," 8, and "Young Indians Work in Old Forms," 635–38; Austin, "American Indian Murals," 380–84; "Indian Artists Take Up Mural Painting," 32; and "Artists with Never a Thought for Fame," 15.

88. Dunn, "The Studio of Painting," 19.

89. For a critique of the controversy surrounding the pedagogy of the Studio and its successors, see Snodgrass-King, "In the Name of Progress, Is History Being Repeated?" 27–35.

Dunn, "The Studio of Painting," 18.

90. Dunn, "The Development of Modern American Indian Painting," 336.

91. Dunn, "The Studio of Painting," 20–22.

92. Dunn's view of the works as "in character with the old" seems to have been limited primarily to form, less frequently to content, and apparently never to purpose of the image. For further discussion of this issue, see Brody, *Indian Painters and White Patrons*, 129.

For development of Native American painting in Oklahoma, see Jacobson, "Indian Artists From Oklahoma"; Dunn, *American Indian Painting*, 219–24; Brody, *Indian Painters and White Patrons*, 120–26, 132–38; Snodgrass, *American Indian Painters*; and Silberman, "A Selection of Native American Art," 47–87, and *100 Years of Native American Painting*.

93. "French Artist Paul Coze Arranges Show of Indian Watercolors," sec. 2, p. 4. A year earlier a group of students had toured with paintings being shown in the southeastern United States and Washington, D.C. (see "New Mexico Indians Make History," 6.) Other exhibitions included ones at the Royal College of Art in London, the Museum of Fine Arts at Stanford University, the Art Institute of Chicago, the San Francisco Museum of Art, the *Second National Exhibition of American Art* at the Rockefeller Center in New York, and annual shows at the Museum of New Mexico in Santa Fe.

94. Dunn, "The Studio of Painting," 20–24.

95. Dockstader, "Directions in Indian Art," 10, 16.

96. Snodgrass-King, "In the Name of Progress, Is History Being Repeated?" 28. The exchange prompted Dunn to write Fahs the following year, enclosing a copy of an *El Palacio* article ("The Studio of Painting") in which Dunn defended herself against the accusations. Dunn requested that the published response be filed in the Rockefeller office with papers concerning the conference "for setting the record straight insofar as possible" (Dorothy Dunn to Charles Fahs, 25 February 1960, Rockefeller Foundation Archives, RF 1.2, Series 200 R, Box 430, Folder 3708).

CHAPTER 2

1. Lloyd New to Charles B. Fahs, telephone call, 27 July 1959, Rockefeller Foundation Archives, RF 1.2, Series 200 R, Box 430, Folder 3708; Lloyd New to Charles B. Fahs, 28 September 1959, Rockefeller Foundation Archives, RF 1.2, Series 200 R, Box 430, Folder 3708.

2. Lloyd New to Charles B. Fahs, 28 September 1959, Rockefeller Foundation Archives, RF 1.2, Series 200 R, Box 430, Folder 3708.

3. Ibid. New obviously chose to exclude from his accounting the arts curriculum

directed by Geronima Montoya at the Santa Fe Indian School, Apache artist Allan Houser's artist-in-residency at the Intermountain Indian Boarding School in Utah, Fred Kabotie's classes at Oraibi High School in Arizona, as well as the Art Department at Bacone College headed by Cheyenne artist Dick West (among other scattered programs).

4. "A Proposal for An Exploratory Workshop in Art for Talented Younger Indians," 15 October 1959, p. 3, Rockefeller Foundation Archives, RF 1.2, Series 200 R, Box 430, Folder 3708; as it turned out, d'Harnoncourt was unable to attend the conference and so Lloyd New spoke at the banquet instead.

The University Committee on Indian Art by now consisted of Emil Haury, chairman; David Patrick, University of Arizona director of research; Sidney W. Little, dean of the College of Fine Arts; Clara Lee Tanner, professor of anthropology; and Andreas Andersen, head of the Department of Art. For further discussion of the committee's work subsequent to the Rockefeller conference, see Emil Haury to Charles B. Fahs and attached resolutions, 27 April 1959, Rockefeller Foundation Archives, RF 1.2, Series 200 R, Box 430, Folder 3708.

5. "A Proposal for An Exploratory Workshop in Art for Talented Younger Indians," 1.

6. The exact statement regarding Hopi art read: "I would like to see a revival in Hopi art. We are indebted to any organization which promotes Indian art and culture" ("A Proposal for An Exploratory Workshop in Art for Talented Younger Indians," 5; see also Dockstader, "Directions in Indian Art," 24).

7. "A Proposal for An Exploratory Workshop in Art for Talented Younger Indians," 4; see also Dockstader, "Directions in Indian Art," 28.

8. A "nominating committee," consisting of Indian educators, traders, museum personnel, adult Indian artists and craftsmen, anthropologists, and tribal officials interested in the arts, was to be appointed for the purpose of selecting participants so as to ensure representation from throughout the southwestern region. The nominees were then to be screened by the University Committee on Indian Art and the finalists interviewed by committee representatives. The Indian faculty involved with the project were to advise the committee in their evaluation of nominees. The actual selection process seems to have been far more haphazard than the proposal would suggest. Lloyd New remembers the participants as having been chosen rather randomly: "Somebody would know somebody and say, 'Well, we think he should come.' And all of us in the Project just thought of people that we thought might work . . . and there was a sense of trying to strike a balance in terms of the geography of the country that we didn't get everybody from the state of Arizona" (*Shared Visions*, 80–81).

9. The original proposal stated that Charles Loloma was being considered to teach metalwork, Lucy Lewis ceramics, and Fred Kabotie painting. Only Loloma actually participated in the workshops ("A Proposal for an Exploratory Workshop in Art for Talented Younger Indians," 8).

10. "A Proposal for an Exploratory Workshop in Art for Talented Younger Indians," 9–10.

11. This must be qualified only because of the large numbers of Indian peoples who had suffered culture loss at this time due to the ravages of boarding schools, relocation programs, and discrimination, in addition to the cultural cost of substance abuse on some reservations.

12. Excerpt from John P. Harrison's diary, Phoenix, Arizona, 13 January 1960, Rockefeller Foundation Archives, RF 1.2, Series 200 R, Box 430, Folder 3708; Lloyd Kiva (New) to John P. Harrison, 29 January 1960, pp. 1–2, Rockefeller Foundation Archives, RF 1.2, Series 200 R, Box 430, Folder 3708.

13. Lloyd Kiva (New) to Harrison, 3.

14. Interviews: John P. Harrison with Fred Dockstadter *[sic]*, Director, Museum of the American Indian, 5 February 1960, Rockefeller Foundation Archives, RF 1.2, Series 200 R, Box 430, Folder 3708.

15. Janet M. Paine to Richard A. Harvill, March 2, 1960, Rockefeller Foundation Archives, RF 1.2, Series 200 R, Box 430, Folder 3708; see also Resolution RF 60039, February 26, 1960, Rockefeller Foundation Archives, RF 1.2, Series 200 R, Box 430, Folder 3708.

16. Resolution RF 60039, p. 60180. The acceptance form participants signed included the following passage: "I also agree that the University may retain one work of its choice produced by me during the period of the workshop for its permanent collections, and may also retain for the period of one year such other works as it may choose for exhibition purposes" (Patrick et al., *Southwest Indian Art*, 39).

17. Resolution RF 60039, p. 60182.

18. Patrick et al., *Southwest Indian Art*, 31, 6.

19. For further discussion of Herrera's career and work, see Rushing, "Authenticity and Subjectivity in Post-War Painting," 12–19. See also Dunn, "The Art of Joe Herrera," 367–73, and Brody, *Indian Painters and White Patrons*, 152–53. Though other sources report that Herrera's work was shown during the 1950s at the Museum of Modern Art, Rushing states that he has found nothing to substantiate this claim (19).

20. Dockstader Report, 20 September 1960, p. 2, Rockefeller Foundation Archives, RF 1.2, 200 R, Box 430, Folder 3708.

The artists attending the 1960 session were Richard Caje, Lydia M. Cosen, Ernest Franklin, Wilkie Gregg, Helen Hardin, Bobby Hicks, Michael Kabotie, Gordon Keahbone, Anderson Lesansee, Vera Lizer, James Lujan, Mary Morez, Ruth Ella Morris, Bob Porter, James Singer, Terry Talaswaima, Richard Taliwood, Roger Tsabetsaye, Ernest Whitehead, and Tom Yazzi. Those who participated in the 1961 session were Thomas Badonie, Jimmie Begay, Henrietta Bobb, George Burdeau, Elmer Chavarria, Roberta Colehay, Jimmie Carol Fife, Bernando Lalo, Shirley Martin, Peter Mitchell, James Natatches, Michael Penrod, James Redcorn, Fritz Scholder, Gibson R. Smith, and Patronella Smith. Seven students attended both sessions: Frank Austin, Jerome Begay, Chester Kahn, Christino Pena, Manfred Susunkewa, Emiliana Vigil, and Antowine Warrior.

21. Patrick et al., *Southwest Indian Art*, 3–4, 36–37.

22. Dockstader Report, 2.

23. Beatty, *Education for Cultural Change*, 474–76.

24. *Shared Visions*, 76.

25. Dockstader Report, 4, 3.

26. Ibid., 5, 10.

27. Ibid., 3, 4, 7.

28. Ibid., 8. This was a philosophy shared by George Boyce, first superintendent of the Institute of American Indian Arts; see chapter 3.

29. Ibid., 11.

30. *Shared Visions*, 75.

31. Dockstader Report, 6, 11.

32. Patrick et al., *Southwest Indian Art*, 14–15.

33. Ibid., 15–17, 20–21.

34. Ibid., 12–21.

35. Ibid., 23–24.

36. Ibid., 1–2, 12.

37. *Shared Visions*, 80; Lloyd Kiva (New) to John P. Harrison, 12 April 1962, Attachment (Comments on Southwest Indian Arts and Crafts Project, University of

Arizona, 2d year, 1961), p. 1, Rockefeller Foundation Archives, RF 1.2, Series 200 R, Box 431, Folder 3709.

38. New cited in Kiva (New) to Harrison, attachment, 1, and *Shared Visions*, 80; Scholder cited in Self, "City Fair," 42.

Scholder's account of how he came to be a participant in the Southwestern Indian Art Project is a bit surprising, particularly given the fact that the organizers stressed the tightening of the selection process in the second year. The final report claims that "the recruitment of new students for the 1961 session was accomplished entirely by personal interview on two trips into the Eastern Arizona and New Mexico areas. As a result, a higher level of capability was secured" (Little et al., *1961 Southwestern Indian Art Project*, 6). Scholder describes his childhood as being disconnected from his Indian heritage: "I really had a non-Indian background. I spent my first 14 years in a small North Dakota border town. We lived on the Indian school campus, because my father (who is half Luiseno) worked for the Bureau of Indian Affairs. But we went to public schools. There were no Indian objects in the house. We never thought of ourselves as Indians." He was studying at Sacramento State College with artist Wayne Thiebaud when he received a letter of invitation to the program in Tucson: "It was really a bad time in my life. I was literally scrounging for both food and materials when, in 1961, out of the clear blue, I got a letter from the Rockefeller Foundation. They were just beginning a new project for Indian artists. My name is on the rolls in Washington which makes me an official Indian I guess and they looked up the rolls and saw that I was both an Indian and an artist. So they sent a letter asking me if I wanted an all-expense-paid trip to the University of Arizona for a summer-long program. To a starving artist that offer looked pretty good. So I went to Arizona" (Self, "City Fair," 41–42).

39. *Shared Visions*, 79–80.

40. "Exhibition: Student Work, Second Annual Southwest Indian Art Project 1961," University Art Gallery, 21 July 4 August 1961, Rockefeller Foundation Archives, RF 1.2, 200 R, Box 431, Folder 3709.

41. Little et al., *1961 Indian Art Project*, 8–9.

42. Kiva (New) to Harrison, attachment, 2–3.

43. Little et al., *1961 Indian Art Project*, 11.

44. Ibid., 13.

45. Ibid., unnumbered prefatory page.

46. The three students listed as recipients of the awards in one newspaper account were James Redcorn, Frank Austin, and Van Tsihnojinnie. However, there is no "Van Tsihnojinnie" on the roster of students who attended the 1960 or 1961 Southwestern Indian Art Projects (Rockefeller Foundation Archives, RF 1.2, 200 R, Box 431, Folder 3709).

47. *New York Times*, 15 October 1961, E-7, cols. 3–6.

48. Sidney W. Little to John P. Harrison, 4 December 1961, p. 2, Rockefeller Foundation Archives, RF 1.2, Series 200 R, Box 431, Folder 3709. See also Little to Harrison, 18 September 1961, p. 2, Rockefeller Foundation Archives, RF 1.2, Series 200 R, Box 431, Folder 3709.

49. Kiva (New) to Harrison, attachment, 2.

50. Excerpt from: Robert W. July Diary with Dean Sidney W. Little, 27 April 1962, Rockefeller Foundation Archives, RF 1.2, Series 200 R, Box 431, Folder 3709.

51. John P. Harrison to Sidney W. Little, 17 May 1962, Rockefeller Foundation Archives, RF 1.2, Series 200 R, Box 431, Folder 3709; Sidney W. Little to John P. Harrison, 24 June 1962, Rockefeller Foundation Archives, RF 1.2, Series 200 R, Box 431, Folder 3709.

52. Interviews: Chadbourne Gilpatric with Sidney W. Little, Dean, College of Fine

Arts, University of Arizona, Tucson, 12 December 1962, p. 1, Rockefeller Foundation Archives, RF 1.2, Series 200 R, Box 431, Folder 3709.

53. Sidney W. Little to Chadbourne Gilpatric, 11 January 1963, Rockefeller Foundation Archives, RF 1.2, Series 200 R, Box 431, Folder 3709. By now Roy Sieber was also leaving to join the faculty of the University of Indiana, and Andrew Rush had decided not to return in 1963, as he felt he had neglected his own painting for the past two summers while teaching in the UA workshops.

54. Resolution RF 60039, 4 February 1963, E 6306, Rockefeller Foundation Archives, RF 1.2, Series 200 R, Box 430, Folder 3708. See also Chadbourne Gilpatric to Richard A. Harvill, 5 February 1953, Rockefeller Foundation Archives, RF 1.2, Series 200 R, Box 431, Folder 3709.

55. Southwestern Indian Art Project, University of Arizona, Tucson: Final Report to the Rockefeller Foundation, 17 March 1965, Rockefeller Foundation Archives, RF 1.2, Series 200 R, Box 431, Folder 3709.

Roger Tsabetsaye had won one of four regional awards in painting at the Philbrook Art Center's *Seventeenth Annual American Indian Artists Exhibition* in 1962. James Redcorn had been awarded a second place. Roy Sieber and Joe Herrera, both instructors for the Southwestern Indian Art Project, served that year on the show's jury, together with Dorothy Field Maxwell ("Art and Artists: Prizes Distributed to American Indians," *Dallas Texas News*, 2 May 1962, Rockefeller Foundation Archives, RF 1.2, Series 200 R, Box 431, Folder 3709).

CHAPTER 3

1. George A. Boyce to Lynne Waugh, 24 July 1972. Cited in Garmhausen, *History of Indian Arts Education in Santa Fe*, 62–67. Boyce was writing Waugh, a reporter for the *Santa Fe New Mexican*, in response to an article written by her that appeared on 23 July 1972 entitled "IAIA Nurtures Indian Art." Waugh had stated that "the Institute of American Indian Art (IAIA) grew out of a Rockefeller-funded school, that Lloyd New, the noted Indian craftsman, established in Scottsdale, Ariz., in the 1950's. The Department of the Interior's Indian Arts and Crafts Board took it over in 1960 and moved it to Santa Fe two years later. Lloyd New came with it and has been its director ever since." Boyce maintained that her statements were "far from the truth" and provided a detailed account of the events, as he knew them, leading up to the establishment of the school.

2. For a thorough discussion of the political machinations by which this Gallup businessman was appointed to the Commissioner of Indian Affairs post, see Burt, *Tribalism in Crisis*, 9–18.

3. In addition to Larry Burt's treatment of the era, the history of termination policy may be found in Fixico, *Termination and Relocation;* Hasse, "Termination and Assimilation"; Orfield, *A Study of the Termination Policy;* Madigan, *The American Indian Relocation Program;* and Officer, "The American Indian and Federal Policy," 45–54, and "Termination As Federal Policy," 114–28.

Under the General Allotment, or Dawes, Act of 1887, title to individual plots of land was to remain in trust with the U.S. government for twenty-five years in order to protect Indians from unscrupulous non-Indian buyers. At the end of this period, Indians were to receive a fee-simple title and be granted citizenship. In reality, the trust periods were frequently extended by U.S. presidents, although the fee patent titles that were granted (sometimes without Native consent) contributed to a quickly eroding Indian land base. In 1934 John Collier made land reform a part of his Indian Reorganization Act, which prohibited further allotment, extended trusts indefinitely, returned lands not allotted under the Dawes Act to the tribes, and made funds available for the acquisition of additional land. See Washburn, *The Assault on Indian Tribalism*; and Philp, *John Collier's Crusade for Indian Reform*, 135–60.

House Committee on Interior and Insular Affairs, *Information on Removal of Restrictions on American Indians*, 88th Cong., 2d sess., Committee Print 38, 41.

4. Fixico, *Termination and Relocation*, 4–8. For a thorough discussion of the impact of World War II on Native Americans, see Bernstein, *American Indians and World War II*.

5. Armstrong, "Set the American Indians Free!" 47–52.

6. Ibid.

7. *Congressional Record*, 20 September 1945, Appendix, A4086.

8. Senate Committee on Indian Affairs, *Aspects of Indian Policy*, 79th Cong., 1st sess., 1945, Senate Report, 92:7998–99.

9. For further discussion of the Indian Claims Commission Act and its significance, see Lurie, "The Indian Claims Commission Act," 56–70.

10. Burt, *Termination and Relocation*, 4–5, 19; Nash, *The American West in the Twentieth Century*, 195–216.

11. Fixico, *Termination and Relocation*, 77.

12. House and Senate Committees on Interior and Insular Affairs, *Termination of Federal Supervision over Certain Tribes of Indians*, 83d Cong., 2d sess., 1954, pt. 5 "California Indians," 457.

13. *Congressional Record*, 29 July 1953, p. 10294.

14. Burt, *Termination and Relocation*, 21.

15. House and Senate Committees on Interior and Insular Affairs, *Termination of Federal Supervision over Certain Tribes of Indians*, 83d Cong., 2d sess., 1954, pt. 1 "Statement of Glenn L. Emmons," 41–43.

16. See Fixico, *Termination and Relocation*, 158–82, and Burt, *Termination and Relocation*, 83–93.

17. For further discussion of the relocation program see Madigan, *The American Indian Relocation Program*; Harmer, "Uprooting the Indians," 54–57; and Ablon, "American Indian Relocation," 362–71.

18. Information about Emmons's meetings with tribal leaders is cited in Burt, *Termination and Relocation*, 78. Emmons was denounced by the National Congress of American Indians at their 1956 annual convention for such practices; see Burt, *Termination and Relocation*, 79–80.

19. Szasz, *Education and the American Indian*, 106, 111; Beatty, *Education for Cultural Change*, 10–11.

20. Beatty, *Education for Cultural Change*, 44.

21. Ibid., 274.

22. Szasz, *Education and the American Indian*, 116.

23. Beatty, *Education for Cultural Change*, 474–76.

24. Ibid., 243–44, 486.

25. Ibid., 475.

26. Ibid., 487.

27. Ibid., 477.

28. Thompson, *Education for Cross-Cultural Enrichment*, 30.

29. Ibid., 33.

30. Ibid., 47.

31. Ibid., 35.

32. This was not a new, post-Sputnik idea; it had been smoldering since the Second World War. In 1947 the American Federation of Teachers' theme for their annual congress was "Strengthening Education for National and World Security." The Office of Education initiated a Zeal for American Democracy program at the time to that same

end; see Guilbaut, *How New York Stole the Idea of Modern Art*, 146–47. The Indian Education Office published articles such as "Education for Democracy" after the war, in which author William H. Hemsing declared, "The Marshall Plan, the radio Voice of America, and CARE packages are only the beginning of our global policy. The mighty disciplined force of a United World brotherhood will win the peace. Let us mobilize this force in every school and community now!" (Hemsing, "Education for Democracy," 138).

33. This statement was made in 1956 by Wesley D'Ewart, assistant secretary of the interior in charge of public land management. D'Ewart was responding to a scathing article by Dorothy Van de Mark published in *Harper's* magazine in March, which had garnered considerable attention and support against the government's termination and relocation policies ("Letters," 4).

34. Thompson, *Education for Cross-Cultural Enrichment*, 111.

35. Collier, "Back to Dishonor?" 578–80; Burt, *Termination and Relocation*, 66–67; and Fey, "Indian Winter," 265–67, and "Navajo Race with Tragedy," 617–19. See also the account of Oliver LaFarge's speech at the annual meeting of the Association on American Indian Affairs, in which LaFarge cited greed for Indian resources and land as the motivation behind termination ("LaFarge Charges U.S. Breaks Indian Trust," 604–5).

36. Van de Mark, "The Raid on the Reservations," 49.

37. Harmer, "Uprooting the Indians," 54; Rowan cited in Burt, *Termination and Relocation*, 84; "The American Stranger," *Kaleidoscope*.

38. Department of the Interior Information Service, "News Release on Indian Policy," Press Release for 15 September 1958, Folder-BIA (articles), Box 9, Fred Seaton Papers, Ewald Research Files, Dwight D. Eisenhower Library, cited in Burt, *Termination and Relocation*, 113.

39. Report to the Congress of the United States by the Comptroller General of the United States, "Review of Certain Aspects of the Program for the Termination of Federal Supervision over Indian Affairs, Bureau of Indian Affairs, Department of the Interior," March 1961, p. 18, cited in Officer, "Termination as Federal Policy," 127; Hank Adams's commentary about doubling enrollment cited in Philp, *Indian Self-Rule*, 240; Deloria, "The Era of Indian Self-Determination," 191.

40. Glenn Emmons, "Freedom for the First Americans," notes for a proposed book manuscript, Folder 15, Box V, Glenn Emmons Papers, University of New Mexico General Library, cited in Burt, *Termination and Relocation*, 127. Emmons had first proposed this plan for gradual termination in 1956.

41. It is interesting to note that Emmons subsequently displayed considerable pride in his role in establishing this arts center. Charles Minton reported that at the open house in 1960 he took great exception to Oliver LaFarge's implication that the Indian Arts and Crafts Board had been responsible for the program. Emmons claimed that the IACB had done nothing and that he had specifically not sent the funding request "upstairs" to the Department of the Interior but instead had handled it himself so as to assure its success (Charles Minton, "Material for Monthly Report for August 1960," p. 7, Charles Minton Papers, Box 1.)

42. Boyce to Waugh cited in Garmhausen, *History of Indian Arts Education in Santa Fe*, 63. Boyce made a point of stating for the record that "the Rockefeller Foundation and Lloyd New's activities at that time were never mentioned or considered, although I have personally known Lloyd New and his activities in Phoenix and Scottsdale for some 30 years." See also the "Report of the Executive Director of the Commission on Indian Affairs," June 1960, p. 2, Charles Minton Papers, Box 2. The Pueblo Market, which functioned as a sales intermediary for Pueblo artists, was originally established as a "rehabilitation" program for Tesuque Pueblo but had been transferred to the Santa

Fe Indian School, where it was administered by school employees. In 1959 it was returned to the pueblo.

43. Charles Minton, "Report of the Executive Director of the Commission on Indian Affairs," December 1960, pp. 1–2, Charles Minton Papers, Box 1.

44. Philleo Nash, Commissioner of Indian Affairs, to Clinton P. Anderson, Chairman, Committee on Interior and Insular Affairs, United States Senate, 10 August 1962, p. 1, George Boyce Papers.

45. The vocational programs in metalsmithing, welding, carpentry, leather, and farming had been discontinued in 1956. Though the government attributed the declining enrollment to increased opportunities for Indian students to attend public or day schools closer to home, some Pueblo Indians claim that the reduced numbers were due to pressure on students to transfer to public schools or to the Albuquerque Indian School. The boarding school's closing was unpopular with the Pueblos, many of whose families had long traditions of attendance. See Hyer, *One House, One Voice, One Heart,* 57, 66–69. This issue, and how it affected the Institute of American Indian Arts, is discussed more fully later in this chapter.

46. Boyce to Waugh cited in Garmhausen, *History of Indian Arts Education in Santa Fe,* 64. Boyce stated that Thompson had to resubmit the proposal several times, as it was removed on a number of occasions from the budget request.

47. Ibid. See also "Jefe Named for SF Indian Arts School," 1.

48. Boyce to Waugh cited in Garmhausen, *History of Indian Arts Education in Santa Fe,* 64.

49. George A. Boyce, "The Indian Tribal Mind: A Study of Social Concepts for Indian Rehabilitation," Manuscript, October 1957, p. 128, George Boyce Papers.

50. Ibid., 97, 111–13.

51. Ibid., 61.

52. "Indian Art Institute Chief Tackles Big Job," 1, 2.

53. "Buildings OK'd for Indian Art Center," sec. 2, p. 9.

54. George Boyce to Commissioner, Bureau of Indian Affairs, 12 December 1961, p. 4, George Boyce Papers. An earlier letter to the commissioner had also stressed similar benefits: "the amazing expressions of sincere interest in the Institute are of such 'political worth,' in the broader meaning, as to be of possible special interest to the Secretary, the Commissioner, and other national leaders. This little project could become of inestimable significance" (George Boyce to Commissioner, Bureau of Indian Affairs, 17 October 1961, p. 2, George Boyce Papers). These sentiments were to find their way into the school's basic statement of purpose (see the introduction).

55. George Boyce to Clinton P. Anderson, U.S. Senate, 12 January 1962, George Boyce Papers; Boyce to Commissioner, 17 October 1961, p. 1; George Boyce's personal notes, n.d., George Boyce Papers. Promotional letters and introductory brochures describing the institute were sent to members of Congress, clergy, BIA Area Offices, and many other parties with an interest in Indian affairs in early 1962.

56. In addition, Boyce met with the full Indian Arts and Crafts Board during the fall to discuss basic goals, principles of operation, and curriculum (Boyce to Commissioner, 12 December 1961, p. 2).

57. George Boyce to Theodore A. Randall and Attachment ("General Objectives, Institute of American Indian Arts"), 25 October 1961, p. 2, George Boyce Papers.

58. "Notes for Possible Staffing and Recruiting Art Department," Attachment to George Boyce to Hildegard Thompson, 12 December 1961, pp. 1–2, 4, George Boyce Papers; George Boyce to Hildegard Thompson, 7 December 1961, p. 3, George Boyce Papers.

59. George Boyce to Allan Houser, 8 December 1961, George Boyce Papers; George Boyce to James A. McGrath, 16 January 1962; Boyce to McGrath, 29 January 1962,

George Boyce Papers; George Boyce to Area Director, Gallup Area Office, Memorandum, 12 March 1962; see also George Boyce to Louis W. Ballard, 23 April 1962; and George Boyce to Area Director, Gallup Area Office, Memorandum, 16 March 1962, George Boyce Papers. Otellie Loloma was chosen for one of two ceramics positions two months later; see George Boyce to Area Director, Gallup Area Office, Memorandum, 28 May 1962, George Boyce Papers.

60. George Boyce, For the Record, Memorandum, 14 March 1962, p. 1, George Boyce Papers.

61. George Boyce to Martin N. B. Holm, 13 April 1962, George Boyce Papers.

62. Ibid.

63. George Boyce to Area Director, Gallup Area Office, Memorandum, 26 March 1962.

64. "Confidential Report of the Executive Director to Edwin L. Mechem, Governor of New Mexico," New Mexico Commission on Indian Affairs, April 1962, p. 6, Charles Minton Papers.

Subsequent quotations concerning the institute's aims and objectives are from the press release unless otherwise noted. This press release distributed at the New Mexico Commission on Indian Affairs March meeting appears to be identical to one reproduced in Indian Education, with the exception of the reference to the student body at the institute being comprised of the "arts elite of American Indian youth." This one phrase raised the hackles of a number of individuals and was avidly quoted by the school's opponents. The words do not appear in the Indian Education version. Minton later referred to the controversy over the wording of the press release in a report issued in September: "The Bureau . . . made it appear that the Pueblos had invented the phrase, 'arts elite,' but this was in the Bureau release from the Institute. Proof of this can be seen in the column of Helene Monberg, Washington correspondent for the Gallup Independent, who, in a dispatch to that paper, quoted what she called the 'purple prose' in the press release and said that it stated the plan was to provide 'an opportunity for self expression in the whole rainbow of the arts. . . . On campus one will meet the arts elite of American Indian youth'" (Minton, "Supplement Number Two," 3). For commentary on the press release distributed to commission members, see Minton, "Supplement on the Institute of American Indian Art," 6–8. For the Indian Education version, see Warren, "Institute of American Indian Arts to Open at Santa Fe," 139–41.

65. Indian Employees of the Santa Fe Indian School to Martin Vigil, 21 May 1962, George Boyce Papers.

66. Ibid.

67. "Confidential Report of the Executive Director to Edwin L. Mechem, Governor of New Mexico," New Mexico Commission on Indian Affairs, June 1962, pp. 8–10, Charles Minton Papers.

The commission at that time consisted of Tom Wiley, chairman; Paul Jones of the Navajo tribe; Martin Vigil of Tesuque Pueblo; Fred Pellman, a Mescalero Apache; Mrs. Walter K. Marmon of Laguna Pueblo; Dr. W. W. Hill; Garfield C. Packard; Paul Brink; and Ed Junker, with Gov. Edwin Mechem as an ex officio member and Charles Minton as executive director.

68. Minton, "Supplement on the Institute of American Indian Art," 10.

69. Ross, "Opposition Made to Closing of Indian School," 1, 3. Minton refuted Boyce's criticisms of the report in the July issue of Indian News. "If Dr. Boyce had read the report carefully," snapped Minton, "he would know that it is based on documentary material, as the report stated." Minton was most disturbed about Boyce's denial that there were large numbers of Indian children without any school to attend: "In the interview with the reporter from the Santa Fe New Mexican, Boyce said that 'they don't state where the 3,000 to 5,000 [Indian children] are, how old they are, and why

they are not in school.' This was expected to dispose of that criticism. As everyone acquainted with Indian education knows, the figure was very conservative, but if Dr. Boyce really wants an authoritative answer to his question, he will find it in *Statistics Concerning Indian Children (1961)*, a fiscal report published by the Bureau of Indian Affairs that Boyce works for." According to this document, Minton continued, 9,691 Indian children were not in school, including 5,779 Navajos, "about whom Dr. Boyce would be expected to know better than anyone else because of his many years' work in Navajo education" (Minton, "The Institute of American Indian Art," 15–16).

70. Joe Trujillo to Clinton P. Anderson, 15 June 1962, George Boyce Papers. See also Joe M. Montoya to Philleo Nash, 26 June 1962; John O. Crow to Joseph M. Montoya, 9 July 1962; Dennis Chavez to Philleo Nash, 26 June 1962; and John O. Crow to Dennis Chavez, 9 July 1962, George Boyce Papers.

Geronima Montoya to John F. Kennedy, 18 June 1962, George Boyce Papers. Montoya remembers a period of harassment of SFIS faculty once the institute take-over was assured. She was called into the office and accused of having not attended to certain responsibilities related to her job, when, in fact, she had completed all the requirements. She was asked to retire. She was told she couldn't teach at the institute because she didn't have a degree. It was clear to her that the harassment was directed at forcing her out (interview by author with Geronima Montoya and Romancita Sandoval, 14 January 1987).

71. George Boyce's personal notes, 7 June 1976, George Boyce Papers.

72. Press Release from the All-Pueblo Council, p. 2, n. d., Martin Vigil to Carl Hayden, 5 July 1962, Attachment, George Boyce Papers.

73. John A. Carver Jr. to Carl Hayden, 31 July 1962, George Boyce Papers. See also "Interior Official Defends Art Plans," p. 5, cols. 3–4; and Carver to Joseph M. Montoya, 31 July 1962, George Boyce Papers.

74. "Pueblos Protest Replacement of Santa Fe Indian School," p. 3, cols. 1–4. It should be noted that the *Navajo Times* coverage of the institute was reported in Santa Fe. See "Institute, Nash Get New Blast." "Navajo Boy Hopes to Enter Art School," p. 8, col. 1.

75. "Enthusiastic about New Art School," p. 8, cols. 2–5. Boyce quoted directly from selected student application letters in his own correspondence with congressmen and other potential supporters of the school and utilized these letters frequently in his press releases. For an earlier example of this type of "news" article, see "Indians See Opportunity in Institute," p. 2, col. 3. Here Charlie Long is also quoted, together with Donna Mae Whitewing, a Winnebago-Sioux, and Douglas Crowder, a Choctaw from Oklahoma. Whitewing poignantly writes, "I know we have a place in society. Some one of us must find it. Through your school and with the advancement of my talents I believe I can find my place in the world, and in so doing encourage others to do the same." Crowder tends to the practical: "So far, art to me has been a hobby, but now I find it may be a way of making a living just as auto mechanics is to the fellows in my class."

76. "Santa Fe School of Indian Arts Presents New Concept in Teaching." Subsequent quotations from the *Navajo Times* reporter are from this article unless otherwise noted.

77. Paul Jones to Philleo Nash, 20 July 1962, George Boyce Papers.

78. Philleo Nash to Paul Jones, 2 August 1962, George Boyce Papers.

79. Finney, "New Indian Art Institute Faces an Investigation," D-7; "Complaints Studied against SF School." Crow, like John Carver, handled many complaints about the school. His defense of the institute was perceived as particularly hypocritical by Martin Vigil. "It is too bad that other Indians in the Bureau are blind to the real needs in Indian education," wrote Vigil to Crow, after the latter had responded to Geronima Montoya's letter to President Kennedy. "Indians will remain second-class citizens so

long as they are at the level of the fifth grade. I think you will agree that you wouldn't have your present job if you had not gone beyond the fifth grade. So why not work to advance the level of Indian education by providing seats in school and educational opportunities such as you have enjoyed" (Martin Vigil to John O. Crow, 10 July 1962, George Boyce Papers). See also John O. Crow to Geronima Montoya, 3 July 1962, and John O. Crow to Martin Vigil, 2 August 1962 [Crow's five-page response to Vigil], George Boyce Papers.

80. Collins, "Boyce Shoots Back." Boyce had also made available to the newspaper positive comments from student application letters, which were published on the same day (see note 75 above). Subsequent references to Boyce's response to the critics are taken from Collins's article unless otherwise noted.

81. "Chairman Opposes Institute." This press release from the All-Pueblo Council was reprinted in the *Navajo Times*, 22 August 1962.

82. "Don Quixote Rides Again," p 4, cols. 1–2.

83. Collier, "Why Presume Idiocy?" p. 4, cols. 1–2.

84. Rush, "Thoughts on Indian Art," p. 4, cols. 1–2.

85. "Dorothy Dunn Favors Arts for Indian Institute Here," p. 11, cols. 1–3.

86. Ibid.

87. "Opposition to Art Institute Termed Tragic by Taoseno," p. 6, cols. 6–8; Hesch, "LaFarge Wonders about Opposition to Indian Institute."

88. Nash to Anderson, 10 August 1962, p. 8. See also "Institute Objections Answered," For response to the report from the opposing camp, see Minton, "Supplement Number Two, Institute of American Indian Art." It is not clear if this report is the same one discussed on Joe Herrera's radio show of 25 November 1962. Boyce was greatly agitated by reports that Herrera, broadcasting in the Keresan language, read from a statement by Nash that intimated that the commissioner was not responsible for the institute, as the decision to establish the school had been made before he took office, and that he felt the Pueblo people should have been consulted before that decision was made. Furthermore, Nash was said to have implied that if the Pueblos continued to oppose the school, he might reconsider the use of the Santa Fe facility (see George Boyce to Area Director, Gallup Area Office, Memorandum, 27 November 1962, George Boyce Papers).

89. "Super of Indian Art Institute Open to Advice on School," p. 10, cols. 5–6.

90. "Schedule of Group Meetings, Institute of American Indian Arts," 20–31 August 1962, George Boyce Papers.

91. "Newsletter No. 2 to Students," Institute of American Indian Arts, 15 August 1962, George Boyce Papers. Subsequent quotations in this chapter are from the newsletter unless otherwise noted.

CHAPTER 4

1. George Boyce to Area Director, Gallup Area Office, Memorandum, 1 October 1962, George Boyce Papers; *Institute of American Indian Arts: A Basic Statement of Purpose*.

2. School Superintendent to Students and Staff, Memorandum, "Responsibility Code for Students," 26 October 1962, George Boyce Papers.

Considering that sixty-nine different tribal groups were represented on the campus, "socially acceptable customs" could not have referred to each student's own cultural norms, thus it must be assumed that the "socially acceptable customs" the students were to model were those of the dominant non-Indian society. This is likewise true of the "discreet adults" to be emulated.

3. Ibid.

4. *Institute of American Indian Arts: A Basic Statement of Purpose;* interview by author with Sherman Chaddleson, 2 June 1989.

5. George Boyce to Area Director, Gallup Area Office, Memorandum, 8 November 1962, George Boyce Papers.

6. The Student Body to Dr. Boyce, 8 November 1962, George Boyce Papers.

7. Student Petition, 8 November 1962, George Boyce Papers.

8. Ibid., attachment.

9. George Boyce to Area Director, Gallup Area Office, Memorandum, 26 November 1962, George Boyce Papers.

10. George Boyce to Elmer Anderson, 15 November 1962, George Boyce Papers.

11. George Boyce to Mr. and Mrs. Solomon Whitewing, 15 November 1962, George Boyce Papers.

12. George Boyce to Charles J. Rives, 12 October 1962, George Boyce Papers; George Boyce to Mr. and Mrs. Douglas Skye, 12 October 1962; George Boyce to Catherine Johnson, 14 November 1962, George Boyce Papers.

13. See School Superintendent to Miss Merry, Miss Victor, Mr. New, Memorandum, 21 November 1962; George Boyce to Anne Spivey, 11 December 1962, George Boyce Papers.

14. School Superintendent, Institute of American Indian Arts to Public Health Service, Division of Indian Health, Department of Health, Education, and Welfare, Memorandum, 12 December 1962, George Boyce Papers.

15. School Superintendent to Area Director, Gallup Area Office, Memorandum, 12 October 1962, George Boyce Papers. One former student relates that he used to call the school the "Heartbreak Hotel," as so many of his colleagues were orphans or came from other difficult home situations (interview by author with Parker Boyiddle, 3 June 1989).

16. George Boyce, "A Few Thumbnail Sketches on the Character and Problems of the Institute of American Indian Arts Student Body," 12 October 1962, p. 2, George Boyce Papers.

17. At least one showing of student work had been mounted locally prior to the Department of Interior exhibit, but it was specifically limited to one purposeful theme. In October 1963 an open house was held at the institute at which the artwork made for the Miccosukee Project was displayed. The project was a summer program wherein selected students worked for six weeks designing and completing paintings, textiles, ceramics, and sculpture for Miccosukee tribal buildings in Florida. Students viewed films and slides, reviewed published materials, and listened to two Miccosukee guest speakers, Calvin and Buffalo Tiger, in their research toward a "Seminole look" for the art forms submitted. Lloyd New also arranged in the design studio a display of shells, postcards, corals, fabrics, dolls, palmetto fronds, palm fiber, moss, and costume designs collected on a trip to Florida for student use. The resulting ceramic lighting fixtures, handprinted drapes, inlaid door pulls, decorative screens, sculptures, and more than one hundred paintings were shipped to Florida for permanent installation following the open house. "The Miccosukee Project," concluded New, "gave the student an opportunity to learn about production demands, man-hour requirements, in general, what it means to hold a job; promptness and serious application, how to meet designated design requirements without sacrificing individuality." See School Superintendent to Area Director, Attention: Area Education, Memorandum, 23 September 1964; Arts Department, Institute of American Indian Arts to Dr. George Boyce, Superintendent, Memorandum, 19 September 1963, George Boyce Papers; and "Tamiami Trail Project for Bureau of Indian Affairs Miccosukee Agency Site 128 Structure," 13 October 1962–1 November 1963, The Gallery on the Campus, Institute of American Indian Arts, Institute of American Indian Arts Archives. A similar program, the Crown Point Project,

was conducted the following summer, with some forty students working on paintings, mosaics, sculpture, ceramics, weaving, textiles, and lighting for the new administration building at the Navajo Subagency at Crown Point, New Mexico. See "The Crown Point Project," The Gallery of the Institute of American Indian Arts, 18 January–9 February 1965, Institute of American Indian Arts Archives.

Udall was, in fact, a champion of government sponsorship of the arts in general and that same spring penned an article for the *Saturday Review* suggesting "guidelines for moving toward a new Augustan Age" in American culture. "The United States is a powerful nation," the Interior secretary declared. "If she is to become a noble nation in the sense that Greece and Rome were, for a season, noble art and philosophy must flourish, so that the outward ripple of our cultural influence will be welcomed on distant shores and will leave a deposit there" (Udall, "The Arts as a National Resource," 14–17).

18. Marlow, "Students Impress Washington," 1.

19. *First Annual Invitational Exhibition of American Indian Paintings*, 1.

20. All the student works mentioned here and in the following pages are currently housed in the Honors Collection of the Institute of American Indian Arts Museum in Santa Fe, New Mexico.

21. *First Annual Invitational Exhibition of American Indian Paintings*, 2.

22. Foreign visitors frequented other bureau schools, as well. See "African Educators Visit Albuquerque Indian School," p. 5, col. 1.

"An Evening of American Indian Art," In honor of His Excellency The President of the Republic of Upper Volta and Mrs. Yameogo, Monday, 29 March 1965, The White House, Institute of American Indian Arts Archives. The dances, performed as "entertainment at dinner," were a Swan Dance, Hopi Buffalo Dance, Tail Feather Dance, Hoop Dance, and the Apache Mountain Spirit Dance. The gifts presented President Yameogo by President Johnson included a Cochiti drum, described as an "Authentic Indian Artefact," and an "Authentic Indian Necklace of silver and turquoises by Navaho Indians of New Mexico." See "State Dinner in Honor of His Excellency, The President of the Republic of Upper Volta and Mrs. Maurice Yameogo," Press Release, Office of the Press Secretary to Mrs. Johnson, White House, 29 March 1965, Institute of American Indian Arts Archives.

23. "SF Indians Tremendous Hit at White House," p. 8, cols. 4–6. See also Wieck, "35 Indian Dancers Charm Guests at White House," D-1.

24. Charles Minton, "Report of the Executive Director of the Commission on Indian Affairs," August 1959, pp. 1–2, Box 1, Charles Minton Papers.

The State Department Indian projects of the early 1960s were consistent with the Kennedy administration's shift from reactionary anti-Communist policies to emphasis on Third World development in the interest of promoting the United States as a champion of progressive change and democracy. See Lasch, "The Cultural Cold War," 81, and Kozloff, "American Painting during the Cold War," 49.

25. Charles Minton, "Report of the Executive Director of the Commission on Indian Affairs," April 1960, p. 1, Box 2, Charles Minton Papers; "Visitors from Africa," 7.

26. "Voice of America Broadcasts Navajo Story to the World," p. 4, cols. 1–4; "Navajo Tribe Life and Customs Featured in Magazine for Russia," p. 8, cols. 1–3; "Russian News Agency Chief Visits Navajo," p. 5, cols. 1–2; "Navajo and Nigerian . . . Experience Counsels Youth," p. 2, cols. 1–2.

27. "LBJ Orders GIs to 'Bama.'"

28. For further discussion of Meinholtz's play, *Moqwina*, see "Northwest Pacific Indian Culture Basis for Experimental Drama Here," Pasatiempo sec., p. 7, cols. 1–4; and *American Indian Performing Arts Exhibition*, 30–31.

29. McClendon, "Santa Fe Indian Art Receives Jubilant Reception at Capital," . See also "Indian Arts Institute Students Frequent D.C.," A-1, cols. 1–7.

30. *American Indian Performing Arts Exhibition,* 10.

31. Ibid., 33; interview by author with James McGrath, 20 June 1989.

32. *American Indian Performing Arts Exhibition,* 28.

33. Lloyd New, "Using Cultural Difference As a Basis for Creative Expression," 10–11. In the school's basic statement of purpose, New had, however, reiterated his commitment to the diversity of Indian expression, paraphrasing his own evaluation of the Southwestern Indian Art Project: "No single approach to the individualistic requirements of the student body is possible. Those students who are a part of a strong living tribal culture will be helped to express themselves in terms of the customs and manners of their group." As before, he qualified his acceptance of this diversity by adding that "such expressions will be recognized as a group-type expression and may be expected to be less personally creative" (*Institute of American Indian Arts: A Basic Statement of Purpose*).

34. *American Indian Artists Exhibition,* 5–31 May 1964, Philbrook Art Center, Call for Entries, Institute of American Indian Arts Archives.

35. *Young American Indian Artists,* 1.

It should be noted that the Riverside Museum had a history of strong support for abstract art. The American Abstract Artists held their third annual show there in 1938 and the "Bombshell Group" responded to Kootz in this setting in 1942.

In addition to being appointed to the Indian Arts and Crafts Board in 1961 (at the same time as he was being considered for the position of arts director at IAIA), New was given a Merit Award in 1962 by the Museum of Modern Art and was invited to show his textiles there.

36. Ongoing controversy concerning the Honors Collection is discussed later in this chapter.

37. Stahl, "Recent Exhibitions," 52–54.

38. *Young American Indian Artists,* 2.

39. "The Institute of American Indian Arts Design Syllabus," n.d. (Santa Fe, New Mexico: Institute of American Indian Arts), Institute of American Indian Arts Archives; interviews by author with Linda Lomahaftewa, 18 May 1989, and Kingsley (King) Kuka, 6 June 1989.

40. "Riverside Museum," *Pressman-Ryan Report.*

41. Ibid.

42. New, *Young Indian Painters from the Institute of American Indian Arts.*

43. "An Evening with the Young Indian Painters from the Institute of American Indian Arts," printed program, Museum of New Mexico, Santa Fe, 11 March 1966, pp. 2–3, Institute of American Indian Arts Archives.

44. Ibid., 1.

45. "The Rain Cloud Callers," illustrated paper prepared as an adjunct to the exhibition by the Museum of New Mexico, Santa Fe, 5 June 24 July 1966, Institute of American Indian Arts Archives. See also "Rain Callers Exhibit Opens," Pasatiempo sec., p. 8, cols. 1–2.

46. "The Institute of American Indian Arts," U.S. Department of the Interior, Bureau of Indian Affairs, n.d., Institute of American Indian Arts Archives.

47. "Mrs. Johnson Praises Local Indian School," D-1–2. See also "Friend of Santa Fe," 12.

48. "Senegal President, IAIA Arts Director Talk Shop," A-1, cols. 6–7.

49. An announcement of the show was made in the Indian Arts and Crafts Board's *Smoke Signals.* (See "Institute of American Indian Arts Sends Exhibition to International Events.")

50. Department of State to Berlin, Edinburgh, and London, Airgram Regarding Educational and Cultural Exchange: Americans Abroad, American Specialists: Indian Sand Painters, 11 July 1966, Institute of American Indian Arts Archives; for travel arrangements see "Transportation Information," Department of State, 24 June 1966, Authorization No. 620695; and Special Order TA-4559," Louis Leibel, Colonel, U.S. Air Force, Headquarters U.S. Air Forces in Europe, 19 October 1966, Institute of American Indian Arts Archives.

51. Virginia E. Orem to James McGrath, 21 July 1966, Institute of American Indian Arts Archives.

52. James McGrath, "News Release Notes," August 1966, Institute of American Indian Arts Archives.

53. James McGrath to Mrs. E. H. Massey and Mrs. Stewart Udall, 23 August 1966, Institute of American Indian Arts Archives.

54. *Glasgow Herald,* 31 August 1966, "News Release Notes," Institute of American Indian Arts Archives.

55. *Evening News and Dispatch,* 1966 Edinburgh Festival, Edinburgh, Scotland, 7 September 1966, news clipping excerpts, Institute of American Indian Arts Archives.

56. *Der Tagesspiegel,* 1966 Berlin Festival, Berlin, West Germany, 9 October 1966, news clipping excerpts, Institute of American Indian Arts Archives; *Indianische Kunst und Kunsthandwerk: Tradition und Gegenwart,* Catalog, Amerika House, Berlin, 10 September 10 October 1966, Institute of American Indian Arts Archives; American Embassy Ankara to U.S. Mission Berlin, Telegram, 13 October 1966, Institute of American Indian Arts Archives.

57. Exhibicion de Obras de Arte y Artesania de los Indios Norteamericanos y de los Esquimales (Buenos Aires, Santiago, and Mexico City: U.S. Department of State and Department of the Interior, 1968), p. 1. It is interesting to note that McGrath kept the review separate from his own introductory essay in the German catalog, reserving the last page for a lengthy direct quote.

58. "European Festivals Exhibition," at the Institute of American Indian Arts, 8 January 1967–3 February 1967, mimeographed sheet, Institute of American Indian Arts Archives. This commentary is repeated in the Alaskan catalog, *Indian and Eskimo Arts and Crafts Exhibition* (Anchorage: Bureau of Indian Affairs, 1967), Institute of American Indian Arts Archives.

59. "European Festivals Exhibition." A local review of the show also emphasized this point. "The discovery that young American artists, who happen to be Indians, are in the beginning stages of creating a contemporary art form which is based on their unique heritage was very exciting to Europeans," wrote Robert Ewing, curator of the Fine Arts Collection of the Museum of New Mexico, concluding that the show "provided a progress report on an art form which has great promise and which shows every sign of developing into an extremely important part of the whole of American Art" (Ewing, "The European Festivals Exhibition of Arts of Indian America," 1, 6).

60. Coates, "Our Far-Flung Correspondents," 102.

61. Ibid., 104. It should be noted that Coates was one of the first to popularize the term "abstract expressionism" in 1946.

62. Ibid., 106–7, 104. In IAIA publications Ted Palmenteer's name is variously spelled "Palmenteer," "Palmanteer," and "Palmateer."

63. Richman, "Rediscovery of the Redman," 62. The IAIA feature was part of a curious section of the article devoted to the counterculture interest in things Indian. The students' "discovery" of their cultural heritage was counterposed to "white Indians'" popular appropriation of Native spirituality, governing styles, environmental knowledge, and art forms at "Happy Hippie Hunting Ground" communes where non-Indian youth formed "tribes" and likened their "be-ins" to powwows and their drug use to

the ritual consumption of peyote. The author seemed surprised that Indian students found hippie attire "incomprehensible" and that on the IAIA campus the sounds of "tom-toms" were mingled with the strains of Diana Ross and the Supremes.

64. Coates, "Our Far-Flung Correspondents," 110; "Apartment Living Course at School," A-11, col. 4.

65. Powers, "Indian Arts and Crafts," 24; "Policy Statement Regarding Production, Acquisition, and Sales of Student Art Product," n.d., Institute of American Indian Arts Archives; "Student Sales IAIA Plan of Operation," n.d., Institute of American Indian Arts Archives.

66. "Policy Statement Regarding Production, Acquisition, and Sales of Student Art Products," n.d., Institute of American Indian Arts Archives; interview by author with James McGrath, 20 June 1989.

67. Interview by author with Rowena Dickerson, 6 June 1989.

68. Administrative Manager to Arts Department, Guidance Department, Academic Department Directors, Memorandum, "Procedure for Students Acquiring Own Art Work," 26 May 1967, Institute of American Indian Arts Archives.

69. "Student Sales IAIA Plan of Operation," 12 December 1964, Institute of American Indian Arts Archives.

70. "Policy Statement Regarding Production, Acquisition, and Sales of Student Art Products," p. 1.

71. Ruth Curtis through Mr. McGrath to Mr. New, "Hookstone," Memorandum, 20 August 1968, Institute of American Indian Arts Archives.

72. Taubman, "Two Cultures Meet in Santa Fe," 32. See also Taubman, "Indians in Santa Fe 1," and "Indians in Santa Fe 2."

73. New, "Cultural Difference as the Basis for Creative Education."

74. Senate Committee on Labor and Public Welfare, *Policy, Organization, Administration, and New Legislation Concerning the American Indians,* pt. 1, "Statement of Lloyd H. New," 91st Cong., 1st sess., 1969, p. 226. See also pp. 229, 233, 234.

75. Ibid., p. 226.

76. Ibid., pp. 230, 231.

77. Interview by author with Oleta Boyce, 2 March 1987.

CONCLUSIONS

1. LaRiviere, "New Art by the Oldest Americans," 23.

2. See Clifford, "Histories of the Tribal and the Modern," 190. Clifford's characterization seems reminiscent of Roland Barthes's essay, "The Great Family of Man," in his *Mythologies,* 100–102. The latter reviews the Museum of Modern Art's 1955 photo exhibition, *The Family of Man.* For another perspective of this ideological tack, see Price, "The Universality Principle," in her *Primitive Art in Civilized Places,* 23–36. For further discussion of the process of canon formation, see Schor, "Patrilineage," 58–62.

3. The reference here is to Picasso's characterization of African art as confirmation rather than revelation: "The African sculptures that hang around . . . my studios are more witnesses than models"; see Rubin's introduction to *"Primitivism" in Twentieth-Century Art,* 1:17.

4. Fisher, "Rockefeller Philanthropy and the Rise of Social Anthropology," 7.

5. Price frames this part of the primitivist equation as follows: "It goes something like this: While Primitive societies, like Ours, can nurture the production of certifiable artistic Masterpieces, and while the sheer aesthetic power of Primitive Masterpieces penetrates linguistic and cultural boundaries to reach sensitive art lovers in the West, the members of these societies (including the most artistically endowed among them)

are themselves handicapped (whether by education or genetic heritage is not specified) to participate in supracultural aesthetic experiences." Native artists are, thus, consigned to play a "European game with high cultural stakes, a game in which primitives are pawns, unable to grasp the rules and unable to win" (*Primitive Art in Civilized Places*, 35). See also Torgovnick, *Gone Primitive*, 96.

6. For further discussion of this contradiction, see Clifford, "Histories of the Tribal and the Modern," 201, and McEvilley, "Doctor Lawyer Indian Chief," 92–93.

7. Barthes, "The Great Family of Man," 151.

8. Clifford has noted that the Western discourses of art and anthropology both presuppose "an underlying set of attitudes toward the 'tribal'" which "assume a primitive world in need of preservation, redemption, and representation" ("Histories of the Tribal and the Modern," 200).

9. Deloria "The Era of Indian Self-Determination," 193.

10. Altbach and Kelly, *Education and Colonialism*, 3–4.

11. Cajete, *Look to the Mountain*, 219.

Selected Bibliography

ARCHIVES

Boyce, George. Papers. Collection of Oleta Boyce. Santa Fe, New Mexico.

Institute of American Indian Arts Archives. Santa Fe, New Mexico.

Minton, Charles. Papers. Collection of Alfonso Ortiz. Santa Fe, New Mexico.

Rockefeller Foundation Archives. Rockefeller Archive Center. Pocantico Hills, North Tarrytown, New York.

SECONDARY SOURCES

Ablon, Joan. "American Indian Relocation: Problems of Dependency and Management in the City." *Phylon* 26 (1965): 362–71.

"African Educators Visit Albuquerque Indian School." *Navajo Times*, 5 January 1962.

"All-American Art." *Art Digest* (1 January 1941): 17.

"All-Pueblo Council Voices Opposition to Art Institute." *Navajo Times*, 22 August 1962.

Altbach, Philip, and Gail P. Kelly, eds. *Education and Colonialism.* New York and London: Longman, 1978.

American Indian Performing Arts Exhibition. Washington, D.C.: U.S. Department of the Interior, 1964.

"The American Stranger." *Kaleidoscope.* NBC broadcast, 16 November 1958.

"Apartment Living Course at School." *Santa Fe New Mexican*, 19 December 1965.

Archuleta, Margaret, and Rennard Strickland, eds. *Shared Visions: Native American Painters and Sculptors in the Twentieth Century*. Exhibition catalog. 2d ed. Phoenix: Heard Museum, 1991.

Armstrong, O. K. "Set the American Indians Free!" *Reader's Digest* 47 (1945): 47–52.

"Artists with Never a Thought for Fame." *Literary Digest* 116, no. 11 (1933): 15.

Austin, Mary. "American Indian Murals." *American Magazine of Art* 26, no. 8 (1933): 380–84.

Barr, Alfred H., Jr. Introduction to *The New American Painting*, 15–19. New York: Museum of Modern Art, 1959.

———. "Is Modern Art Communistic?" *New York Times Magazine*, 14 December 1952, 22.

———. "Letters to the Editor." *College Art Journal* 15, no. 3 (1956): 184–85.

Barthes, Roland. "The Great Family of Man." In *Mythologies*, trans. Annette Lavers. New York: Hill and Wang, 1972.

Beatty, Willard W., ed. *Education for Cultural Change: Selected Articles from Indian Education, 1944–1951*. N.p.: U.S. Department of the Interior, Bureau of Indian Affairs, 1953.

Berlo, Janet Catherine. "Introduction: The Formative Years of Native American Art History." In *The Early Years of Native American Art History: The Politics of Scholarship and Collecting*, ed. Janet Catherine Berlo, 1–21. Seattle and London: University of Washington Press, 1992.

Bernstein, Alison R. *American Indians and World War II: Toward a New Era in Indian Affairs*. Norman: University of Oklahoma Press, 1991.

Braden, Thomas. "I'm Glad the CIA Is 'Immoral.'" *Saturday Evening Post* 20 (May 1967): 10.

Braun, Barbara. "Art from the Land of the Savages, or Surrealists in the New World." *Boston Review* 13, nos. 5–6 (1988): 18–19.

———. *Pre-Columbian Art and the Post-Columbian World: Ancient American Sources of Modern Art*. New York: Harry N. Abrams, 1993.

Brody, J. J. *Indian Painters and White Patrons*. Albuquerque: University of New Mexico Press, 1971.

Brophy, William A., and Sophie Aberle. *The Indian: America's Unfinished Business*. Report of the Commission on the Rights, Liberties, and Responsibilities of the American Indian. Norman: University of Oklahoma Press, 1966.

"Buildings OK'd for Indian Art Center." *Santa Fe New Mexican*, 8 October 1961.

Burt, Larry W. *Tribalism in Crisis: Federal Indian Policy, 1953–1961*. Albuquerque: University of New Mexico Press, 1982.

Cajete, Gregory. *Look to the Mountain: An Ecology of Indigenous Education*. Durango, Colo.: Kivaki Press, 1994.

"Chairman Opposes Institute." *Santa Fe New Mexican*, 6 August 1962.

Charlot, Jean. "All-American." *Nation* 152, no. 6 (1941): 165–66.

Clifford, James. "Histories of the Tribal and the Modern." In *The Predicament of Culture*. Cambridge: Harvard University Press, 1988.

Coates, Robert M. "Our Far-Flung Correspondents: Indian Affairs, New Style." New Yorker, 43, no. 17 (1967): 102–12.

Cobbs, Elizabeth A. *The Rich Neighbor Policy: Rockefeller and Kaiser in Brazil.* New Haven: Yale University Press, 1992.

Cockcroft, Eva. "Abstract Expressionism, Weapon of the Cold War." *Artforum* 12 (1974): 39–41.

———. "Mexico, MoMA, and Cultural Imperialism." *Art Workers News* 10, no. 7 (1981): 12–15.

Collier, John. "Back to Dishonor?" *Christian Century* 71 (May 1954): 578–80.

———. "Why Presume Idiocy?" *Santa Fe New Mexican,* 10 August 1962.

Collier, Peter, and David Horowitz. *The Rockefellers: An American Dynasty.* New York: Holt, Rinehart and Winston, 1976.

Collins, Jim. "Boyce Shoots Back." *Santa Fe New Mexican,* 5 August 1962.

"Complaints Studied against SF School." *Santa Fe New Mexican,* 26 July 1962.

Congressional Record. Washington, D.C., 20 September 1945, Appendix.

———. Washington, D.C., 16 August 1949.

———. Washington, D.C., 29 July 1953.

———. Washington, D.C., 22 April 1954.

———. Washington, D.C., 23 May 1955.

Cowling, Elizabeth. "The Eskimos, the American Indians, and the Surrealists." *Art History* 1, no. 4 (1978): 484–500.

Deloria, Philip S. "The Era of Indian Self-Determination: An Overview." In *Indian Self-Rule: First-Hand Accounts of Indian White Relations from Roosevelt to Reagan,* ed. Kenneth Philp, 191–207. Salt Lake City, Utah: Howe Brothers, 1986.

D'Ewart, Wesley. "Letters." *Harper's Magazine* 212, no. 1272 (1956): 4–10.

d'Harnoncourt, Rene. "Challenge and Promise: Modern Art and Modern Society." *Magazine of Art* 41, no. 7 (1948): 251–52.

———. Foreword to *The New American Painting,* 5. New York: Museum of Modern Art, 1959.

Dockstader, Frederick J. "Directions in Indian Art." In *Proceedings of a Conference Held at the University of Arizona, 20–21 March 1959.* Tucson: University of Arizona Press, 1959.

"Don Quixote Rides Again." *Santa Fe New Mexican,* 7 August 1962.

"Dorothy Dunn Favors Arts for Indian Institute Here." *Santa Fe New Mexican,* 28 August 1962.

Douglas, Frederic H., and Rene d'Harnoncourt. *Indian Art of the United States.* New York: Museum of Modern Art, 1941.

Dunn, Dorothy. *American Indian Painting of the Southwest and Plains Areas.* Albuquerque: University of New Mexico Press, 1968.

———. "The Art of Joe Herrera." *El Palacio* 50, no. 12 (1952): 367–73.

———. "The Development of Modern American Painting in the Southwest and Plains Areas." *El Palacio* 58, no. 11 (1951): 331–53.

———. "The Studio of Painting, Santa Fe Indian School." *El Palacio* 67, no. 1 (1960): 16–27.

"Enthusiastic about New Art School." *Navajo Times,* 11 July 1962.

Ewing, Robert A. "The European Festivals Exhibition of Arts of Indian America." *Quarterly of the Southwestern Association on Indian Affairs* 4, no. 2 (1967): 1–6.

Exhibicion de Obras de Arte y Artesania de los Indios Norteamericanos y de los Esquimales. Buenos Aires, Santiago, and Mexico City: U.S. Department of State and Department of the Interior, 1968.

Fey, Harold. "Indian Winter." *Christian Century* 72 (March 1955): 265–67.

———. "Navajo Race with Tragedy." *Christian Century* 72 (May 1955): 617–19.

Finney, Ruth. "New Indian Art Institute Faces an Investigation." *Albuquerque Tribune*, 26 July 1962.

First Annual Invitational Exhibition of American Indian Paintings. Washington, D.C.: U.S. Department of the Interior, 1964.

Fisher, Donald. "Rockefeller Philanthropy and the Rise of Social Anthropology." *Anthropology Today* 2, no. 1 (1986): 5–8.

Fixico, Donald L. *Termination and Relocation: Federal Indian Policy, 1945–1960.* Albuquerque: University of New Mexico Press, 1986.

"French Artist Paul Coze Arranges Show of Indian Watercolors." *Santa Fe New Mexican*, 27 October 1935.

"Friend of Santa Fe." *Santa Fe New Mexican*, 23 September 1966.

Garmhausen, Winona. *History of Indian Arts Education in Santa Fe: The Institute of American Indian Arts with Historical Background, 1890 to 1962.* Santa Fe: Sunstone Press, 1988.

Goldwater, Robert. *Primitivism in Modern Art.* 1938; New York: Vintage Books, 1967.

Gritton, Joy. "Cross-Cultural Education vs. Modernist Imperialism: The Institute of American Indian Arts." *Art Journal* 51, no. 3 (1992): 28–35.

———. "The Institute of American Indian Arts: A Convergence of Ideologies." In *Shared Visions: Native American Painters and Sculptors in the Twentieth Century*, ed. Margaret Archuleta and Rennard Strickland, 22–29. 2d ed. Phoenix: Heard Museum, 1991.

Guilbaut, Serge. *How New York Stole the Idea of Modern Art.* Trans. Arthur Goldhammer. Chicago: University of Chicago Press, 1983.

Harmer, Ruth Mulvey. "Uprooting the Indians." *Atlantic Monthly* 197, no. 3 (March 1956): 54–57.

Hasse, Larry J. "Termination and Assimilation: Federal Indian Policy, 1943 to 1961." Ph.D. diss., Washington State University, 1974.

Hellman, Geoffrey T. "Imperturbable Noble." *New Yorker* 36 (1960): 49–112.

Hemsing, William H. "Education for Democracy." In *Education for Cultural Change: Selected Articles from Indian Education, 1944–1951*, ed. Willard W. Beatty, 134–38. N.p.: U.S. Department of the Interior, Bureau of Indian Affairs, 1953.

Hesch, Bill. "LaFarge Wonders about Opposition to Indian Institute." *Albuquerque Journal*, 12 August 1962.

Hewett, Edgar Lee. "Native American Artists." *Art and Archaeology* 13, no. 3 (1922): 103–12.

Holm, Thomas. "The Discovery of Indian Art: Awareness or Choices." In *Sharing a Heritage: American Indian Arts*, ed. Charlotte Heth, 67–74. Contemporary American Indian Issues Series, no. 5. Los Angeles: Regents of the University of California, 1984.

Hyer, Sally. *One House, One Voice, One Heart: Native American Education at the Santa Fe Indian School.* Santa Fe: Museum of New Mexico Press, 1990.

"Ike Likes the Arts, So—U.S. May Export Culture." *U.S. News and World Report* (28 January 1955): 68.

Indian and Eskimo Arts and Crafts Exhibition. Anchorage, Alaska: Bureau of Indian Affairs, 1967.

"Indian Art Institute Chief Tackles Big Job." *Santa Fe New Mexican,* 13 September 1961.

Indian Art in the United States and Alaska: A Pictorial Record of the Indian Exhibition at the Golden Gate International Exposition. Prepared by the Indian Arts and Crafts Board of the U.S. Department of the Interior at the Federal Building on Treasure Island, San Francisco, 1939. Ann Arbor, Mich.: University Microfilms.

"Indian Artists Take Up Mural Painting." *Art Digest* 7, no. 7 (1933): 32.

"Indian Arts Institute Students Frequent D.C." *Santa Fe New Mexican,* 22 April 1965.

Indianische Kunst und Kunsthandwerk: Tradition und Gegenwart. Amerika House, Berlin, 10 September 10–October 1966. Institute of American Indian Arts Archives.

"Indian Tribal Arts Exhibition Starts on Long Tour of Nation." *Art Digest* 16 (1931): 6.

"Indians See Opportunity in Institute." *Santa Fe New Mexican,* 5 August 1962.

"Institute, Nash Get New Blast." *Santa Fe New Mexican,* 17 August 1962.

"Institute Objections Answered." *Santa Fe New Mexican,* 15 August 1962.

Institute of American Indian Arts: A Basic Statement of Purpose. Santa Fe: Institute of American Indian Arts, 1962.

"Institute of American Indian Arts Sends Exhibition to International Events." *Smoke Signals* 50–51 (fall–winter 1966): 36–37.

"Interior Official Defends Art Plans." *Santa Fe New Mexican,* 5 August 1962.

Jacobson, Oscar B. "Indian Artists from Oklahoma." *University of Oklahoma Museum of Art Bulletin* 7, no. 5 (1964).

"Jefe Named for SF Indian Arts School: Noted Educator Gets Local Post; Bureau to Air Plans." *Santa Fe New Mexican,* 27 July 1961.

Jewell, Edward Alden. "The American Indian Exhibition: A Tradition Lives On." *New York Times,* 6 December 1931, sec. 9, p. 18.

Jonaitis, Aldona. "Creations of Mystics and Philosophers: The White Man's Perceptions of Northwest Coast Indian Art from the 1930s to the Present." *American Indian Culture and Research Journal* 5, no. 1 (1981): 1–45.

Kelly, Lawrence. *The Assault on Assimilation: John Collier and the Origins of Indian Policy Reform.* Albuquerque: University of New Mexico Press, 1983.

Kozloff, Max. "American Painting during the Cold War." *Artforum* 11 (1973): 43–54.

"LaFarge Charges U.S. Breaks Indian Trust." *Christian Century* 71 (May 1954): 604–5.

LaRiviere, Anne L. "New Art by the Oldest Americans." *Westways* 65, no. 5 (1973).

Larson, Gary. *The Reluctant Patron: The United States Government and the Arts, 1943–1965.* Philadelphia: University of Pennsylvania Press, 1983.

Lasch, Christopher. "The Cultural Cold War: A Short History of the Congress for Cultural Freedom." In *The Agony of the American Left*, 63–113. New York: Random House, 1968.

"LBJ Orders GIs to 'Bama.'" *Santa Fe New Mexican*, 21 March 1965.

Levi-Strauss, Claude. "The Art of the North West Coast at the American Museum of Natural History." *Gazette des Beaux-Arts* 24 (1943): 175–82.

Little, Sidney, et al. *1961 Southwestern Indian Art Project, June 12 through July 22, 1961: Report to the Rockefeller Foundation.* Tucson, Arizona: University of Arizona Press, 1961.

Lurie, Nancy Oestreich. "The Indian Claims Commission Act." *Annals of the American Academy of Political and Social Science* 311 (May 1957): 56–70.

Lynes, Russell. *Good Old Modern: An Intimate Portrait of the Museum of Modern Art.* New York: Atheneum, 1973.

Madigan, LaVerne. *The American Indian Relocation Program.* New York: American Association of Indian Affairs, 1956.

Marlow, Sigrid. "Students Impress Washington." *Santa Fe New Mexican*, 27 May 1964.

Mathews, Jane De Hart. "Art and Politics in Cold War America." *American Historical Review* 81, no. 4 (1976): 762–87.

Mauer, Evan. "Dada and Surrealism." In *"Primitivism" in Twentieth-Century Art: Affinity of the Tribal and the Modern*, ed. William Rubin, 541–84. Vol 2. New York: Museum of Modern Art, 1984.

McClendon, Sarah. "Santa Fe Indian Art Receives Jubilant Reception at Capital." *Santa Fe New Mexican*, 22 April 1965.

McCray, Porter. "As the Critics Saw It." In *The New American Painting*, 7. New York: Museum of Modern Art, 1959.

McEvilley, Thomas. "Doctor Lawyer Indian Chief." In *Art and Otherness: Crisis in Cultural Identity.* Kingston, N.Y.: McPherson, 1992.

Meriam, Lewis, et al. *The Problem of Indian Administration.* Baltimore: Johns Hopkins Press, 1971.

Minton, Charles. "The Institute of American Indian Arts." *Indian News* (July 1962): 15–17.

———. "Supplement Number Two, Institute of American Indian Art." *Indian News* (September 1962).

———. "Supplement on the Institute of American Indian Art." *Indian News* (June 1962).

"Mrs. Johnson Praises Local Indian School." *Santa Fe New Mexican*, 23 September 1966.

Museum of Modern Art. *Rene d'Harnoncourt 1901–1968: A Tribute.* New York: N.p., 1968.

Nash, Gerald D. *The American West in the Twentieth Century: A Short History of an Urban Oasis.* Albuquerque: University of New Mexico Press, 1973.

"Navajo and Nigerian . . . Experience Counsels Youth." *Navajo Times*, 23 May 1962.

"Navajo Boy Hopes to Enter Art School." *Navajo Times*, 11 July 1962.

"Navajo Tribe—Life and Customs Featured in Magazine for Russia." *Navajo Times,* 9 May 1962.

New, Lloyd. "Cultural Difference as the Basis for Creative Education." In *Native American Arts, 1,* issued by U.S. Department of the Interior, Indian Arts and Crafts Board. Washington, D.C.: U.S. Government Printing Office, 1968, pp. 4–12.

———. "Using Cultural Difference as a Basis for Creative Expression." *Journal of American Indian Education* 4, no. 3 (May 1965): 8–12.

———. *Young Indian Painters from the Institute of American Indian Arts.* Santa Fe: Museum of New Mexico, 1966.

Newman, Barnett. *The Ideographic Picture.* New York: Betty Parsons Gallery, 1947.

———. *Northwest Coast Indian Painting.* New York: Betty Parsons Gallery, 1946.

"New Mexico Indians Make History." *Santa Fe New Mexican,* 11 October 1934.

"Northwest Pacific Indian Culture Basis for Experimental Drama Here." *Santa Fe New Mexican,* 21 March 1965.

Officer, James E. "The American Indian and Federal Policy." In *The American Indian in Urban Society,* ed. Jack O. Wadell and O. Michael Watson, 45–54. Boston: Little, Brown, 1971.

———. "Termination as Federal Policy: An Overview." In *Indian Self-Rule: First-Hand Accounts of Indian White Relations from Roosevelt to Reagan,* ed. Kenneth Philp, 114–28. Salt Lake City, Utah: Howe Brothers, 1986.

"Opposition to Art Institute Termed Tragic by Taoseno." *Santa Fe New Mexican,* 12 August 1962.

Orfield, Gary. *A Study of the Termination Policy.* Denver: National Congress of American Indians, 1965.

Paalen, Wolfgang. *Dyn* 4–5 (1943): unnumbered prefatory page.

Pach, Walter. "The Art of the American Indian." *Dial* 68 (January 1920): 57–65.

———. "Notes on the Indian Water-Colours." *Dial* 68 (March 1920): 343–45.

———. "The Indian Tribal Arts: A Critic's View of the Significance of a Unique American Asset." *New York Times,* 22 November 1931, sec. 8, p. 13.

Patrick, David, et al. *Southwest Indian Art: A Report to the Rockefeller Foundation Covering the Activities of the First Exploratory Workshop in Art for Talented Younger Indians Held at the University of Arizona in the Summer of 1960.* Tucson, Arizona: University of Arizona, 1960.

Philp, Kenneth. *Indian Self-Rule: First-Hand Accounts of Indian-White Relations from Roosevelt to Reagan.* Salt Lake City: Howe Brothers, 1986.

———. *John Collier's Crusade for Indian Reform, 1920–1954.* Tucson: University of Arizona Press, 1977.

Pollock, Jackson. "My Painting." *Possibilities* 1, no. 1 (winter 1947–48): 78–83.

Powers, Marcella. "Indian Arts and Crafts." *New Mexico Magazine* 43, no. 8 (1965): 22–25.

Preston, Stuart. "To Help Our Art: Council Will Circulate Exhibitions Abroad." *New York Times,* 30 December 1956, sec. 2, p. 15.

Price, Sally. *Primitive Art in Civilized Places.* Chicago and London: University of Chicago Press, 1989. Reprint, 1991.

"Pueblos Protest Replacement of Santa Fe Indian School." *Navajo Times,* 11 July 1962.

"Rain Callers Exhibit Opens." *Santa Fe New Mexican*, 5 June 1966.

Richman, Robin. "Rediscovery of the Redman." *Life* 63, no. 22 (1967): 52–70.

"Riverside Museum." *Pressman-Ryan Report. 6th Hour News Show*. WNBC-TV, New York, 1966.

Roosevelt, Franklin. "Radio Speech Attendant upon the Dedication of the New Building of the Museum of Modern Art, New York City, 10 May 1939." *New York Times*, 11 May 1939, p. 29.

Rose, Barbara. *Readings in American Art Since 1900*. New York: Frederick A. Praeger, 1968.

Ross, Sally. "Opposition Made to Closing of Indian School, Opening of Art Institute in SF." *Santa Fe New Mexican*, 7 June 1962.

Rubin, William, ed. *"Primitivism" in Twentieth-Century Art: Affinity of the Tribal and the Modern*. 2 vols. New York: Museum of Modern Art, 1984.

Rush, Olive. "Indian Murals at Santa Fe, New Mexico." *Contemporary Arts* (November–December 1932): 8.

———. "Thoughts on Indian Art." *Santa Fe New Mexican*, 15 August 1962.

———. "The Young Indians Work in Old Forms:" *Theatre Arts* 17, no. 8 (1933): 635–38.

Rushing, W. Jackson. "Authenticity and Subjectivity in Post-War Painting: Concerning Herrera, Scholder, and Cannon." In *Shared Visions: Native American Painters and Sculptors in the Twentieth Century*, ed. Margaret Archuleta and Rennard Strickland, 12–21. 2d ed. Phoenix: Heard Museum, 1991.

———. "Marketing the Affinity of the Primitive and the Modern: Rene d'Harnoncourt and 'Indian Art of the United States.'" In *The Early Years of Native American Art History: The Politics of Scholarship and Collecting*, ed. Janet Catherine Berlo, 191–236. Seattle and London: University of Washington Press, 1992.

———. *Native American Art and the New York Avant-Garde*. Austin: University of Texas Press, 1995.

———. "Ritual and Myth: Native American Culture and Abstract Expressionism." In *The Spiritual in Art: Abstract Painting, 1890–1985*, 273–95. Los Angeles: Los Angeles County Museum of Art, 1986.

Rushing, W. Jackson, and Bruce Bernstein. *Modern by Tradition: American Indian Painting in the Studio Style*. Santa Fe: Museum of New Mexico Press, 1996.

"Russian News Agency Chief Visits Navajo." *Window Rock (Ariz.) Navajo Times*, 23 May 1962.

Sandler, Irving. *The Triumph of American Painting: A History of Abstract Expressionism*. New York: Harper and Row, 1970.

"Santa Fe School of Indian Arts Presents New Concept in Teaching." *Navajo Times*, 11 July 1962.

Schor, Mira. "Patrilineage." *Art Journal* 50, no. 2 (1991): 58–62.

Schrader, Robert. *The Indian Arts and Crafts Board: An Aspect of New Deal Indian Policy*. Albuquerque: University of New Mexico Press, 1983.

Self, Winke. "City Fair: Cutting through Indian Romanticism." *San Diego* 24, no. 9 (1972): 41–42.

"Senegal President, IAIA Arts Director Talk Shop." *Santa Fe New Mexican*, 30 October 1966.

"SF Indians Tremendous Hit at White House Reception." *Santa Fe New Mexican*, 30 March 1965.

Shared Visions: Native American Painters and Sculptors in the Twentieth Century. Proceedings of a Conference Held at the Heard Museum, 8–11 May 1991. Phoenix: Heard Museum, 1992.

Silberman, Arthur. *100 Years of Native American Painting.* Oklahoma City: Oklahoma Museum of Art, 1978.

———. "A Selection of Native American Art." *Tamaqua* 2, no. 2 (1991): 47–87.

Sloan, John, and Oliver LaFarge. *Introduction to American Indian Art.* New York: Exposition of Indian Arts, 1931.

Snodgrass, Jeanne. *American Indian Painters: A Biographical Directory.* Contributions from the Museum of the American Indian, Heye Foundation. Part 1. New York: Museum of the American Indian, 1968.

Snodgrass-King, Jeanne. "In the Name of Progress, Is History Being Repeated?" *American Indian Art* 10, no. 2 (1985): 27–35.

Stahl, Harvey. "Recent Exhibitions." *Arts Magazine* 40, no. 4 (1966): 52–54.

"A Statement on Artistic Freedom." *College Art Journal* 14 (winter 1955): 195.

Stocking, George W., Jr. "The Santa Fe Style in American Anthropology: Regional Interest, Academic Initiative, and Philanthropic Policy in the First Two Decades of the Laboratory of Anthropology, Inc." *Journal of the History of the Behavioral Sciences* 18 (1982): 3–19.

"Super of Indian Art Institute Open to Advice on School." *Santa Fe New Mexican*, 30 August 1962.

Szasz, Margaret Connell. *Education and the American Indian: The Road to Self-Determination Since 1928.* 2d ed. Albuquerque: University of New Mexico Press, 1977.

Taubman, Howard. "Indians in Santa Fe—1: Students in Federally Run School Analyze Their Burning Problems." *New York Times*, 16 May 1967, p. 42.

———. "Indians in Santa Fe—2: Youths Find Unexpected Freedom in Arts Workshop in U.S. School." *New York Times*, 18 May 1967, p. 55.

———. "Two Cultures Meet in Santa Fe." *Think* 33, no. 6, 1967: 27–32.

Thompson, Frank. "Are the Communists Right in Calling Us Cultural Barbarians?" *Music Journal* 13 (July–August 1955): 5.

Thompson, Hildegard, ed. *Education for Cross-Cultural Enrichment: Selected Articles from Indian Education, 1952–1964.* Haskell, Kans.: Haskell Institute Press for the Bureau of Indian Affairs, U.S. Department of the Interior, 1964.

Torgovnick, Marianna. *Gone Primitive: Savage Intellects, Modern Lives.* Chicago: University of Chicago Press, 1990.

Udall, Stewart L. "The Arts as a National Resource." *Saturday Review*, vol. 47, pt. 1 (March 1964): 14–17.

U.S. Congress. House. Committee on Education and Labor. *Hearings on Various Bills Relating to Awards of Medal for Distinguished Civilian Achievement, and Cultural Interchange and Development.* 84th Cong., 1955–56.

———. House. Committee on Education and Labor. *Report on the Relationship of the Federal Government to the Arts: Hearings on H.R. 3541.* 85th Cong., 1st sess., 1958.

———. House. Committee on Education and Labor. *Statement of Lloyd Goodrich, Chairman, the Committee on Government and Art, New York City: Hearings on H.R. 3541.* 85th Cong., 1st sess., 1958.

———. House. Committee on Interior and Insular Affairs. *Information on Removal of Restrictions on American Indians.* 88th Cong., 2nd sess., 1964. Committee Print 38.

———. House and Senate. Committees on Interior and Insular Affairs. *Termination of Federal Supervision Over Certain Tribes of Indians: Hearings on S. 2749 and H.R. 7322.* Part 1, "Statement of Glenn L. Emmons, Commissioner of the Bureau of Indian Affairs (accompanied by H. Rex Lee, Associate Indian Commissioner; and Lewis Sigler, Program Counsel, Bureau of Indian Affairs." 83d Cong., 2d sess., 1954.

———. House and Senate. Committees on Interior and Insular Affairs. *Termination of Federal Supervision Over Certain Tribes of Indians: Hearings on S. 2749 and H.R. 7322.* Part 5, "California Indians." 83d Cong., 2d sess., 1954.

———. Senate. Committee on Indian Affairs. *Aspects of Indian Policy. Harry S. Truman. Report for the Committee on Indian Affairs.* 79th Cong., 1st sess., 1945. Senate Report.

———. Senate. Committee on Labor and Public Welfare. Subcommittee on Indian Education. *Policy, Organization, Administration, and New Legislation Concerning the American Indians.* Part 1, "Statement of Lloyd H. New, Director, Institute of American Indian Arts, Santa Fe, N. Mex." 91st Cong., 1st sess., 1969.

Van de Mark, Dorothy. "The Raid on the Reservations." *Harper's Magazine* 212, no. 1270 (March 1956): 48–53.

"Visitors from Africa." *Navajo Times,* 9 August 1961.

"Voice of America Broadcasts Navajo Story to the World: Communist Propaganda Denied." *Window Rock (Ariz.) Navajo Times,* 7 March 1962.

Wade, Edwin. "The Ethnic Art Market and the Dilemma of Innovative Indian Artists." In *Magic Images: Contemporary Native American Art,* ed. Edwin L. Wade and Rennard Strickland, 9–17. Norman: Philbrook Art Center and the University of Oklahoma Press, 1981.

Warren, Alvin C. "Institute of American Indian Arts to Open at Santa Fe." In *Education for Cross-Cultural Enrichment: Selected Articles from Indian Education, 1952–1964,* ed. Hildegard Thompson. Haskell, Kans.: Haskell Institute Press for the Bureau of Indian Affairs, U.S. Department of the Interior, 1964.

Washburn, Wilcomb E. *The Assault on Indian Tribalism: The General Allotment Law (Dawes Act) of 1887.* Philadelphia: J. B. Lippincott, 1975.

Waugh, Lynne. "IAIA Nurtures Indian Art." *The Arts—'72: An Annual Report,* a special section in *Santa Fe New Mexican,* 23 July 1972.

Whitney, John Hay. Foreword to *Masters of Modern Art.* New York: Museum of Modern Art, 1954.

Wieck, Paul R. "35 Indian Dancers Charm Guests at White House." *Albuquerque Journal,* 31 March 1965.

Young American Indian Artists. Exhibition catalog. New York: Riverside Museum, 1965.

INDEX

Loloma, Otellie, 8, 49, 61, 83, 171n59
Long, Charlie Chee, 92, 173n75
Long, Frank, 10
Lovato, Delfin, 149

Mackey, Howard, 149
Malone, George, 70
Man of Time (Hyde), *136*
Man Spirit in the Wind (Palmenteer), 139, *142*
marketing, of Indian arts and crafts: d'Harnoncourt's efforts at, 4, 17–19, 24; Directions in Indian Art conference, discussed at, 14–15, 41–42; of IAIA student work, 145–147; for modern living uses, 15, 17–18, 24; at Southwestern Indian Art Project, 61; during 1920s and 1930s, 14–15, 22–23, 161n43
Martinez, Julian, 164n87
Martinez, Maria, 36
Martinez, Miguel, 164n87
Martinez, Richard, 164n87
McCray, Porter, 32–33, 34
McGrath, James, 84, *142*; and *American Indian Performing Arts Festival*, 116, 117–118; and *European Festivals*, 135, 136–137, 141, *142*, 143, 178n57; and "An Evening with the Young Indian Painters . . . ," 134; and Hookstone, 145, 146, 147; on modern art correlated to primitive, 122, 127, 141, 143
McKay, Iliff, 72
Mechem, Edwin, 87, 89
Meinholtz, Rolland, 116
Menominees, 67, 69, 77
Menta, Joe, *136*
Meriam Report, 14, 35–36
Merry, Oleta, 91, 99, 100
Miccosukee Project, 175n17
Michaels, Joseph, 127–129
Miller, Dorothy C., 34
Minotaure, 20
Minton, Charles, 35, 78, 87, 88–89, 172nn64, 69
Mitchell, Mary, 78, 84
modern adaptations, of Indian arts and crafts. *See* adaptation *vs.* tradition
modern art (*see also* adaptation *vs.* tradition): abstract art (*see* abstract art); correlated to primitive art, 19–22,

23–26, 122, 127–130, 152–153, 159nn28, 34, 179nn3, 5; in the cultural Cold War, 4, 27–28, 29–34; education, MoMA style, 4, 26, 27, 34–35, 127, 163n80; surrealists, 19–20, 26, 159n31
modern living skills, for Indians, 2, 73–74, 81–82, 104–106, 144–145
MoMA (Museum of Modern Art). *See* Museum of Modern Art (MoMA)
Monberg, Helene, 172n64
Montoya, Geronima, 2, 38, 90, 164n3, 173n70
Montoya, Joseph M., 90
Montoya, Tommy, 144; *San Juan No. 2,* *132*
Moon Woman Cuts the Circle (Pollock), 26
Moqwina (Meinholtz), 116
Morris, Thomas, 90
Morrison, George, 111
Morrow, Dwight W., 16
Morrow, Mable, 49
Moss, Frank, 117
Motherwell, Robert, 28
Mural Guild, 36
murals, 8, 17, 24, 36
Museum of Modern Art (MoMA): and abstract expressionists, 26, 27; and the cultural Cold War, 4, 27, 28, 29, 32–34, 162n59; d'Harnoncourt's influence on, 4, 12; education in modernism, 4, 26, 27, 34–35, 127, 163n80; film programs, 50, 57, 127, 163n80; "Indian Art of the United States" exhibition, 22–25; International Program, 32–34; Merit Award, to New, 177n35; and surrealists, 20
Museum of New Mexico, 129
music, Indian, 84–85, 99, 116, 137, 158n15
Myer, Dillon S., 71

Nailor, Gerald, 38
Nash, Philleo, 90–91, 94–95, 98, 110, 117, 119, 174n88
Native American Arts, 147–148
Navajo language, use of, 74
Navajo Special Education Program, 73–74, 79
New, Lloyd "Kiva," 9; on adaptation *vs.* tradition, 2, 8–9, 15, 27, 118–119, 129–130, 177n33; on arts education,